Feasts and Celebrations
in North American Ethnic Communities

FEASTS

and

Celebrations

in North American Ethnic Communities

Edited by
Ramón A. Gutiérrez and
Geneviève Fabre

University of New Mexico Press
Albuquerque

Library of Congress Cataloging-in-Publication Data

Feasts and celebrations in North American ethnic communities/edited by
Ramón A. Gutiérrez and Geneviève Fabre. — 1st. ed.

   p. cm.

Selected papers from the English presentations given at a conference
at the Institut d'anglais Charles V, Paris, Dec. 14–16, 1989.

Includes bibliographical references and index.

ISBN 0-8263-1593-3

1. Festivals—United States—Congresses.
2. Ethnic festivals—United States—Congresses.
3. Rites and ceremonies—United States—Congresses.
4. United States—Social life and customs—Congresses.

I. Gutiérrez, Ramón A., 1951–   .
II. Fabre, Geneviève.
III. Institut d'anglais Charles V.

GT4803.A2F43   1995

394.2'6'08693—dc20

   94-42710

   CIP

Designed by Sue Niewiarowski

Contents

Contents

Preface

Ramón A. Gutiérrez

This book had its origins in an international symposium on "Festivals and Celebrations in North American Ethnic Communities," convened by Professors Geneviève Fabre and Rachel Ertel, through the *Centre Interdisciplinaire de Recherches Nord-Américaines* (CIRNA) of the University of Paris 7. Held December 14–16, 1989, at the *Institut D'Anglais Charles V* in Paris, France, the conference brought together over sixty American, European, and Latin American scholars from the disciplines of art, anthropology, history, politics, and sociology, as well as from the emerging and hybrid fields of cultural studies, ethnic studies, women's studies, and performance studies. Precipitated largely by the celebration and pageantry associated with the Bicentennial of the French Revolution, the symposium organizers asked participants to consider festivals and celebrations as "total social facts," which encoded the histories and memories of ethnic groups, as well as their resistance to cultural assimilation and the civic projects of nation-states.

The result was a stimulating interdisciplinary symposium with papers and cultural presentations that examined the celebrations and rituals of African Americans, Haitians, Cubans, West Indians, Mexican Americans, Chicanos, Filipinos, Puerto Ricans, Cambodians, Laotians, Asian Americans, and Anglo Americans living primarily in the United States. From family reunions to pilgrimages, from religious feasts to life-cycle rites, the participating scholars intensely informed, contested, and synthesized the dimensions of the known and the as yet unknown about festivals and celebrations.

The sheer number of excellent essays generated by the symposium made it quite impossible to publish all of them. The best essays written originally in

French, German, and Spanish, were published in France as a special issue of the academic journal, *Revue de L'AFEA* 51 (January 1992) edited by Geneviève Fabre and Rachel Ertel. A selection from the essays written in English are herein collected. Space limitations in the present volume meant that excellent essays by Wayne Ashley, Dolores Rivas Bahti, Juan Bruce-Novoa, Francine García-Hallcom, Andrée-Ann Kekeh, Hélene Le Dantec, Joan M. Martin, Stephan Palmié, Robert Orsi, Margaret Ripley Wolf, and Stan Yogi, all of whom were participants in the symposium, could not be included here. The theoretical and empirical contributions made by these scholars throughout the symposium sharpened the intellectual quality of the essays published here.

The present volume is organized into three sections, with each one focused on various aspects of the relationships between celebrations and ethnic communities in the United States. The first section, "Colonialism and Festival: The Art of Resistance," examines a set of rituals and celebrations initially introduced into what is now the United States during colonial times, which came to be identified with particular ethnic groups. Geneviève Fabre's essay, "Pinkster Festival, 1776–1811: An African-American Celebration," traces the history of one religious festival originally introduced into New Amsterdam by the Dutch as a spring fertility ritual that affirmed communal ethnic identity. Gradually, Pinkster was appropriated by African Americans as a festival that reflected the complex power relations in which slaves and ex-slaves lived, and which intermixed voices, forms, and symbols drawn from various African and New World cultural traditions. Professor Fabre documents the historical representations and interpretations of Pinkster Festival in popular journalism, poetry, and fiction, noting the enduring paradox of slave societies: "For societies where the weight of puritanism was strong, and in which the highest values were work, industriousness, sobriety, the freedom and amusements of their members was also of great concern." Pinkster allowed African Americans both to confirm the "black image in the white mind," while contesting those images and in the process constructing powerful self-identities.

Anthropologist Alessandra Lorini deepens our historical understanding of New York African-American culture in her essay, "Public Rituals and the Cultural Making of the New York African-American Community." In comparing the uses of ritual public space by African Americans during the period between the 1825 festivities inaugurating the Erie Canal and the 1909 Hudson-Fulton Festival, in honor of Henry Hudson and Robert Fulton—the discoverer and the first navigator of the Hudson River, respectively—Professor Lorini shows different segments of the African American community displaying different attitudes toward what to celebrate and exactly how. These divergent views reflected attitudes within the African-American community toward emancipation, the uses of freedom, and the confrontation with and struggle against racism. By staging their own parades and spectacles, African Americans invented images of themselves that contested white stereotypes of their race, thus creating public images of their full participation as citizens and their respectability in civil society.

Much as African Americans transformed the original meanings of European festivals and rituals in a colonial context, so, too, in the southwestern United States rituals and celebrations that were initially introduced by the Spanish colonizers to dominate, humiliate, and educate the colonized indigenous populations are still performed, albeit in transmogrified forms and with profoundly different meanings. María Herrera-Sobek studies one such form, the *pastorela*, a Christmas shepherd's play first introduced in Mexico by the friars to Christianize the Indians. In "The Mexican/Chicano *Pastorela*: Toward a Theory of the Evolution of a Folk Play," Professor Herrera-Sobek describes how the *pastorela* was transformed into a site of resistance, a ritual place where the colonized could contest their own domination by profaning the play's language through eschatological, erotic, and raunchy humor. Professor Norma Cantú further expands our understanding of the Spanish colonial experience in what is now the United States in "Los Matachines de la Santa Cruz de la Ladrillera: Notes toward a Socio-literary Analysis.." The Matachines, a religious dance drama of humiliation, which depicts the Indians' acceptance of the cross and their conversion to Christianity, is one of the oldest religious dramas still enacted in the United States. Professor Cantú maintains that today the festival performance of Matachines in the south Texas town of Laredo can be read as a cultural text that succinctly encapsulates the history of cultural resistance among Mexicans living in the southwestern United States. By venerating the cross in the Matachines dance, residents of two barrios in Laredo, Texas, affirm their identities as mestizos, renew their historical ties to Mexico, and create a sense of religious community that is quite distinct from that which is created in Roman Catholic churches.

The second section of this book explores "Rituals of Renewal and Return." One of the most important functions of ethnic rituals and celebrations is to restore, renew, and rejuvenate a personal sense of self tied to a larger community. By traveling to a distant sacred site, by cooking special foods associated with a particular deity or saint, or by enacting ritual performances in a precisely prescribed fashion, the sacred is conjured. Communing with the sacred by traveling to a pilgrimage site is the topic of Professor Ramón A. Gutiérrez's essay, "El Santuario de Chimayo: A Syncretic Shrine in New Mexico." Professor Gutiérrez explores the history of the Santuario de Chimayo, the largest pilgrimage site in the United States, and analyzes the multiple layers of meaning that the shrine possesses for American Indians, Hispanos, and Anglos. The various behaviors displayed by pilgrims at the Santuario, the miracles they ascribe to the shrine, and the ways in which pilgrims imagine the divine are all topics explored in this work.

Much as the Santuario de Chimayo psychically renews body and soul, Mother Christine Hall, far away in New York City, physically renews individuals in her storefront church. In "First You Feed Them, Then You Clothe Them, Then You Save Them: The Hungry and Homeless and the Sunday Feast at a Pentecostal Storefront Church in East Harlem," Professor Anna Lou Dehavenon enters the blight of urban poverty to study the rituals and feasts that Mother Christine Hall's Glorious Church in New York City creates on a weekly basis. Guided by the salvation theology of Pentecostalism, Mother Hall welcomes into her church the poor and homeless Puerto Rican and African-American residents of East Harlem, showering them with bountiful gifts of food, clothes, and shelter, in return for the salvation of their souls.

The salvation of one's soul presupposes a body. In Sybil Kein's essay, "The Celebration of Life in New Orleans Jazz Funerals," she reminds us that in death there is also renewal for the community of the living. Professor Kein analyzes how African-American residents of New Orleans blend elements of the African and West African religious heritage with European Christianity at funerals. Disentangling the various cultural strands that are manifest in funerals, she discovers that Africans deemed death as a rebirth, that at death an American slave was freed in spirit and body for return to Africa, and that the highly erotic voodoo dances at funerals represented the emergence of life from death. The procession structure, the structured church service, and the wearing of black clothing during a funeral all represented the Christian legacy in which jazz funerals occurred.

One of the central themes addressed by many of the essays collected here is the forging and affirmation of ethnic, national, and pan-ethnic identities through the cultural performance of ritual. In the final section of this anthology, "Celebrations and the Creation of Identities," various scholars analyze the creations and messages of such identities. The gargantuan feats of heroes, both physical and spiritual, often become, in complex societies, icons on which to anchor local sentiments, national identities, and resistance to mass culture. José Rizal, the Philippine hero executed by the Spanish in 1896 for advocating national independence, is just such an icon. In their essay "Celebrating Rizal Day: The Emergence of a Filipino Tradition in Twentieth-Century Chicago," Roland L. Guyotte and Barbara M. Posadas focus on the ways in which Rizal Day celebrations fostered a cross-class sense of Filipino identity between students and workers in the United States during the early part of the twentieth century. Guyotte and Posadas carefully trace the transformation of the Rizal Day celebration over time. As Filipinos went from being temporary migrants to permanent immigrants and gradually acculturated, accepting the dominant culture of American society, Rizal Day celebrations in Chicago changed from being patriotic events of nationalist resistance to American colonialism, which tied Filipinos to their island, to becoming elaborate class-stratified social balls that simply mirrored the signs and symbols of American popular culture.

Expanding on the ways in which local and regional identities often clash with mass culture to produce new identities, Ted Ownby shifts our gaze to the study of Anglo ethnic culture in the American South through their emblematic harvest celebrations. In "Harvest Celebrations in the Rural South and the Challenge of Mass Culture, 1865–1920," Ownby traces the historical transition from such local customs as corn shuckings, cotton picking, and hog killings to county fairs that were organized by state and federal governments. Prompted primarily by the mechanization and commercialization of southern agriculture at the turn of the century, county fairs vividly demonstrated the ways in which the national market penetrated the lives of southern rural folk. This market culture disparaged the older masculine culture marked by personal honor and competition, and, instead, celebrated rational scientific management. For women, judged baking and quilting contests at county fairs reinforced the idea that the place of the women was in the home. But it was in the sinful, self-indulgent displays in the fair midways that the assault on southern evangelical sensibilities and rural culture was most profound. Professor Ownby argues that prohibition and moral-purity campaigns developed as a defensive reaction to the intrusion of immoral and sinful modern, urban-based ideas most visible at county and state fairs.

How celebrations can become fields for the creation and enactment of identities is the theme of Jack Kugelmass's essay, "Imagining Culture." Here, the celebration is the Halloween parade in New York City's Greenwich Village. Since the parade's invention in 1987, it has become one of the city's grandest, if not one of its most outrageous, events. Kugelmass shows how the Halloween parade has become a celebration through which members of the gay community affirm their membership in a collective culture and, indeed, create that culture through the performances they enact and view on the streets of New York City.

The New York borough of Brooklyn is the locale studied by Remco van Capelleveen, in his essay "The Caribbeanization of New York City: West Indian Carnival in Brooklyn." As a result of the Hart-Cellar Immigration Act of 1965, large numbers of West Indians of different nationalities have migrated and settled in Brooklyn, and as a result of daily social and spatial interactions, they have developed an African-Caribbean pan-national ethnic identity and consciousness in New York. This African-Caribbean identity, Professor van Capelleveen argues, is most apparent during the West Indian Carnival, which takes place every year during the Labor Day weekend. Employing the motto "We all is one," the carnival blends masking and musical styles to create an egalitarian celebration devoid of flags and national emblems. Though appeals to black unity occasionally punctuate the carnival, the overwhelming theme is one of ethnic solidarity rooted in immigration rather than racial unity based on race.

These are the themes of the essays presented herein. In what follows, Professor Fabre explores the broad theoretical issues that she had in mind when she organized the first international symposium on "Festivals and Celebrations in North American Ethnic Communities."

1

Feasts and Celebrations
Introduction

Geneviève Fabre*

Celebrations have always been vital to the well-being of society. Not only do they punctuate its life with rituals, ceremonies and festive events, they also bring an essential and rich spirit to its everyday existence as well as to its special moments. They are touchstones for its strength and cohesion or for its tensions and conflicts. Solemn or trifling, serious or lighthearted, elaborate or simple, and holding at the same time normative and subversive functions, they are necessary to the pulse of society. Popular pastimes and entertainments, seasonal holidays and calendar customs, religious rites or feasts of misrule, anniversaries and commemorations, national, local, or familial feasts, masques, parades, festivals, and carnivals have always existed. Accepted or tolerated in one place, they may be encouraged and promoted in another or still sanctioned and suppressed elsewhere. Their forms may change and their implications alter with the social order; the object of celebration may suddenly be replaced: the celebration itself still endures. By no means relegated to leisure life, they are central to the political, social, and religious life, and involve major institutions. Historians may deplore the fact that there are now fewer authentic feasts, and there is ample evidence that traditional forms are disappearing. But the celebrative festive spirit is never totally lost. Temporarily submerged, it rises to triumph again. Very much a part of the society in which they were conceived, celebrations nevertheless have a life of their own. Their slow or sudden promi-

*A grant from the Rockefeller Foundation at their center in Bellagio, Italy, enabled me to write the first draft of this essay and the final version of the Pinkster essay.

nence or demise may be determined by ideological trends or cultural fashions, by changing moods of government or public opinion; they still amazingly avoid the pressures of time and policies and, while undergoing constant transformations, manage to survive in what are their most essential characteristics.

A familiar and universal feature in society, celebratory performances are often controversial and surrounded with contradictions. They have their advocates and their critics; simultaneously they can be found necessary and disparaged, be perceived as inconsequential and volatile, or as elevating and sacred, as moral or highly immoral, as legal or as an expression of lawlessness. Considered as moments of freedom, they are also controlled. Their time and space span is carefully planned: no trespassing is allowed and regulations can be severe and restrictive. While they provide occasions for the eruption of violence, they are also used as channels to contain the upsurge of unrestrained elements. They can be simultaneously a threat to, or a warrant of, the social order.

It is because of their complexities and their paradoxical nature that celebrations have retained our attention for the study of ethnic and immigrant communities in the U.S.A., which we have been pursuing over a number of years at our research center, the CIRNA (Center for Interdisciplinary Research on North America). In December 1989, we organized an international conference on this topic at the University of Paris VII. Most of the papers included in this volume were presented at this conference.

It seemed interesting to approach the analysis of these societies from a perspective that could highlight unheeded aspects and would also focus on, and help reconsider, much-discussed issues: their respective history and place in American society; their distinctive modes of insertion and assimilation; the process of their acculturation and their determination to proclaim their difference; their struggles to win recognition and equal rights.

While American society is always planning and reorganizing its calendar of festive events, its national holidays and commemorative celebrations—from Thanksgiving to Halloween, from Independence Day to Washington's or, more recently, Martin Luther King's, birthday—ethnic communities create their own cycle of ritualized events. They do so by evolving different forms of participation: either they seemingly respect major American celebrations, but twist their meaning around; or they impose changes that become officially recognized; or they stage their separate ceremonies in a calendar of alternative, and sometimes counter, celebrations. Christmas and other "holidays" or seasonal events are observed, but they do not receive the same prominence or significance from one group to another. The Fourth of July may be declared a national day, but it is not an "Independence" day for some groups, such as African-Americans to whom 1776 failed to herald the emergence of a new era, or other groups that still do not feel themselves to be an integral part of the nation; their historical experience directs them toward other commemorations. Similarly, the quincentennial celebration of the discovery of America has elicited a hot debate on the significance of 1492 and on the appropriateness of inserting into the national memory an event that brought wrongs and injustices into the history of many peoples. Some groups whetted their weapons, sharpened their rhetoric and their imagination to prepare counter celebrations all over the country; many seized upon the occasion, not for another thanksgiving, but to challenge American democracy, its internal and external policies.

American society has a tradition of pageantry, of public and dramatic—visual and tangible—reenactment of its history, which has been a crucial instrument for the reconstruction and reevaluation of its past and its culture. Combining mass recreation with moral and patriotic education, these civic celebrations have encouraged ethnic groups to enter the public space, and they have been a channel to win more visibility and power. On the one hand, these pageants invited groups to join in a common civic identity and managed to weld together communities divided by ethnic and class affiliations or interests; on the other hand, they provided a "locus" to express their different loyalties, plots to act out their separate and distinctive memories and histories and to shape their individual perceptions and representations. Dissenting voices have been included in these events, which brought together an increasingly diverse population in the midst of many social changes. Thus, historical pageantry can be viewed as a way to reinforce the existing order and the principles on which it is based; as such, it certainly contributes to preserve Anglo-Saxon supremacy. Or, by contrast, it can be perceived as a ritual of democratic participation constructing a civil identity which takes into account the experiences and values of other peoples. A crucial force in the shaping of American culture, it is a major source for the study of American society.

Parades offer the best example of pageantry. Many essays in this volume deal with that tradition, which has had its ebb and flow, but can be traced from colonial times to the present day and has involved many ethnic groups; from the times when slaves and free blacks were organizing public events to elect or to celebrate their own kings and governors to the era when black

musicians and veterans marched in official parades; from the institutionaliza-
tion of the Irish parade on St. Patrick's Day to that of the Puerto Rican Day
Parade. Excluded from, or only partially admitted in the great American pageants—like the annual Mummers parade in Philadelphia or the event celebrating the opening of the Erie Canal—groups have struggled to win admission
into national ceremonies or have evolved their separate rituals. Ethnic associations and organizations display their banners, count their members, and
test their influence in the community as well as in the larger society. Many
well-established celebrations, like Labor Day and Halloween, have their parades and give evidence of the equal importance of sacred and worldly events.
The tradition of parading, stronger in certain cities, like Mobile or New Orleans, New York, or Miami, and pervasive in the Southwest among Mexican
Americans, exists all over the United States. If parades are a firmly entrenched
national tradition, their modes and patterns have been diversified as each
group introduces its own symbols and styles of performance, its display of
ornaments, costumes, and emblems. The occasion for communities to understand and interpret for their members and for others the signs of their identities, pageants are also the place where signs may be exchanged and
transformed, where boundaries may be shifted or marked differently. Finally,
parades sometimes provide the occasion to express grievances and claims,
and can be turned into protest marches. The celebrative spirit and the subversive mood often combine, especially when the object of celebration seems
out of reach or only dimly present. Many militant groups, civil right advocates
and anti-war protestors, have resorted to marches to change the national
consciousness or to stir up dormant memories or forgotten causes.

  If parades are connected with the secular and political culture, they are
closely related to another tradition, initially more religious: that of processions
and pageants organized around Christmas and around pilgrimages, funerals,
and other public or secret rites. Each culture has its own way of honoring the
dead, and ethnic groups have brought a multiplicity of ceremonies—from jazz
funerals to the Mexican Day of the Dead—into American celebrative life, in a
country where death was considered important mostly for the funeral of
major figures, presidents, or war heroes. In these processions, religious symbols or emblems have the capacity to rally masses of people, and they are
often closely associated with political action.

  Significantly, parades and processions are often included in celebrations or
may even become the main celebrative event. Whatever their place, they
have a rich symbolic significance and offer a way of performing experience

and of identifying "sites of memory": events, moments, legendary or historical figures, places and actions stored in the collective memory are thus deliberately called upon and endowed with symbolic significance.

Next to pageants and parades, festivals and carnivals are seen as less serious events, less controlled and controllable, less dignified and ordered, more exotic or exuberant.

The borderline between parades and festivals is hard to define. Ethnic festivals, introduced by cultural groups most remote—geographically and ethnically—from the Anglo-Saxon norm, are often more tolerated than officially accepted and are often categorized among other carnivalesque events. Perceived sometimes as going against the American grain, as alien to the prescribed forms of celebration, they stand apart and separate in the list of festive events. A challenge to the Puritan mind, they have nevertheless entered the American scene: early Negro jubilees, festivals like Pinkster in New York or John Canoe in Carolina, were either ignored, dreaded, or despised, or they were the object of intense curiosity and attraction. Censured, forbidden, and submitted to strict regulations, they managed to survive and, if they seem to have had a short-lived existence, they reemerged under new forms after having gone underground. They always drew large crowds of visitors and onlookers from all social groups.

The festivals examined here are mostly connected with the African or Hispanic Caribbeans, and they are a North American variation of what is happening in the African diaspora, in Brazil, Jamaica, and Trinidad, in Puerto Rico and Cuba, or in the French West Indies. Seen as products of southern cultures, they have now become more firmly rooted in the northern parts of the American continent, in its southern edge (Miami) or in colder northern cities (Toronto and New York). They account for the caribbeanization of the United States, and for its latinization too, since many expressive forms were evolved in Latin America. With the growing influx of immigrants from South America through Mexico, and from the Caribbean, some regions have become sites for the encounter between Latin American and Afro-Hispanic cultures.

Whereas some festivals clearly designate ethnic groups, carnivals and masquerades create a "communitas" that supersedes boundaries. With less decorum but more flourish, animated with the "politics of mirth" and a "will to adorn," and carrying various associations of renewal, fertility, and freedom, carnivals have an exuberance that threatens the social order; they also extend dangerously the area of rejoicings into expanses where instability and ambiguity prevail. Anarchical, wild, nursing lust and intemperance, encouraging public mirth, but also unrestrained, and characterized by unlawful conduct and rebelliousness, their meaning is ambivalent and elusive. They stem from a rich tradition of insolence—unhampered and rash words and actions.

Apparently less formal than civic celebrations, more turbulent, and governed by the principle of "paidia"—which Roger Caillois defined as one of free improvisation and uncontrolled fantasy—they are nevertheless carefully planned. Their extravagance is channeled by complex rules and conventions, which, even if they belong to the world of play, give them a sense of purpose imbued with irony and expressed through mimicry and parody.

Disagreeing with theories that view the carnivalesque as chaotic and loose, spontaneous, childlike, and primitive, we see these celebrations as "framed," structured and sophisticated; and we follow Victor Turner in his emphasis on their dialectical nature, as they move from "structure to antistructure and back again to transformed structure," from hierarchy to equality, from indicative mood to subjunctive mood. Less interested in the escape valve or release theory—which sometimes prevails among anthropologists—we are more concerned with the fact that feasts not only channel but reforge energies and can have a transformative function. They present a wealth of symbols, through a profusion of visual, sensory images that force us to modify our perception of the ordinary world. Through this display of cultural signs, each ethnic group makes itself known, explores its identity, tests its power, and demonstrates the scope of its imagination. In the essays, this symbolic and semantic richness is examined.

Temporally and spatially, there exist close links between carnivalesque performances and religious feasts, even though these two forms are often seen as representing two poles of celebrative life, one more playful and profane, the other more ritualistic and sacred. Carnival often precedes and may follow a period of abstinence and strict religious observance. Rigorous devotions follow license and indulgence. On the other hand, religious feasts often include parades and processions with bands, floats, and banners that may be as flamboyant as those of the civic marches. True, statues and shrines and images of saints replace the ludicrous lampoons and figures, and celebrants are supposed to show more piety and restraint than the sensuous revelers. But religious performances—also sometimes aptly called "festivals"—include activities that generate the same festive spirit as their secular counterparts. Many Italian saints' celebrations display ludic and carnivalesque features. Ethnic festivals have religious overtones; and as religious feasts are moving more frequently out into the public space, rituals of worship have become public spectacles; as a result, it seems more and more difficult to draw the line between these two opposite and highly competing realms of celebratory practice. This extension of the ecclesiastical order and liturgical mode into the rural or urban landscape finds its parodic replica in the satirical lampoon of many carnivals and its more serious duplication in the ceremonial of some festivals and parades.

The use of private and secret celebrative spaces is also examined in some essays. In clubs, homes, and churches, ethnic communities may be freer to maintain customs and practices that are distinctively theirs. In these spaces, groups intensify their membership and kinship ties, and they stage rituals of loyalty, a gathering of the spirits, a coming together, while they simultaneously reenact the various displacements, uprootings, dismemberings. Places of worship, of reflection, or of mere conviviality, they also provide a perspective from which to look at the world—the too-distant or sometimes mythical world of their home country, the more or less hostile world they now live in. In this space, they bring together all the threads of loose ties and lost identities, dramatize and resolve some of their tensions and conflicts, reconstruct their repertory of images and memories around a more cohesive image of the community, and sharpen their tools and rehearse the acts and rituals that they may bring out to the public space.

A strong dialectical relationship develops between the public and the private space, with each echoing, reinforcing, or questioning the other. We have been attentive to this interaction and interpenetration, and to the role it plays in legitimizing and guiding action.

Throughout these essays we have not tried to draw a strict typology of feasts, yet we have considered possible regrouping or differentiation according to common or contrasting features. Many performances presented here are civic or religious celebrations that can be contrasted with more ludic celebrations: the ones belonging to the domain of ritual, the others to the world of play, the former resorting more to metonymy, the latter to metaphor. Ritualistic performances are seen as more conservative, as both adhering to and acknowledging the society and the cultural values it celebrates; the ludic events are more subversive and therefore more open to change. Although such distinctions are useful and attractive, we find that play and ritual may combine, that different poles and modes may coexist and intertwine, and that feasts often elude categorizations. Also, in the case of ethnic celebrations, what would be judged as conservative in a different context can be innovative, inasmuch as it challenges the established order and forces new symbols and images on the national consciousness; conversely, seen in the context of each community, these celebrations can be adamantly opposed to change because of their heavy reliance on tradition. The double threat of being either totally ignored and despised or totally assimilated at the risk of losing one's ethnic identity can lead to fear of change and modernity. Although we are aware in this volume of these conflicting trends and tensions, we see feasts as the place where these tensions are best made manifest and, if not resolved, at least acknowledged; they are sites also where tradition and culture are not only reenacted but reinvented. In this perspective, the issue of modernity is discussed as well as the intrusion of mass culture and the gradual transition from pre- to post-industrial eras.

The way in which certain feasts are attentive to crucial social issues is emphasized in some papers which show that apparently traditional celebrations may have a political relevance. The use of familiar images and symbols, drawn from the ethnic traditions and values, helps to explore and define problems with which groups are confronted; in the process, new modes of representation are created which, in turn, engender new meaning and a better understanding of the situation of each community. Rather than merely reflecting social reality, festive performances are metasocial and offer a comment upon that reality. They express the society and the culture in ways in which they are not otherwise expressed. Feasts often play out an idealized form of society while offering, in their more critical and satirical moments, alternate forms resonant with subversive significance. They can thus generate new "structures of feeling" and verbal and nonverbal language forms that are both celebratory and agonistic, cognitive, and volitional.

Through their dramatic and narrative function, celebrations, which unfold in time and space, represent the development of the group, actualizing memories of its beginnings and of experiences it went through during the stages of its history. In this way, they also reflect upon their own origin and history. Each feast, however unique and singular it may be, bears the memory of, and anticipates, other feasts. But each, finite and ephemeral by definition, also anticipates its own ending or its ultimate disintegration. In this emergence and death may lie its major symbolic significance: in the image it presents of the life process itself. Disruptive, because of the sudden interruption that it brings to the flow of things and its suspension of daily life, it nevertheless participates in the infinite flux of life and in its rhythms.

This volume presents a variety of celebrations—civic and ludic, religious and profane, public and private, popular and more elitist, primitive or traditional and modern, and rural and urban. Although existing categories of cultural performance have proved useful, we have been wary of binary oppositions. The studies offered here show that genres, modes, and moods often overlap, compete with each other, and ultimately interact even within the same festive event. If some ethnic groups have in certain regions, at certain historical moments, privileged specific forms and have thereby been instrumental in establishing a tradition and giving it prominence, they have also found themselves in situations of contact involving conflicts, exchanges, competing loyalties, chosen or imposed acculturation, and more or less radical changes.

We have been attentive to these developments, to power issues and to class differences, to manifestations of authority and claims of legitimacy as celebrations reflect a community's notion of its power (or lack of power) and its prerogatives. Even if some performative events exist only in enclaves, as isolated and separate units, and others create a larger network and extend to create a cultural diaspora, there nevertheless exist many commonalities between apparently distant observances. Our focus has been temporal, regional, topical. Yet we are struck by all the echoes we find from one event to the next, by the permanence and perennial quality, by the constant infusion of new elements and the fascinating circulation of images, structures, and symbols. With the increasing mobility and migration of some groups, the northern part of "the Americas" has become an arena for the interplay between ethnic communities and an important matrix for the emergence of new, invented cultures. It is also the space where new ties and boundaries are being constantly constructed, or deconstructed and "displaced." The encounter between European cultures and indigenous cultures may not be over yet; and while Anglo-Saxon society is still clinging to its assimilationist or hegemonic dream, it is being challenged by the arrival of many other immigrants who bring into its midst newer or older cultures from other continents and confront it with new stakes. Feasts are the templates by which to gauge all these processes: creolization of cultures, syncretism, various degrees of acculturation. As groups devise their strategies for a more or less successful, more or less controlled americanization, one speaks of threats of africanization, caribbeanization, latinization, and now asiatization of the United States. Festivals and celebrations are making all of these trends more perceptible; they create arenas where new forces come into play and, in turn, generate new developments.

Part One

Colonialism and Festivals
The Art of Resistance

2

Pinkster Festival, 1776–1811
An African-American Celebration

Geneviève Fabre

In the post-revolutionary era and through the early years of the nineteenth century, African Americans held, along the Hudson River, in New York and in east New Jersey, a Whitsuntide festival known as "Pinkster." During its years of existence, this festival assumed a greater importance and was attended not only by crowds of free blacks and slaves, but also by many other ethnic groups who, although they were gradually relegated to the role of spectators, participated in varying degrees in its ritual. Pinkster bore much resemblance to other African-American celebrations—to New England governors' elections, to the famous John Canoe festival, or to the earlier Congo Square dances in New Orleans, as well as to other festivities in the diaspora. It also anticipated carnival forms that developed in late nineteenth-century Louisiana: the Mardi Gras Indians or the Zulu parades. Yet it evolved out of a very distinct sociocultural setting and derived its significance from a unique history.

Pinkster, as is attested by the name (the word, meaning Pentecost, was used as early as 1667 in a Dutch Book of Sermons), was originally a Dutch celebration observed at Whitsuntide in New Amsterdam by the early settlers eager to preserve some of their Old World customs (Earle, 196–202). Pinkster was not only a religious gathering; it was also the occasion to reinforce, around the collective memory of the home country, a sense of community and of the new identity in the colony. In the calendar of feasts, Pentecost, also called *Pfingster* in German, was a religious celebration closely associated with seasonal change, which, in turn, was a fit symbol for the Feast of the Holy

Spirit. In cold climates, the advent of spring was a long-expected event. During the ceremonial rituals, much attention was given to the awakening of nature, the blossoming of trees and flowers, and the preparation of new crops. The Azalea, "Pinkster Blummachee," was chosen as one of the emblems, and it was sung and praised for its splendor. With the "blue flag," or iris, it served as an important symbol of the renewal of life: in Albany, the space chosen for the festivities, "Pinkster Hill," was adorned with flowers, and this sudden transformation—conceived as a preliminary ritual—offered "a beautiful contrast with the forbidding nakedness" of the surrounding barren and dusty hills (Earle, 200).

At the turn of the nineteenth century, Pinkster became a mostly black festival. Contemporary accounts made a passing allusion to the Dutch origin or to the Dutch presence, and they described at great length the ceremonial dances, music, and speeches of the "Africs," who were henceforth at the center of the scene, as both the main organizers and participants.

The historical circumstances that transformed an all-Dutch feast into an African-American festival are little known and have not been thoroughly researched. African dance, music, and oratory became essential parts of the ritual. One sees here an example of the way in which black skills were used and welcomed in many feasts of the New World, and they are also exemplary of the process of acculturation, through which European forms were made to serve African functions, or of interesting forms of syncretism and invention of tradition. The change to an all-black festival may be ascribed to different trends: the growing slave population in the New York area and the greater assimilation of the descendants of the Dutch settlers; the steady flow of Africans at a time when the foreign slave trade was not yet officially abolished; and renewed contacts with African customs. Without fully investigating the demographic, economic, political, or cultural factors that might have helped in grasping the complexities of this mutation, scholars have used Pinkster to illustrate their own theories on black or "slave cultures."

At one end of the spectrum, a theory presented by cultural nationalists or proponents of the Afrocentric idea claims that Pinkster offers a clear instance of the recreation of African patterns in the New World, and interprets the festival mainly in its relation to African customs and practices (Stuckey; Williams Myers). Pinkster, "infused with memories of Africa" (Shine) and transplanted into the New World, is perhaps one of the manifestations of a larger phenomenon: the emergence throughout the diaspora, in different historical eras, of black festivals—in Brazil, in Trinidad and other islands, in New Orleans and Mobile (Kinser), in the Carolinas, and, in its more modern forms, in New York and Toronto. At the other end, Pinkster is seen mainly as a black imitation of European celebrations. This serves the purpose of those who wish to emphasize the European origin of black culture, and who view the latter mostly as a distortion or occasionally grant African Americans various degrees of originality and creativity in this process of appropriation and adaptation. If one chooses a middle ground, Pinkster can be seen as the result of the encounter between several cultures and as a form of syncretism, as evidence of the ways in which African Americans appropriated an alien culture and created a truly indigenous form through inventing a new tradition. Pinkster should not be analyzed in terms of the polarization often used to appraise black culture—an opposition drawn along racial (black and white), geopolitical, or geocultural lines (Europe and Africa, North and South of the nation). Instead, one should see it in a more complex configuration, in which a multiplicity of voices, forms, structures, and functions come into play, and resulting in an interaction between groups involving not only power relationships, but reciprocity and competitive pursuits as well. Pinkster provides one of the most interesting examples of this intricate web; and this can best be grasped not so much through the actual experience (there is still insufficient data and material to approach the reality of the feast), as through the "documentary culture" that recorded it or through the "selective tradition," with its special emphasis, omissions, distortions, and the influence of the spirit of the time. (I am using here the distinctions established by Raymond Williams in *The Long Revolution.*) Focusing on these two levels in the analysis of culture, I shall deal mostly with the historical representations and interpretations that exist either in journalistic, in poetic, or in narrative fictional form.

The earliest description of Pinkster probably appeared in *The Albany Sentinel* and was reprinted in 1803 in *The Daily Advertiser* (June 29). In that same year, 1803, the famous "Pinkster Ode" was written.[1] Passing or extended references to Pinkster are to be found in local history or annals,[2] or in the famous description given by James F. Cooper in *Satanstoe*. It is true that in all of these sources, it is not so much the Dutch festival as the African celebration that received attention: "Strangely . . . that observance was chiefly by an alien, a heathen race. Nowhere was it a more glorious festival than at Albany among the sheltered, the cherished slave population in the town and its vicinity" (Earle, 196). It was the African character of the festivities—the style of dancing (even if it was described as "antics"), the music with the Guinea drum, and the specific rituals and general spirit of the event—which produced the difference between Pinkster and other fairs and merry makings (Cooper, 60). Observers saw in Pinkster ceremonies that bore similarities with the African customs of anticipating harvest or were related to rites of passage. This Africanness may explain the attraction of a festival that was perceived as more exotic and tantalizing than the more familiar European feasts. Simultaneously, this exoticism elicited ambiguous reactions ranging from genuine admiration to outright disparagement. "Africs" were praised for their display of talent, the quality of their performance, and their capacity to attract big crowds; but their "bacchanalia" were condemned mainly on moral grounds, for bringing disorder and for encouraging misconduct. The main event, called Toto dance, was shunned by white visitors because its "indecent gesticulations" were too savage or lewd. Descriptions abounded in laudatory or derogatory remarks, in amused or condescending observations, and in equally exaggerated praise or condemnation; and esthetic judgement (with the recurrence of such terms as "horrid," "hideous," or "indecent") was often the expression of moral values (Earle; Eights).

Documentation regarding Pinkster contains a wealth of details, which comprise not only valuable sources for the reconstruction of the festival, but show the degree of careful scrutiny that the rituals received. It also includes abrupt, emphatically negative assumptions that seem to be in contradiction with the admirable precision of some of the observations made. The recorders were overwhelmed by the richness and elaborateness, the esthetic and emotional appeal, of Pinkster, yet they wanted to belittle the effects produced and make sure that spectators would not be carried away and that readers would be given the proper criteria by which to appraise the performance. Hyperbolic terms were immediately corrected by depreciative epithets meant to temper enthusiasm and to reinforce stereotypes.

These texts offer an interesting image of black culture "in the white mind"; this image either gave further evidence of the "happy state" the slaves and free blacks lived in, or contributed to create, in turn, the image of Sambo as entertainer. Feasts were usually referred to as merry frolics, revelry, harmless or jolly amusements, or as great weird saturnalia (Cooper, 55), bacchanalian revels (Earle, 198), and clowning buffoonery (Eights, 198). Dances were seen as lewd, sexually provocative, ludicrous, or indecent (Furman, 267), or as partaking "largely of savage license" (Earle, 198). When this "festival of misrule" was banned by a city ordinance of the Albany Common Council in 1811, after occasional arrests for misconduct, it was charged with bringing too much boisterous rioting and drunkenness (Furman, 268). By then the negative stereotypes prevailed; and the excitement created by the celebration—both among blacks and whites—was perceived as a threat to common morality, which had to be checked for the ancient burghers as well as for the lower classes.[3]

Here lies an enduring paradox. For societies where the weight of puritanism was strong, and in which the highest values were work, industriousness, and sobriety, the freedom and amusements of their members was also of great concern. For that reason, African-American festivals served diverse functions. On the one hand, they were opportunities for "merriment," as a welcomed and necessary relief from work and drudgery; on the other hand, the "darkies" were entrusted with the delicate task of entertaining white spectators, of inducing them to take greater pleasure in life. The sight of a black jubilee served precisely that purpose: In watching black slaves and servants dance and sing, the more "respectable" onlookers could enjoy, by proxy, a liberty and sensuality that they themselves could not reach without losing their dignity and self-respect. Pinkster also reinforced the image that New York society wished to give of its liberalism—its tolerance, the diversity of its cultures, and the intrinsic happiness of even the poorest and assumedly more oppressed among its population.[4]

I have chosen to limit my further remarks to two documents: the Pinkster Ode of 1803, written when Pinkster was still at its peak, and Cooper's description, less contemporaneous to the event, although it claimed that the feast, banned in Albany, continued to be observed in other places. A comparison between the two texts may help to clarify the processes of interpretation mentioned earlier. The Ode, one of the earliest descriptions of a folk festival in the United States, differs from some of the more straightforward accounts. Dedicated to Carolus Africanus Rex, or King Charles, "by His Majesty's Obedient Servant, Absalom Aimwell, Esq.," the Ode belongs rightly to the ceremonial rite itself. This song of praise, presented by a dutiful servant, significantly called "Aimwell," also provides the most detailed account of the whole Jubilee. The faked or assumed author is both principal actor (an Afric insider) and distant observer. The Ode must be seen in both contexts, as part of the event and as offering a selective interpretation. The festival of Albany[5] became the prototype of all Pinkster celebrations, its most popular and famous form, centered around the impressive figure of King Charley, the accomplished master of ceremonies, who is said to have died at the age of 120 in 1824. An occasion to give praise in which the community, gathered around its self-appointed leader and king, expressed in all its regalia its loyalty to its sovereign, Pinkster was a mock-serious reconstitution of a British or of an African court. Conversely, for the king, the feast offered the opportunity to assemble all of his "subjects," in order to sound his authority and to restate his power. The central role given to the king invites a parallel with the governors' and kings' elections in New England, demonstrating how Pinkster belongs to (and perhaps initiated) a long tradition of coronations that started in colonial times and developed through the nineteenth century.[6]

Charles the King, "nobly born, well made and tall," placed by the celebrants above King George or Bonaparte, was famous "from Hudson's stream to Niger's wave." His unusual stature and status—"for a sceptre he was born"—elicited respect from whites and blacks alike. His African origin and royal birth made him unique among his peers (he was a Guinea man from Angola; and Earle tells us that nearly all African-born men who became leaders were Guineans): "you will never see his like again" (Pleat and Underwood, 34). Servant and ruler and excelling in both, he was depicted as graceful, polite, and pleasant. These characteristics, when found in ordinary slaves, were interpreted as signs of obedience and submissiveness. Not so with Charles, who was neither Uncle Tom nor Sambo; he commanded respect, wielded authority, and acted as mediator between two racial worlds. His harangue was not the act of an Uncle Tom, speaking in the interest of white rulers, but a speech full of double entendre, infusing in black listeners a sense of dignity, power, cohesion, and solidarity, while it tried to placate, not black insurgency, but white minds that were uneasy and fearful in front of such a display of autonomy and sense of community. The king's costume, combining elements drawn from a variety of backgrounds—a British brigadier's jacket of scarlet, a tricorned cocked hat, and yellow buckskins (Eights, 325)—further demonstrated the blending and syncretization of cultural memories and the range of effects that a ceremonial garb worn by an African slave could create: from humour to parody, from irony to seriousness.

The king's main functions, from a white point of view, were to control events that could get out of hand or become subversive; The king could also facilitate the acculturation of his fellow slaves and free blacks: this "civilized" Negro could bring composure and refinement. One witnesses here the unusual reversal of stereotypes—the official recognition of African royalty and gentility, instead of the more common association of Africanness with savagery or lack of culture.

For the slaves who elected him, the king represented all that was denied to the enslaved: nobility, freedom, power, leadership, and authority. We know that slaves, selected as leaders or representatives, were Africans of noble birth and of impressive physical stature. The authority of Pinkster kings—just as that of New England governors—operated beyond the festive occasions and was respected by whites; the existence of a black king with high functions also attested to the capacity of African Americans to organize their own society and to reach a degree of self-government. Whether these social organizations had their origins in African customs or in European courts, or were conceived as parodies or caricatures of such practices, does not diminish their importance as acts of civic life.

The king or "prince" was also a justice maker, who could intercede to right the wrongs done to an oppressed people and lead the fight against tyranny. It behooved him therefore to interpret the idea of freedom for "Pinkster's sons," who were also called the "sons of Ham." His harangue to the crowd—an essential part of the ceremony and the only moment when music could be stilled—was a hymn to freedom. This slave "whose soul was always free" was best fitted to speak of liberty, but in a way that did not trespass the limits set by white authorities. His speech was meant to temper the fiery spirit of those who might be tempted to carry the idea of liberty too far. In line with the milder tradition of the black church, the king preached for respectability, good behavior, restraint, gratefulness, endurance of pain, and humility: "Let us with grateful hearts agree / not to abuse our Liberty . . . Yet nobly let us still endure / the ills and wrongs we cannot cure" (35). The king will not let the "happy jubilee" go astray. He must prevent unruliness, misbehavior, or rioting if he wants to continue to reign unmolested on merry grounds. This image of respectability became a major concern for many African Americans throughout the nineteenth century in the organization of similar feasts, as is evidenced by the comments made in the black press.[7]

Although, according to the Ode, many other groups participated in the festival—Indians, Germans, French, Dutch, Anglo Saxons, and Jews—and other cultural heroes "mounted the stump" to address the crowd—Jack the Rover and Jo the Politician, who waged an unending war on speculation, corruption, Democrats, and all of the enemies of liberty—the king remained the undisputed master of ceremonies, the most powerful figure around which all praises converged, all energies crystallized.

Thus, as documented by the Ode, Pinkster exemplified two important trends in the role granted to feasts at the turn of the century: the official recognition of blacks' special gift, not only for maintaining or creating a festive spirit, but for infusing it into other groups; and the willingness to find occa-

sions for the harmonious integration of all groups and classes and for con-
vivial interaction. Feasts offered the best opportunity, erasing conflicts and
tensions, releasing suffering caused by inequalities, and enduring restraints
on freedom. Thus, a society where many political and social strifes were
being led (between Federalists and Democrats, between pro- and anti-sla-
very factions, and for or against the abolition of the slave trade) allowed
itself spaces where it could dream of the utopian reconstruction of a pluralistic, multiethnic order, in which freedom and liberty could be granted to all.

At a time when the issue of slavery was more and more debated, observers of Pinkster and similar feasts chose to displace this too-acute problem.
They focused their attention not on the ordinary daily life and hardships of
slaves, but on those privileged moments when Africs could take a glimpse of
freedom. The fact that blacks were chosen as those who excelled most in
organizing a celebration of freedom, and that their ability to do so was officially acknowledged, tells much about the paradoxes of American society and
its stereotyped image of black life. The sight of what was interpreted as merriment and glee among the enslaved was a welcomed release from the guilt
generated by the "peculiar institution." The Ode also presented an interpretation of black entertainment, which, in many ways, still persists today: blacks
entertaining themselves, but also entrusted with the entertainment of whites,
who were less inclined or less "naturally" gifted for enjoyment and failed to
perceive the note of irony and parody in these celebrative performances.

Written ten years after the Ode, *Satanstoe* emphasizes both the African
element and the unique character of the festival. Cooper tells us that Pinkster,
widely observed in New York City, Hall Park, and Long Island, could only
occur in New York and not in New England: "no man ever heard of a festival
in New England that had not some immediate connection with saints or
politics, where even Blacks are so ground down in the Puritan mill, that they
are neither fish, flesh nor red herring, as we say of a nondescript" (60). What
struck the observer was the animation, the importance of the gathering—
people coming from forty miles away—the diversity of activities, and the
strict ordonnance of events. Preparations started weeks in advance and engaged blacks in much trading, in Brooklyn or New York, "to sell sassafras,
swingle tow," to dance for eels, to earn money for Pinkster, and to buy ginger-
bread and rum, two staple foods for a black festival. Either because Cooper
chose to minimize the political aspects of Pinkster and to insist on its more
folkloric features, or because his memories brought him back to a time when
the feast was already commercialized, his description focused on rather su-

perficial observations that one could make about any fair, with booths and sports and diverse attractions, as well as a lot of dancing, drinking, and eating. Yet Pinkster is definitely presented as a black festival, where whites were mostly spectators: "hundreds of whites were walking through the fields, amused spectators." While festivities began on Monday (Episcopal Whitsunday), blacks, the principal actors, only appeared on Tuesday. We know, from another account (Eights, 326) that the order of appearance of each group was carefully planned and staged, with due respect to rank and hierarchy: "it was considered vastly ungenteel by the colored nobility to make their appearance on the commencing day."

What was most striking about Pinkster, for Cooper as well as for the author of the Ode, was that it was one of the rare occurrences when not only all races but all classes met and interacted freely: blacks and whites; servants and masters; middle-class, respectable blacks and the mass of the enslaved.[8]

If Cooper's narrative acknowledges the roles of blacks in "keeping" the festival, it provides very few keys for a better understanding of its meaning. The visitor, whose interest and curiosity are raised by the exoticism of the black "frolics," betrays the usual condescension and prejudice toward these simple but "coarse" amusements: "the blacks were collected in thousands in those fields, beating banjoes, singing African songs, drinking and *worst of all* laughing in a way that seemed to set their very heart *rattling with their ribs.* Everything wore the aspect of good humor, though it was good humor in its *broadest and coarsest* forms" (60). Although we are told that a Negress "jabbered away explaining the meaning of different ceremonies to a cluster of very interested visitors" (62), these meanings are left unexplored. Cooper's narrator is more anxious to approach a party of young white girls in order to have a romantic adventure than to learn about the customs that the "wrinkled grayheaded negresses," the girls' "confidential servants," know so well.

In trying to account for the special quality of black and white relationships, Cooper prefers to dwell on the distinctive and milder form of slavery that developed under Dutch rule; he insists on the trust and respect that household servants and field slaves received and on the major role they came to play in a domestic as well as in an agricultural economy: "New York never had slaves on the system of the Southern planters. . . . All or nearly all our household servants were and still are black, leaving the department of domestic economy almost exclusively in their hands. Among the Dutch in particular, the treatment of the negro was of the kindest character, a trusty field slave often having as much to say on the subject of tillage and the crops as the man who owned the land he worked" (64). Both races, we are told, were part of the same family. Unusual ties were contracted through special practices and rites: Dutch families would give their white child a young slave who was of the same age and sex, and associate their fortunes "in the limits of their respective pursuits and positions" (65).

Descriptions of Pinkster thus offered an opportunity to discuss the issue of slavery and, in the case of Cooper, to present the system under its favorable aspects. Attention given to slave merriments, as black festivities were commonly viewed, brought more weight to the pro-slavery argument, demonstrating, as in *Satanstoe,* the excellence of white–black relations. (This, incidentally, may be one of the reasons why historians who plead for the evils of slavery are so reluctant to mention these festivals, and why this span of slave culture has not been thoroughly researched.)[9]

Interestingly, Cooper's text alludes to an often overlooked aspect of black life: the interaction between the African and the American born; the role played by the former "as ambassadors from the land of their ancestors" (65), carriers of African customs. The process of imitation, usually ascribed to blacks in their emulation of whites, is here displaced. American- and African-born slaves and free blacks are shown in their grave and serious endeavour to recapture the spirit of their forebears and to perpetuate tradition: "nothing was done in the way of caricature, but much in the way of respect and affection. . . . Though the attempt was often ludicrous, it never failed on the score of intention and gravity" (66). The reinvention of tradition through a creative process is underestimated by Cooper, who, if he grants the Africs seriousness of purpose, denies them artistic achievement.

Cooper's text, for all its sympathy toward blacks, presented as respectable human beings who rarely misbehaved (a drunken slave was a rare sight, and slave misconduct was also uncommon), is nevertheless full of the most common stereotypes: blacks portrayed as "glistening, smooth-faced, laughing, red-lipped, pearl-toothed, black-eyed" (65). Their ability to innovate and to create a new syncretic culture is not considered. The serious purpose that these playful and good-natured people lent to their Jubilee is not even investigated.

It was more important for Cooper, and to a certain extent for the author of the Ode, to demonstrate how the North had evolved milder forms of slavery and taken the lead in the abolition movement. Writing in a state that had abolished slavery in 1827, Cooper turned his back on the contemporary scene and on the upheavals tearing the nation apart; he portrayed idyllic scenes and chose the nostalgic mode to speak of slavery times. Unaware that blacks observed similar celebrations in the South, where slavery was harsher, he saw Pinkster—just as the Ode had viewed it earlier—as emanating from a rather unique situation, and as a privileged space where different processes of acculturation and unusual modes of interaction could take place, involving the various classes, ethnic and racial groups, and native and foreign cultures. The much-sung "Pinkster grounds" became a symbol of liberty, where each group could inscribe its own past and history and perform its difference while acknowledging that of others.

In Albany, the geographic situation of the festival held a particular symbolic significance for African Americans. Pinkster Hill—which was later to become the seat of the state government—provided for this popular feast a place of eminence from which to look at the world. As in many feasts, we find here the inversion pattern, where the low occupy a higher position and temporarily wield power. This status had ironic and satirical implications for the African king who held his court on high—in mock imitation or in anticipation of other rulers who choose to establish their government on prominent spots or on Capitol Hills.

Pinkster Hill was also the site of "instructive ceremonies"—executions and other punishments involving unruly slaves—which drew huge crowds for the "show." In 1794, a massive execution was staged there when blacks were accused of setting a fire that had almost burned the entire city of Albany in 1793. When the "ceremony" was cancelled, there was a violent reaction from the spectators who had traveled some distance to see the show (Mather, 587). Images and memories of reprisals and chastisement were thus constantly present, reminding blacks that the liberty they were allowed to enjoy on Pinkster grounds would always be short-lived. Conversely, memories of black insurgency were also lingering in the minds of whites.

The proximity of Pinkster to two other historical sites was even more revealing: the Hill was close to two burial grounds, a military cemetery and an old black cemetery. The military space indirectly brought to mind blacks' heroic participation in the nation's past and in its fight against its enemies—a role that was often disregarded. If white society was prompt in chastizing blacks for their ill-doings, it seldom acknowledged their honorable contribution to the nation's history, which should have entitled them to certain civic rights. The black cemetery, on the other hand, far from pleading for the integration of blacks, was a reminder of their separate status and fate within American society. It also established links, not with white America, but with Africa—with African burial rites and reverence for the dead and the ancestors, with black forefathers and foremothers, with the first to be enslaved, and with the first slaves to fight for freedom. The cemetery—where, incidentally, the African origin was often indicated on grave epitaphs—testified to the existence of a strong culture grounded on age-old institutions and beliefs, and to the slaves' capacity to establish their own cultural autonomy; on the negative side, it was the result of discrimination and segregationist practices, of which the dead and the living were equally victims. The continuity between past and future was both a source of pride and of anxiety. And, ironically, cemeteries were an appropriate choice of space: the ultimate freedom sites—since only in death could blacks hope to find the freedom they were celebrating.

These contradictory aspects account not only for the paradoxes, but also for the complexities of the site. On those grounds, American society was staging its democratic and pluralistic ideal, performing its sense of community and difference; here, all groups could apparently meet freely, interact, and freely invent their own culture in mutual respect of others. On these same grounds, African Americans, overwhelmingly present during the festival, reminded their countrymen of the limits set on their freedom outside Pinkster. In a sense, their appropriation of the site was a symbolic act, justified by long years of historical, even if invisible, presence. The pomp and high seriousness, which presided over the homage paid to their king and was seen as ludicrous and burlesque by some, was an ironic comment on a republic dedicated to freedom that could enslave authentic kings and their subjects. Pinkster ceremonies also offered a statement on a history that could allow such reversal of fate, on the indignity of those who dared to establish their power on the subjugation of others, and on the resilience of their victims whose spirit would not be crushed.

Although it is difficult to find approximations of what the lived experience of Pinkster was for blacks, who took such an important part in the organization and invention of its various rituals, one could displace all of the suggested interpretations of the texts we examined to reach totally different meanings; merriment and glee were not the expression of carelessness or of a carefree "happy" state, but evidence that body and mind refused to be destroyed by a cruel condition, and that the will to live and the idea of freedom could triumph.

Harmless amusements could turn into violent occasions and lead to insurrectionary acts. The recorders of Pinkster chose to emphasize order and harmony over disruption and conflict, and they preferred to ignore aspects that were a serious concern to some white authorities and might have led to the banning of Pinkster. We know that the potential for violent outbreaks was always there; that African feasts played an important role in the history of black insurgency and resistance, and that appearances could give the lie and hide immense tensions. The image of freedom reenacted could become intolerable for whites; the temptation to trespass the frontier set between freedom performed and actual acts of liberation was always a strong one for blacks.

As a final analysis, one must see Pinkster and other feasts through the fundamental functions they served. Typically, contemporary accounts offered descriptive elements, but never looked into the possible meanings for the celebrants themselves.

Festive events performed multiple functions. They helped the community build its self-image and the image that it wanted to present to the global society. This was done, in the case of African Americans, in constant confrontation with the "black image in the white mind." In this representation, blacks played with the paradoxical aspects of their situation, as well as with certain stereotypes—endorsing or rejecting them, constructing and deconstructing meanings and identities. They did so, at times, to placate white society; at other times, to challenge its basic assumptions and premises; or to convey certain messages and statements (as, for example, with Pinkster, on American slavery–African freedom, and on black and white–enslaved and ruler relations). Celebrations were also symbolic acts through which the group dealt with its history, its memory, and its collective imagination, and created its own value system and worldview. They called attention to the social structure and to inner diversification: status conferred by African origin and ancestry, values attached to certain qualities—physical and moral—and to forms of authority. This became all the more important as the dominant group tended to ignore these distinctions as well as to lump all blacks in a racial category defined by its absolute difference from the white race, or to use these distinctions to divide and create tensions. The white–black opposition was thus challenged.

In antebellum America, black ceremonial life constructed an image of Africa as the homeland and a land of freedom, despite all historical claims to the contrary. This central and prestigious place given to Africa is also to be found in black folklore. The figure of the king can be related to other figures, like the Flying Africans—another impersonation of the image of freedom—who could fly back to their home country like High John the Conqueror; even if Pinkster emphasized not so much the legendary power as the social status that the Africans received.

Furthermore, Pinkster and similar events, like the coronations of kings and governors, give evidence of the early development of African-American thought. Any study of black leadership should start with these early models of self-appointed leaders, and follow them up to the present political figures. Elections and festivals afforded an opportunity to give visibility, but also, most importantly, legitimacy, to the black presence in white America. These appearances in public spaces, the ability to rule over that space during the time allotted, enabled African Americans to emphasize—visually and verbally— aspects of their lives or potentialities, which would otherwise never have been considered or heeded and which could engender various degrees of admiration, amused curiosity, or fear.

Finally, celebrations provided occasions to develop expressive modes and complex art forms—visual and kinetic (costumes, colors, banners, and dance steps and movements), auditive (sounds and rhythms) and verbal (oratory, lyrics)—which combined distinctive African styles of performance with styles borrowed from other cultures, and they presented artistic and ironic statements on the existing order. In these eighteenth- and nineteenth-century celebrations, one can find the genesis of a poetics that attempted to create a syncretism of different cultures and to find a dialectical expression of their interaction. Devices and strategies were evolved: some were openly disclosed, while others were subtly hidden yet implicitly present. Feasts developed an inner code, which was best understood by the community alone, whereas another more predictable meaning was offered to outsiders. Celebrations thus display a wealth of signs whose significance is open to diverse (mis)interpretations, but which encapsulate certain essential truths for the participants. Through their dramatized performance of some ideas or concepts—those of liberty or social justice—they hold a definite political significance.

Celebrations, because of the complexities of their features and their functions, should be considered important sources for historians and scholars. Their careful analysis may highlight crucial aspects of society: acculturation processes (cross-cultural exchanges as well as the invention of distinctive cultural patterns), race relations and power dynamics, and the role of ideas and representations, of "mentalities" but also of "structure of feeling."[10] African-American festive rituals should not be seen as marginal occurrences, parentheses inserted in the flow of history, but as major events that can offer determinant indices for the study of society and that fully belong to its creative, critical culture. Not only did they bear upon certain issues, but they could become crucial agents of change. Shaped as they were by some fundamental beliefs, convictions, or motivations, they, in turn, could transform these in fundamental ways. They challenged society by celebrating its potential more than its faked realizations, its disconcerting failures and flaws more than its imperfect achievements; they staked out legitimate claims, thus forcing the collective imagination to invent and perform alternative forms and to experiment with new ideas of freedom and democracy.

Notes

1. *A Pinkster Ode for the Year 1803, Most Respectfully Dedicated to Carolus Africanus, Rex . . . by His Majesty's Obedient Servant, Absalom Aimwell, Esq.* (Albany: Printed Solely for the Purchasers and Others, 1803).

2. Stiles, 1869; Furman, 1874; Watson, 1846; Eights, 1867; Munsell, 1867; De Voe, 1862; Earle, 1896; Cooper, 1845.

3. The ban on Pinkster might have been a reaction of the upwardly mobile population against a popular form of entertainment, and might have resulted from the degradation which followed its increased commercialization.

4. New York prided itself on having a merrier spirit than New England, and when Pinkster and the "Negro elections" were compared, the latter were seen as more staid and serious.

5. Albany, in 1790, had the largest black population of the region: 3,929 slaves, 170 free blacks. Although the percentage of blacks was higher in New York city and county, there were there only 2,369 slaves and 1,101 free blacks out of a total of 33,131 inhabitants. Evarts B. Greene and Virginia D. Harrington, *American Population before the Federal Census of 1790* (1932; repr., Gloucester, Mass.: Peter Smith, 1966), 105.

6. Melvin Wade, "Shining in Borrowed Plumage. Affirmation of Community in Coronation Festivals of New England: 1750–1850," *Western Folklore* 40 (3) (1981), 211–31.

7. Mostly in the *Freedom's Journal*. The debate on the appropriateness of certain celebrations was carried on through the first half of the nineteenth century.

8. Yet Eights again tells us that each class or group played a different role each day: the upper class on the third; the humbler classes on the fourth and fifth; the poorer lingering on the last day to receive unpurchased material; on the second day, "the crowd was far more circumspect . . . and orderly in their demeanor, as all the more respectable members of the community were there to witness any disreputable act and ever afterward be sure to reward their transgressors with their most severe indignation and contempt" (Eights, 325).

9. Conversely, the study of black celebrations could be used to discredit the abolitionist movement. When the Virginian William B. Smith described a beer dance in his native state with Negroes "clapping juber" to the music of a priestlike banjo man, he did so to demonstrate that "Virginia slaves were the happiest of the human race", declaring that "if a northern abolitionist, with his pocket filled

with inflammatory documents and resolutions, could have witnessed such a
scene in Virginia, he would, in my opinion, have consigned them to the flames."
Smith's account of the "wild fantastic dance," with its "ludicrous twists, wry jerks
and flexible contorsions of the body and limbs," displays the usual mixture of
curiosity and condescension, and the same misunderstanding of black festive
events as is to be found in whites'—native or foreigner—reports. *Farmer's Register* (Shellbanks, Va.), 6 (April 1838), 58–59.

10. This concept was developed by Raymond Williams in *The Long Revolution* (New
York: Columbia University Press, 1961).

References

Cooper, James Fenimore. *Satanstoe*. New York: Burgess, Stringer, 1845.

De Voe, Thomas F. *The Market Book: A History of the Public Markets of the City of New York*, Vol. 1. New York: B. Franklin, 1862.

Earle, Alice Morse. *Colonial Days in Old New York*. New York: Scribner's, 1896.

Eights, James. "Pinkster Festivals in Albany Sixty Years Ago." In *Collections on the History of Albany*, comp. Joel Munsell, Vol. 2 (1867), 323–27.

Furman, Gabriel. *Antiquities of Long Island, New York*. New York: J. W. Bouton, 1874.

Kinser, Samuel. *Mardi Gras at New Orleans and Mobile*. Chicago: University of Chicago Press, 1990.

Pleat, Geraldine R. and Underwood, Agnes. "Pinkster Ode: Albany 1803." *New York Folklore Quarterly* 8 (1952), 31–45.

Stiles, Henry R. *A History of the City of Brooklyn*. Brooklyn: City of Brooklyn, 1869.

Stuckey, Stirling. *Slave Culture: Nationalist Theory and the Foundation of Black America*. New York: Oxford University Press, 1987.

Watson, John F. *Annals of Philadelphia and Pennsylvania. In the Olden Time. Being a Collection of Memoirs, Anecdotes, and Incidents of the City and its Inhabitants*. Philadelphia: J. M. Stoddart, 1846.

Williams, Raymond. *The Long Revolution*. New York: Columbia University Press, 1961.

Williams Myers, A. J. "Pinkster Carnival: Africanisms in the Hudson River Valley." *Afro-Americans in New York Life and History* 9 (January 1985), 7–18.

3

Public Rituals and the Cultural Making of the New York African-American Community

Alessandra Lorini

If celebrations and their rituals are seen through the lens of a cultural anthropologist, they appear as the "stories people tell about themselves" (Clifford Geertz) or the "proper, ideal pattern of social life" (John Skorupski).[1] These insights, together with the concepts of "invention of tradition" (Eric Hobsbawm) and "selection of traditions" (Raymond Williams),[2] can be fruitfully applied to the reading of the few sources available on the community life of blacks in nineteenth-century New York, and to the interpretation of the largely unexplored records of public celebrations in that city.

This essay looks at race as a historical product and an ideological construction through the study of festivals and celebrations among black New Yorkers in the nineteenth and early twentieth centuries. It will be argued that acts of invention and reinvention of selected traditions, far from being exclusive products of hegemonic groups, are part of the broader process of cultural circularity between "high" and "low" cultures.[3]

In November 1825, New York witnessed the grand celebration for the inauguration of the Erie Canal conceived, in the words of the Committee of the Corporation and of the Merchants and Citizens of the City of New York, as "a proud monument of the intelligence and powers of a free people." Trade societies, mechanics, artists, manufacturers, merchants, and all professions and citizens were represented in the land procession, made of seven thousand artisans, journeymen, and apprentices, that passed through the commercial area of lower Manhattan and met at the Battery with the naval parade. This celebration of "the industry and enterprise of our citizens" that had subdued "the wilderness of the West" was also meant to

29

symbolize the victory of civilization over nature: "The land where so lately the wild beast prowled, and the wild man roamed, is occupied by peaceful husbandmen, and now resounds with the industrious hum of man in the industrious pursuits of civilized life." Living evidence were "the aborigines from Lake Erie, with their canoes," who participated in the aquatic parade. The celebration of a work that "will serve to consolidate the Union of the states, and to preserve inviolate our republican institutions . . . national and individual prosperity."[4] was exclusively a male business, except for the participation of a special boat of the governor's wife and a few other ladies who were there exclusively as the women of important men. No real woman appeared in the four divisions of trades, arts, and others, which bore on their banners, however, symbolic female figures: Wisdom, Minerva, Plentifulness, and so on.[5] The city's free blacks did not participate in the parade as barbers, coachmen, or the representatives of any other job they were doing at that time; but in official reports, mention is made of the presence of a few blacks with the Saddlers and Harness Makers: "a white charger, fully caparisoned, led by two black grooms in rich Moorish dress"; there were also a few blacks with the Firemen Eagle Company no. 13, whose engine was mounted on a stage drawn by "four milk white steeds elegantly caparisoned, and led by four Africans dressed in rich Moorish costume."[6] What does this representation mean?

In a celebration of the new republic, whose national unity was based on the work of independent men, no reference was made to the existence of slavery; during the highly structured ceremonial, no gesture or word served as a reminder of the constitutional compromise, and no banner of the trade societies included any symbol of the moral evil of the "peculiar institution" of the South that contributed to the wealth of the merchants in the North, who, together with other social components, celebrated the Erie Canal as a symbol of a united and homogeneous new republic. Those few exotic black servants were not meant to represent their condition; as in a Renaissance court festival, they were mere ornamental figures. In the selective process of inventing tradition, the relatively homogeneous population and the still solid artisan system of New York tacitly accepted the tradition of slavery in the South, and made invisible the presence of an existing black community that, in Manhattan in 1825, counted around fifteen thousand people.[7]

In 1825, more than one-fifth of Manhattan blacks lived in the Sixth Ward, which spread from the area of the Five Points—the intersection of Cross, Anthony, Little Water, Orange, and Mulberry streets—north and west to the Hudson river.[8] What characterized New York blacks as a community was the

existence in their neighborhoods of important organizations such as the Ab-
yssinian Baptist Church, the St. Philip's Protestant Episcopal Church, the Bethel
African Methodist Episcopal Church, the African Society for Mutual Relief, the
African Free School, and the African Grove.[9]

In 1827, there began to circulate in this community the *Freedom's Journal*,
the first African-American paper in the country, run by black ministers, teachers, and a few other professionals, which was devoted to "the dissemination
of useful knowledge"; to moral and religious improvement; to the opposition
to the colonization schemes, discussed at that time, which advocated the
deportation of all free blacks to Africa; and to the defeat of any form of
"misrepresentation of the race."[10] The paper appeared in the year in which
slavery was officially abolished in New York State, an event that the black
community heralded with two separate celebrations, on July 4 and July 5. The
intense debate, in the *Freedom's Journal*, about how to celebrate this event
reveals the existence of cultural conflicts within the African-American community over the creation and use of public ceremonial space.

On June 22, 1827, the African-American paper published a series of articles, letters, and statements, generally anonymous, on the "propriety" of
celebrating Emancipation day with a parade in the public space. Leaders of
the African-American community who thought of themselves as "guardians
for the public welfare" of their community "brethren," felt that it was their
"imperious duty" to enter their "protest against all public procession." The
argument of the opposition was mainly grounded on a fear that the unavoidable outcome of a public parade would be some riotous behavior seriously
damaging the image of the entire African-American community. Another argument held that processions were of no benefit to African-Americans: "do
they make us richer, or better? Have they not rather a tendency to injure us,
by exciting prejudice, and making the public believe we care for nothing so
much as show?" Although the fear of being assaulted by members of the
white lower classes was indeed rather appropriate—as the riot of 1834 demonstrated—it was not the most important aspect of this debate.

The editors of the paper had informed their readers that on the occasion
of the State Emancipation there were going to be two celebrations: "one
party will celebrate the Fourth of July, without any public procession, and the
other, the Fifth, with a grand Procession, Oration and Public dinner." One
editor was pleased to learn that "most of the Societies of colour have refused
to join in the contemplated procession," and strongly hoped that "those who
resolved upon it, will calmly re-consider the subject . . . and that a more

matured examination of it ... will prevail with them, to give over the idea of parading the streets on the occasion, and to join with their brethren in celebrating the proper day in a proper manner."[11] Thus, the real issue seems to be what was considered at that time to be the proper public behavior for African Americans.

The New York press did not mention the parade of July 5, in which a large part of the black community participated. But in the memoir of that day composed years later by black physician James McCune Smith, one can find a detailed description of that event which captures the spirit of involvement of the black community:

A magnificent, inspiring, international pageant ... full-voiced shouting for joy, and marching through the crowded street ... First of all Grand marshal of the day was Samuel Hardenburgh, a splendid-looking black man, in cocked hat and drawn swords, mounted on a milk-white steed; then his aids on horseback ... then the orator of the day ... then in due order, splendidly dressed in scarfs of silk with gold-edgings, and with colored bands of music, and their banner appropriately lettered and painted, followed: The New York Society for Mutual Relief, the Wilberforce Benevolent Society; then the people of five or six abreast, from grown men to small boys. The side walks were crowded with the wives, daughters, sisters, and mothers of the celebrants ...[12]

In a sense, this parade was an act of inventing tradition for a separate republic whose values, however, reflected those celebrated in the Erie Canal parade: the entrance of the public space was a male prerogative, a statement of power embodied in the figure of the marshal of the day on a white steed, a status reversal of the exotic grooms of the 1825 parade. It was a provocative statement of racial pride, which symbolically reversed the image of the black exotic grooms of the Erie Canal parade, and therefore cannot be read simply as an imitation of the white men's parade.

The debate over the propriety of organizing parades for the celebration of the anniversary of the State Emancipation and other events continued for two more years in the pages of the Freedom's Journal, and then passed on to those of the Colored American. In 1828, the Freedom's Journal stressed the "orderly manner" of the parade in Manhattan, led on July 5 by the same marshal of the day; but a few days later, the paper heavily criticized a public parade of African Americans in Brooklyn as "foolish exhibitions of ourselves." The writer had heard of the "insolence of certain coloured females," and of "debasing excesses" that had occurred during the event; no mention was

made of what had really happened, and one was left to believe that, according to the writer, "nothing is more disgusting to the eyes of a reflecting man of
colour than one of these *grand processions,* followed by the lower orders of
society," which reminded him of "a shabby representation of Hannibal and his
hardy legions." The writer also complained of "many a hard day's earnings
being expanded to prepare and purchase the cast off garments of some field
officer, or the sash and horse trappings of some dragoon serjeant," to dress
up as general, marshals, and admirals on these occasions and be "complete
and appropriate laughing stocks for thousands of our citizens, and to the
more considerate of our brethren, objects of compassion and shame."[13] The
brethren of Brooklyn defended themselves against what they considered a
"misrepresentation" of the "rational" object of their parade, and the accusa-
tion of "excesses" that they considered "unavoidable among a vast con-
course of people."[14]

This concern for public behavior reflects the need among educated Afri-.
can Americans to defeat the racist stereotype of the notorious unruly behavior of black people, in which the guilt of one single individual of their race was
indiscriminately extended to all blacks. Accordingly, the value of *respectability,*
as one of those fundamental values of the new republic that made work and
self-improvement the pillars of the American society, became a paradigm
with which one's sense of worthiness was defined and measured. Public behavior became then a crucial issue within the African-American community in
which the papers broadly circulated, creating a dichotomy between the "high"
and the "low," between those who gave priority to knowledge and self-improvement and those who indulged in expensive and immoral pastimes such
as the theater, considered by many as the first step down the path of vice.[15]

During the first part of the nineteenth century, educated black New Yorkers sought in vain to be rid of prejudice that attributed the same negative
characteristics to all members of their race. Racial stereotyping accompanied
rapid urbanization, and the city—and its poorest residents—became the symbol of all evils. In the eyes of urban reformers and city observers who wrote
hundreds of reports on the Five Points—the first slum in America where
most blacks and Irish immigrants lived—the visibility of the poor seemed to
have made obsolete the republican value of economic independence. The
language of these reports, in which characters living in that area are presented to a middle-class public as though they were grotesque caricatures of
the horrors of urban degradation, reveals a complex interaction between the
observers' anxiety to explain the unknown sides of city life and the preexis-

tent racial and ethnic stereotypes. Impressionistic descriptions of the stench of the sewage and the strange food, the filth, the dark, the pigs and rats that decorated the "dens" of the poor, and the vivid scenes of sexual promiscuity, gambling, and other forms of vice and crime were obsessively repeated in the reports of contemporary observers who toured the Five Points, accompanied by policemen.[16]

The role played by the established institutions in black neighborhoods since the early nineteenth century passed almost unnoticed in the night tours of most American contemporary observers, whose depictions of blacks living at the Five Points represents the central paradox of nineteenth-century American thought: the coexistence of the ideology of individualism, according to which every person is judged for individual accomplishments, and the strong belief that individual characteristics as predetermined by the race and ethnic group to which that person belongs. In this light, the appeal of educated black New Yorkers to respectability and morality, based on a firm condemnation of any public misbehavior, can be better understood as an attempt to establish a tradition for their community whose first step was the abolition of slavery as the fulfillment of the original republican values of the American Revolution.

Throughout the first half of the nineteenth century, black New Yorkers, with the financial help of white abolitionists, had created many associations for the "mental and moral uplifting" of their race and for improving the "useful knowledge" of members whose literacy was granted by the extensive programs of the free schools. In the listing of hundreds of meetings in the African-American press, one can locate the value given to knowledge as racial pride and the key to economic improvement and political citizenship in the country. At the same time, the issue of whether to celebrate national holidays such as the Fourth of July, given the existence of slavery in America, is often debated in these newspapers.

In the North, the sharp words of black abolitionist Frederick Douglass expressed the prevalent feelings among African Americans for the Fourth of July:

What, to the American slave, is your 4th of July? I answer: a day that reveals to him, more than all other days in the year, the gross injustice and cruelty to which he is the constant victim. To him, your celebration is a sham; your boasted liberty, an unholy license; your national greatness, swelling vanity; your sounds of rejoicing are empty and heartless; your denunciation of tyrants, brass fronted impudence; your shouts of liberty and equality, hollow mockery; your prayers and hymns, your sermons and thanksgivings with all

your religious parade and solemnity are, to him, mere bombast, fraud, decep-
tion, impiety, and hypocrisy—a thin veil to cover up crimes which would
disgrace a nation of savages.[17]

Those black New Yorkers who thought that the Fourth of July was mainly
a noisome affair of white crowds celebrated, instead, August 1, the anniversary of the West Indian Emancipation of 1834. August 1, 1839, for example,
was celebrated "not as the anniversary of American Independence is celebrated, with rioting and dissipation, and scenes which make man, originally
created 'but a little lower than the angels' to become lower than the demons." There was no firing of cannons, no drinking of rum, no fighting or
gambling, and "no horrid oaths at which the fiends themselves, would tremble
to listen," for the day was celebrated "with prayer and thanksgiving," the editors of *Colored American* proudly stated. In New York, there were morning
prayer meetings and an evening concert of sacred music at the Presbyterian
church, and an evening meeting at the Political Association, in which several
addresses and an ode were delivered.[18] This was the pattern of most August
1 celebrations among northern black communities until the 1850s, although
there was no common agreement on the significance of that day. In West
Indian emancipation, the masters had received payment as compensation for
their loss of slaves.[19]

Apparently, different attitudes toward what and how to celebrate corresponded to different strategies for emancipation and the use of freedom
among northern African-American communities. The emphasis given to *respectability* seemed to imply an ambivalent need of blacks to be recognized as
worthy of freedom by whites, while the emphasis on *confrontation and struggle*
against racism, in both its explicit and subtle forms, expressed a denial of any
deferential attitudes toward authorities and a notion of freedom as exclusively the result of self-conquest. This cultural conflict within the New York
black community would persist well after the Civil War and lead to different
strategies for political, economic, and social achievements.

Although the debate over "rational amusements" for the moral uplifting of
the lower classes strictly paralleled the one among white urban reformers in
the same period, the debate within the African-American community was
more related to the emergence and consolidation of a black middle-class
style based on the creation of an acceptable public image.

In the proliferation of benefit societies, literary associations, and other
cultural organizations whose meetings were regularly announced in the Afri-

can-American press, Masonic lodges played a significant role in the definition and practice of black middle-class respectability and the use of public ceremonial space. Based on the strong internal cohesion of their members, and secret rituals that only apparently can be seen in conflict with the use of a public ceremonial space, African-American Masonic lodges of New York and Brooklyn usually organized turn-outs on festive occasions, with processions and the display of their emblems.

Why did Freemasonry appeal to African Americans? Its secrecy and its rituals seemed to respond to their need to create a separate republic based on the respectability and social achievement of their worthy members. To be admitted to a lodge, a black man needed to be nominated or recommended by a member and to show some measure of economic success and popularity in the community, all of which were seen as evidence of good moral character.[20] In a way, it provided the experience of belonging to a select group of people. Hence the pride of entering the public ceremonial space in full regalia and with emblems whose meanings were known, however, only to their bearers. This is clear evidence of a distinctive class style within the African-American community, whose ostentatious display, however, met the criticism of some black abolitionists. Frederick Douglass, for example, saw the white interest in encouraging the involvement of blacks in these organizations. In fact, involvement in fraternal activities drained energy from civil rights activities that were threatening to the white status quo. "We are imitating the inferior qualities and examples of white men, and neglecting superior ones," Douglass remarked, pointing to "the weak and glittering follies of oddfellowship and freemasonry."[21]

Both Gunnar Myrdal and Franklin Frazier seem to agree that the black bourgeoisie aspired to "imitate" the white bourgeoisie.[22] But how much was this a conscious imitation and how much was, instead, the result of what W.E.B. Du Bois would call the "two-ness" of African Americans, namely, the conflict of being both black and American? One could look at blacks' entrance into the public ceremonial space as an attempt to overcome this conflict by placing African-American traditions within American society. Accordingly, African-American parades could be read, together with other parades in the city space throughout the nineteenth and early twentieth centuries, as texts of inventing and reinventing traditions. The question is not whether black Americans adopted white middle-class values in shaping their separate republic, but how the existing racial attitudes in the general society, which excluded from them the benefits of full American citizenship, influenced the

cultural responses that black Americans gave in facing the stereotypes attributed to their race. In this perspective, the creation of a public ceremonial
space can be seen as the creation of an African-American public image based
on respectability as a counterpoint to the image of blacks that emerged in
nineteenth-century reports on the dark sides of city life.

In examining the New York African-American press from the 1870s to the
early 1900s, one is struck by the mushrooming of social activities whose goals
were more secular than those in the period preceding the Civil War. What
appears is an ongoing process of cultural remaking of the New York African-American community as a separate republic—but one in which economic and political goals are redefined within the changes of American
society generally.[23]

In the first half of the 1880s, the *New York Globe* listed an astonishing
number of announcements of Masonic lodge celebrations. From this source,
one learns about the extraordinary capacity of Masonic parades to attract
crowds with their ostentatious display of exotic masquerades. For example,
in 1884 the paper described a masquerade reception and two grand parades
held by the Hamilton Lodge, which apparently was the most conspicuous in
its grandiosity and exoticism. In fact, when the carriages arrived at Wendell's
Hall, "bearing with them masked visages that excited the admiration and
wonderment of the onlookers at the door for their diversified character, no
two being alike," it was clear that it was going to be "one of the best masked
balls ever given in this city." And when the procession took place, "it brought
to mind the recent *Mardi Gras* festival at New Orleans.[24] But the year after
the festival overshadowed "any and all attempts in this particular direction
ever made by any organized body among us," the *Globe* commented. The
presence of eighteen hundred people in the ball room reminded the writer
"of some Eastern tale or almost forgotten dream of the Arabian Nights":
they wore silks and satin, and jewels ornamented the costumes of the "Indians, counts, cavaliers, judges, priests, devils, queens, witches" who mingled
"in graceful confusion" with friars, goblins, cowboys, Quakers, and angels.[25]

These carnivalesque scenes, far from providing examples of "saturnalia,"
symbolized the prestige and high social status of the participants. When they
were placed within the universe of a segregated group, scenes of a "world
turned upside-down" and of status reversal, which these masked balls seemed
to portray, became a symbolic appropriation of themes of Western culture
and folklore. At the same time, the carnivalesque themes of "plentifulness
and excess" ruling these festivals were meant to celebrate the recent gain in

material wealth by a small but growing portion of the black population, those who could feel a part of the American myth of the "self-made man."

It is quite interesting that in 1883, a few days before the Hamilton Lodge festival, there had been a meeting of the Bethel Literary and Historical Society, held at the Bethel Church, to discuss the following subject: "Resolved, We Need Wealth More Than We Do Education." According to the *Globe,* both sides of the subject were so well argued that the president concluded that wealth and education "went hand in hand" and that "our people should strive to acquire both."[26] From such thin evidence it is possible to imagine within the New York black community the existence of different positions concerning the emphasis given to economic and educational improvement, or the priority of the acquisition of material wealth in spite of the lack of civil rights that educated black New Yorkers most cherished. At the turn of the century, these issues became extremely complicated because of the cultural fracture that resulted from the arrival of European immigrants and southern blacks in the midst of the process of remaking the New York African-American community.

At the turn of the century, the more than sixty thousand blacks living in the New York area were most heavily concentrated in Manhattan. Around five thousand of them were foreign-born and had come from the British West Indies and the Caribbean islands. Although they were a small proportion of the general population, there were more foreign-born blacks in New York than in any other American city.[27] By 1900, for the first time in New York history, more than one-half of the black population was born outside the state.[28] Almost all of the southern blacks who had migrated to New York in the early 1900s had settled in the already densely populated area of the Tenderloin district—from west of the twenties to the low forties—and San Juan Hill—in the west sixties. In 1910, of the more than ninety thousand blacks in the metropolis, the majority was southern-born.[29]

In the 1890s, together with the new waves of immigration from southern and central Europe, and the slow but steady beginning of black migration from the South, came the new theories, to whose establishment American social scientists contributed—theories that shared the common premise of an assumed racial inferiority of blacks and new immigrants. Race became a broad idea with no scientific evidence to support its ideological construction, in which human qualities were graded according to selected standards of superiority and inferiority. After the Spanish war in Progressive America, cultural nativism and imperialism, the offsprings of social Darwinism, coexisted with the ideal of equality of opportunities. At the same time, the fears of urban degradation expressed by Progressive reformers reestablished earlier stereotypes of city evils based on the behavior and life-style of the new immigrants. The bulk of documents left by New York reformers who worked in city slums offers a variety of attitudes and perceptions of these middle-class observers. In contrast to the earlier generation of reformers who visited the Five Points, Progressive observers read urban poverty by using the conceptual framework that the American social sciences had made available.

At the beginning of the twentieth century, the school of cultural relativism of anthropologist Franz Boas had already influenced many Progressive reformers who, in 1905, collaborated to a special issue of *Charities* dedicated to blacks in American cities. According to Boas, studies of traits on African culture as they were observed in aboriginal homes showed that there was nothing to prove that "licentiousness, shiftless laziness, lack of initiative, are fundamental characteristics of the race." He argued that these qualities were the result of social conditions rather than of hereditary traits. In fact, the tearing away from the African soil and the consequent loss of the traditional life-style were replaced by the dependency of slavery and followed by a period of disorganization and a severe economic struggle.[30]

In taking an opposite view, John R. Commons—another extremely influential Progressive social scientist actively involved in many state and government commissions on labor issues—wrote that "race differences are established in the very blood and physical constitution. They are the most difficult to eradicate, and they yield only to the slow processes of the centuries."[31]

This cultural tension between heredity and environment permeated the "Americanization Movement" that Progressive reformers organized in the late nineteenth century. One of the most important ideological aspects of Americanization was the cultural attempt to reinvent those traditions of the early republic that culminated in the great celebration of the opening of the Erie Canal in 1825. More than eighty years later, Progressive reformers in the city reinterpreted those traditions and staged a gigantic celebration, the Hudson-Fulton Festival of 1909, in which the history of the American republic was taught to and performed by the new immigrants, white and black alike. What kind of public ceremonial space was designed by this celebration? How did class, race, and gender play into it? What did its parades say, and who did they represent?

The Hudson-Fulton Festival's main goal was "to promote the assimilation of our adopted population." The celebration, accordingly, had to be "educational, not commercial"; "everything should be as educative as possible and . . . the greatest number of people possible should freely see the public spectacles."[32]

Progressive New York seemed to be very aware of the value of traditions. The festival was conceived, in fact, as a reading of the past of the American republic in order to establish a linear form of progress in the development of American civilization:

The power of tradition has been one of the most fundamental and conservative forces of all people of all times . . . a people naturally tends to follow the impulses of the past and to adhere to tradition unless turned therefrom by other influences. Therefore the ingrained history of a nation which in a broad sense we call tradition, serves as a balance wheel, tending to restrain sudden and spasmodic departures from the normal mode of progress. Historical culture thus materially promotes the welfare of the Commonwealth.[33]

This one-million-dollar celebration in commemoration of the discovery of the Hudson River by Henry Hudson in 1609 and the inauguration of steam navigation on that river by Robert Fulton in 1807 was conceived as "a rational festival of patriotic sentiment." The traditions to pass to immigrants were selectively chosen and represented in pageants to be intellectually convincing and emotionally compelling. Pageantry, as a form of representation of American traditions, was largely used within the "Sane and Safe Fourth of July" movement, which the American Playground Association of America saw as an attempt to reform what in the eyes of many Progressives had become "the Barbarous Fourth," namely, a boisterous holiday of merrymaking and no patriotic meaning. Many reformers researched historical records of the early republic and proposed to revive the "glorious Independence Day"; it was conceived as a reinvention of an early tradition that combined recreation, patriotism, and the renewal of civic and community pride, and urged the new immigrants to participate in the festival and place their own heritage within the context of American values.[34] The magnificent Hudson-Fulton Festival was a fruit of this spirit.

What kind of public ceremonial space was designed by the great parades that, from September 25 to October 9, 1909, filled Manhattan and the other boroughs? How did representation work in this festival? What was the role played by blacks this time, compared to their decorative-exotic role in the Erie Canal celebration? Can this festival and its parades be read as a text of ideological continuity that the organizers wanted to establish between the values of nationalism in the early republic and those related to the Americanization of immigrants in the early twentieth century?

The festival opened with a naval parade, and continued with a historical parade, aquatic sports, a children's festival, and a carnival parade.[35] Manhattan, Brooklyn, the Bronx, and the Hudson Valley were all invested with these events, which, according to the local press, attracted between two and three million people.

The organization of the parades started as early as 1905. The goal of the historical parade was to illustrate, by moving tableaux, "memorable scenes in the history of the City and the State for public education and entertainment." This educational aim was connected to the other aim of uniting in the procession "the representatives of as many as possible of the nationalities composing the cosmopolitan population of the State, so as to make them feel that the heritage of the State's history belonged to them as well as to those more distinctively American."[36] In the list of more than twenty nationalities represented in the marching bodies, there were seventy "real Iroquois Indians . . . who were secured from the Indian reservations," who took the characters of the floats representing the Indian period with their exotic costumes and ceremonial dances. "Citizens of African . . . descent" were enlisted among the twenty nationalities of immigrant groups. The historical floats were presented as a sequence of fifty-four scenes that illustrated the progress of the state from the Indian period to the present time.[37]

The carnival parade did not mean merrymaking; it was designed to teach the sense of universality of poetry, myth, legend, and allegory by offering a vision of human nature in which the traditions of the Enlightenment and Romanticism were combined. All of these myths and legends were overwhelmingly northern European.[38] In fact, the commission had asked the help of German societies to reproduce the pageantry of their fatherland. There were 12,500 participants in the parade of northern European folklore, which was meant to teach American civilization to immigrants from southern and central Europe and to blacks from the southern states.

The children's festival was the most telling of all celebrations. It would have been inconceivable in 1825, when children as "apprentices" represented their arts and crafts in the Erie Canal parade. The thousands of children participating in the Hudson-Fulton Festival, who came from the schools of the Lower East Side, from Sunday schools, missions, and settlements, were given roles in the play as "the background of American history, with emphasis on prominent personalities and events."[39] The effort was extraordinary and required a high level of preparation and mobilization; well in advance of the event, many pastors of churches, superintendents of Sunday schools, playground teachers, presidents of clubs, societies, and settlements, and others were contacted and asked to cooperate in training the children for participation in the pageants.

The spectacle was extraordinary. More than 500,000 children were involved in the festival in greater New York. Children were organized into forty divisions and dispersed throughout the city's parks and avenues. All did the same exercises, sang the same songs, gave the same salutes, declared the same allegiance to the flag, and produced their dance tableaux, which told the story of different periods in New York history since Henry Hudson had sailed up the river. The same scheme of festival was followed throughout the city; parades formed at public schoolhouses, churches, clubrooms, and private schools.[40] Among the many tableaux were those performed at Fort Green Park by black children from the Lincoln Settlement: "Negro celebration," "Negro Sailor Girls drill," and "Negro cadets drill."[41] And the colored girls from the Abyssinian Baptist Church successfully performed a Japanese dance in Fifth Avenue that "brought such a round of cheers that it was repeated."[42]

The New York African-American press extensively reported on the Hudson-Fulton celebrations. The New York Age, the leading African-American paper, fully described the historical parade, the floats, and the other phenomena of the great festival of Americanization and democracy. According to the Age, nearly three hundred Negro citizens took part in the historical parade, preceded by the New Amsterdam band. Nevertheless, on the same front page of the paper, near favorable comments about the magnificent programs of the festival, one can read an article on racial discrimination that depicts the dark side of the Progressive era, when blacks in the South were lynched and heavily discriminated against in other parts of the country where Jim Crow laws apparently did not exist.[43] Ironically, a few days later, the headlines of the Age had to report open discrimination toward Negro sailors, who were not allowed to participate in the big naval parade and assigned, instead, to duty in battleships. It was reported that Filipino sailors paraded with the other sailors, and that other instances of discrimination toward Negro sailors apparently occurred whenever there was a parade.[44] According to the Age, this exclusion aroused a storm of criticism from African-American residents in greater New York as well as a more general condemnation.

How can one interpret the exclusion of black sailors from the public ceremonial space during a festival that was meant to celebrate the progress of

American civilization as the unity of all ethnic groups? What did the presence of black participants in the festival represent? It may be enlightening to compare how Indians, African Americans, and women were represented in the 1909 festival of American democracy with their representations in the Erie Canal celebration of 1825.

The history of American Indians was allotted a great space in the historical parade; seventy "real" Indians from the reservations were there to represent a glorious past that concealed their inglorious present and their hopeless future of permanent confinement on reservations. By contrast the Indians in the Erie Canal celebration were represented as proud "savages" and dangerous enemies not completely tamed but with no history to tell; Indians in the Hudson-Fulton Festival were there to tell their legends, myths, and history, for they were given only a past: they were perceived as a "dying race" whose culture enchanted early twentieth-century anthropologists. In contrast to the decorative and symbolic role given to women in the Erie Canal celebration, women in the 1909 festival were fully present on the floats of the historical and carnival parades. Dressed in the colorful costumes of their immigrant mothers, young white women represented themselves by making an entrance in the public space that acknowledged their relevant presence in the work spaces of factories and department stores. Middle-class women were among the organizers of the festival, and they had already given life to those many committees, clubs, Sunday schools, settlements, and other groups that populated the lively panorama of Progressive-era New York. There were still female symbols in the parades, just as there were in the Erie Canal celebration; but now, according to early twentieth-century romantic views, these symbols were intended to represent the power of myth in history. Whereas there were only few blacks dressed up as exotic servants in the Erie Canal celebration, the three hundred African-American participants in the Hudson-Fulton Festival were there to represent one immigrant group among many others; black children, like all the other immigrant children, skillfully performed their tableaux and drills. In the ideal society designed by the festival, all were equally given the right to fully enjoy American citizenship; but the exclusion of black sailors from the aquatic parade brought all of the participants back to the ugly reality of racial discrimination in the Progressive era, an age in which the ideology of progress could hold together humanitarianism and social engineering, equalitarianism and racist philosophies.

Notes

1. See Clifford Geertz, *The Interpretation of Culture* (New York: Basic Books, 1973); and John Skorupski, *Symbol and Theory: A Philosophical Study of Theories of Religion in Social Anthropology* (Cambridge: Cambridge University Press, 1976).

2. "'Inventing tradition' is taken to mean a set of practices, normally governed by overtly or tacitly accepted rules and of a ritual of symbolic nature, which seek to inculcate certain values and norms of behaviour, which automatically implies continuities with the past." Eric Hobsbawm, "Inventing Traditions," in *The Invention of Tradition,* ed. Eric Hobsbawm and Terence Ranger (Cambridge: Cambridge University Press, 1983), 1. According to Raymond Williams, a selective tradition is "an intentionally selective version of a shaping past and a pre-shaped present, which is then powerfully operative in the process of cultural definition and identification. . . . What it offers in practice is a sense of *predisposed continuity.*" Raymond Williams, *Marxism and Literature* (New York: Oxford University Press, 1977), 115–16.

3. Mikhail Bakhtin was able to study popular culture in pre-industrial Europe by employing as his main source Rabelais's masterpiece of French literature, *Gargantua and Pantagruel.* This approach is implicit in Carlo Ginzburg's suggestion to consider popular culture in light of an indissoluble relationship between folkloric and official culture, that is, in terms of circularity and exchange. See Mikhail Bakhtin, *Rabelais and His World* (Cambridge: M.I.T. Press, 1968) and Carlo Ginzburg's introduction to Peter Burke, *Cultura popolare nell'Europa moderna* (Italian trans., Milano: Mondadori, 1980), vii.

4. Cadwallader D. Colden, *Memoir Prepared at the Request of the Committee of the Common Council of the City of New York and Presented to the Mayor of the City at the Celebration of the New York Canals* (New York: Corporation of New York, 1825), 129, 153, 155, 173, and 174.

5. For an interpretation of simultaneous real exclusion and symbolic representations of women in parades, see Mary Ryan, "The American Parade: Representations of the Nineteenth-Century Social Order," in *The New Cultural History,* ed. Lynn Hunt (Berkeley: University of California Press, 1989).

6. Colden, *Memoir,* 231 and 241; and the *New York Evening Post,* Nov. 5, 1825.

7. In 1820, there were 13,100 blacks in Manhattan and 1,761 in Brooklyn; in 1830, 16,082 and 2,007, respectively; in 1840, 18,595 and 2,846, respectively; in 1850, 16,131 and 4,065, respectively; in 1860, 14,927 and 4,999, respectively; in 1870, 15,755 and 5,653, respectively; in 1880, 22,496 and 9,153, respectively; in 1890, 26,330 and 11,307, respectively; in 1900, 42,299 and 18,367, respectively; and in 1910, 69,700 and 22,702, respectively. See George E. Haynes, *The Negro at Work in New York City: A Study in Economic Progress* (New York: Longmans, Green and Co., 1912), 47. In the 1820s and 1830s, this population was composed mainly of free blacks, the descendants of manumitted slaves, and fugitive slaves. Banned from the city trades, black men and women were domestic servants, waiters and waitresses, cooks, barbers, and caterers.

8. In 1820, one-half of the blacks lived in the Fifth, Sixth, and Seventh wards, and

many others lived in the First, Third and Ninth wards. See W. E. B. Du Bois, "Some Notes on the Negroes in New York City," in *Pamphlets and Leaflets by W. E. B. Du Bois*, ed. Herbert Aptheker (New York: KTO Press, 1986).

9. Located on Mercer Street, the experience of this African theater, whose first-rate staging of Shakespearean plays from 1819 to 1823 received ludicrous reviews from some New York papers and harassment from white rowdies, clearly reveals the attitude of northern whites toward the culture of free blacks: any form of uplifting was mocked, for it actually denied the assumed notion of the inferiority of the black race.

10. *Freedom's Journal*, Mar. 16, 1827.

11. Ibid., June 22, 1827.

12. Federal Writers' Project, *Writers' Program of New York City*, reel no. 4, "Negroes in New York" (typescript), 25–26.

13. *Freedom's Journal*, July 11 and 18, 1828.

14. Ibid., Aug. 1, 1828.

15. The early New York African-American press attacked the theater by using the rhetoric of the Calvinist tradition and joined, in so doing, many white reformers who condemned the theater for the passions it stirred and the bad company that it might inspire, thus leading to the ruin of youth.

16. From the 1830s to the 1860s many foreign travelers included a visit at the Five Points in their program. See Alessandra Lorini, "New York City as Text: Nineteenth-Century Representations of the Poor and Their Living Space," *Rivista di Studi Americani* (1990).

17. Frederick Douglass, "The Meaning of July Fourth for the Negro," in *The Life and Writings of Frederick Douglass*, ed. Philip S. Foner (New York: International Publishers, 1950), 2:443.

18. *Colored American*, Aug. 17, 1839.

19. See Benjamin Quarles, *Black Abolitionists* (New York: Oxford University Press, 1969), 128. According to some black abolitionists, the celebration of the downfall of slavery in Haiti or the birthday of Nat Turner were more significant dates than that of West Indian emancipation.

20. The symbols of Freemasonry represented progress and status change: a rough stone was the symbol of man in infancy; a polished stone was the sign of a virtuous man of achievement. See Loretta J. Williams, *Black Freemasonry and Middle-Class Realities* (Columbia, Mo.: University of Missouri Press, 1980), 49–55.

21. Frederick Douglass, "What Are the Colored People Doing for Themselves," in *Negro Social and Political Thought, 1850–1920*, ed. Howard Brotz (New York: Basic Books, 1966), 205.

22. Gunnar Myrdal, *American Dilemma: The Negro Problem and Modern Democracy* (New York: Harper and Bros., 1944); and Franklin Frazier, *Black Bourgeoisie* (New York: Free Press, 1965).

23. Whereas before the Civil War African-American papers were in the hands of the religious leaders of the community and financially supported by white abolitionists—like the *Colored American*, which was fully supported by Arthur Tappan—

after the war the papers became more secular and were connected to political parties. The *New York Globe* was discontinued in November 1884 because of an internal dispute between Thomas Fortune and the Reverend W. B. Derrick. In 1891, Fortune became the director of the *New York Age*, which passed in 1907 to the control of Booker T. Washington. See Martin E. Dann, ed., *The Black Press, 1827–1890: The Quest for National Identity* (New York: Putnam, 1971).

24. *New York Globe*, Feb. 24, 1883.
25. Ibid., Mar. 8, 1884.
26. Ibid., Feb. 24, 1883.
27. There were more black women than men; black women had to work to support themselves much more than did foreign-born and native-born white women. See Gilbert Osofsky, *Harlem: The Making of a Ghetto* (New York: Harper and Row, 1971), 3–4.
28. Ibid., 8.
29. According to a 1907 study, in one group of 240 blacks interviewed in New York City only 18 were born there; only 3 were over forty when they migrated, with the vast majority between the ages of fifteen and thirty; and 96 percent had arrived in New York after 1887. See Helen A. Tucker, "Negro Craftsmen in New York," *The Southern Workman* (October 1907), 545–51.
30. Franz Boas, "The Negro and the Demand of Modern Life," *Charities* (Oct. 7, 1905), 87.
31. John R. Commons, *Races and Immigrants in America* (New York: Macmillan, 1907), 7.
32. Hudson-Fulton Celebration Commission, New York, *The Fourth Annual Report of the Hudson-Fulton Celebration Commission to the Legislature of the State of New York*, 2 vols., prepared by Edward Hagaman Hall (Albany, N.Y.: J.B. Lyon Co., 1910), 1:5–7.
33. Ibid., 7–8.
34. See Julia Ward Howe, "How the Fourth Should be Celebrated," in Robert Haven Schauffler, *Independence Day* (New York: Dodd & Mead, 1934) and Mrs. Isaac Rice, "Our Barbarous Fourth," *Century Magazine* (June 1908).
35. The program of this gigantic festival is fully reported in the pages of the *New York Tribune*, Sept. 25, 1909.
36. Hudson-Fulton Celebration Commission, *Fourth Annual Report*, 283, 287.
37. Ibid., 292–303.
38. *New York Sun*, Sept. 29, 1909.
39. "Children's Festivals, Hudson-Fulton Celebration," *The Playground* 3, no. 8 (November 1909), 1.
40. *New York Tribune*, Oct. 3, 1909.
41. Ibid., 9.
42. Hudson-Fulton Celebration Commission, *Fourth Annual Report*, 507.
43. *New York Age*, Sept. 30, 1909.
44. Ibid., Oct. 7, 1909.

4

The Mexican/Chicano *Pastorela*
Toward a Theory of the Evolution of a Folk Play

María Herrera-Sobek

The Mexican/Chicano *pastorela*, or shepherd's play, has been part of the cycle of religious dramas both in Mexico and the American Southwest for several centuries. In the Southwest, it is part of the religious-drama cycle including in the First Cycle *La comedia de Adán y Eva* and *Caín y Abel o el primer crimen* and is derived from the Old Testament, while the Second Cycle encompasses *Coloquio de San José, Coloquio de Pastores, Auto de los Reyes Magos*, and *El niño perdido*, from the New Testament (Campa). The *pastorela* has been the object of censorship, prohibitions, and hostility from the Catholic church and from other critics who bemoan its often eschatological, erotic, contentious, and downright raunchy humor. However, in spite of the church's constant displeasure and the barbs or complete neglect of literary critics, it has managed to survive and to evolve up to the present decade. In fact, recently there has been somewhat of an interest in the genre on the part of a few scholars and well-known directors both in Mexico and the United States. For example, Miguel Sabido, a highly respected Mexican director, presents a major *pastorela, Pastorela Mexicana*, in Mexico City. For the past few years he has been touring the country and mounting the play in various Mexican cities. Luis Valdez, a Chicano playwright and director, offers a highly successful *pastorela, La Pastorela: The Shepherd's Play*, in San Juan Bautista, California, every other year (Valdez) and has recently produced a video of the *Los Pastores* play. Valdez's *pastorela* was first staged in 1975, with the goal of reviving an ancient tradition. In his program notes, he adds: "It is our belief that *La Pastorela* is one of the masterpieces of the folk theater tradition; and one that deserves to be recreated again and again, as long as people care to make contact with the humanity of centuries of past human generations" (Ibid.).

Because of its longevity and the numerous texts that are currently appearing, the *pastorela* affords an excellent opportunity to analyze the changes it has undergone both diachronically and synchronically. In this essay, I highlight an important vector that has affected changes in both the content and the structure of the genre. It is my position that, more than any other single factor, political events transpiring in Mexico and Europe have been the determining force in the evolution of the genre.

The evolution of the *pastorela* can be explained through the political struggles between those who hold hegemonic power and those who are outside the decision-making process. That is to say, the woof and the loom weaving this particular historical tapestry have been impacted by the realization of the intrinsic political power of both the text and the theatrical representations of *pastorelas* to transform societal structures. The theatrical representation of shepherds' plays, therefore, will fluctuate between the hegemonic institutions holding political power and the folk themselves in a never-ending pendular motion that is present even today. I contend that the evolution of these texts is directly affected by the ideological changes surfacing due to class conflicts and political and religious confrontations. Therefore, when we approach the study of this genre, we must take into consideration and be cognizant of the important factor of power: the power of the pen, the power of folk traditions, the power of literary criticism, and the power of the ruling classes. Through the evolutionary process of this humble genre, we can detect the struggle between the above entities in a battle for survival. Those sectors holding political power will continually try to suppress *pastorelas* written by the folk or the intelligensia and will try to supplant them with their own versions. In turn, shepherds' plays written by the masses will be perceived by the ruling classes as subversive and politically dangerous. The folk, on the other hand, will rejoice in the satire, the sharp stinging wit, and social protest structured within the play. Many *pastorela* texts are characterized by this subversive political streak structured within the confines of a more traditional text.

One of the salient marks of the *pastorela* is its formulaic structure. These folk dramas are composed of basically seven formulae which can be detailed as follows.

(1) Introductory songs, verses, dances, and so on

(2) The appearance of archangels Michael or Gabriel and the announcement of the newborn Jesus to the shepherds

(3) The beginning of the journey to Bethlehem to worship the newborn babe

(4) The attempt by the devil(s) (one or several) to distract the shepherds from their journey to Bethlehem. Generally three attempts are enacted. The devils' temptations are structured by utilizing three of the seven capital sins:

   (a) temptation through gluttony: food is offered to the hungry shepherds

   (b) temptation through lust: enticing young seductive women appear to the male shepherds

   (c) temptation through greed: wealth, jewels, and riches are offered to the shepherds

(5) The appearance of the archangel Michael who saves the shepherds from the clutches of the devil in the nick of time.

(6) The arrival of the shepherds in Bethlehem

(7) The presentation of gifts, songs and dancing in front of the Christ child Jesus

As can be deduced from the above scheme, the *pastorela* has a formulaic structure and can be easily manipulated at the various functions; characters, jokes, songs, speech events, and so on can be added, subtracted, or changed to fit any ideological scheme. The basic moral confrontation between good and evil likewise can be readily manipulated to fit any ideological scheme, since the concept of "good" can stand for anything that those structuring the drama desire it to represent and the concept of evil likewise can represent whatever those writing or enacting these plays wish it to symbolize. Thus, the conceptualization of evil in a recent *pastorela* performed in Mexico City was a corrupt government official; in another, the entrenched ruling political party, the PRI (Partido Revolucionario Institucional), represented evil. Dan Williams, in a review of the play for the *Los Angeles Times,* writes:

MEXICO CITY—Four angels from on high strummed guitars and sang of a miracle, then offered their musical services for baptisms, weddings and other parties.

Two shepherds, one a machete-wielding farmer with a hot temper and the other a feathered Aztec who carried an American Express card, decided that the angels must be part of a marijuana stupor.

The shepherds were not en route to Bethlehem. They were in Mexico City to complain about a corrupt mayor who had stolen their papaya crop. And the mayor, whose sins included the embezzlement of earthquake relief funds and the sale of psychedelic gelatin, sent three demons to waylay the shepherds. (*Los Angeles Times,* Dec. 19, 1985)

Luis Valdez, on the other hand, used a wealthy rancher to represent his conceptualization of evil. A description of the devil as played by Valdez was rendered as follows by Los Angeles Times theatre critic Dan Sullivan:

Satan's commander, Lucifer, played by El Teatro's leader, Luis Valdez—is impressively plain. The black suit and ruffled shirt suggest a wealthy rancher, who started as a field boss and hasn't forgotten how to shape people into line. He wants those shepherds turned around now, and he'll go out to help. (Los Angeles Times, Dec. 24, 1977)

Scholars are not in agreement as to the origins of the pastorelas. The nuclear plot is based on the prophecies of Isaiah and the New Testament. Some studies point to the cult of Mitra as an antecedent, since the cult involves the worship of the sun and has as primary elements the birth of the sun in a grotto and the shepherds worshiping this birth, as well as additional aspects related to the resurrection motif (see Romero Salinas). It is believed that the early Christians found it expedient to incorporate some elements of the Mitra cult in order to successfully disseminate the teachings of Christianity (ibid., 23). And it is here, then, that we first encounter the sproutings of the pastorela as a propagandistic tool in disseminating a particular ideology.

Byzantine culture spread throughout Europe and other parts of the world during the Middle Ages. By 1223, St. Francis of Assisi had introduced the representation of the Nativity scene similar to the iconography popular in Byzantine culture, which was spreading throughout the Italian peninsula (ibid., 24).

In this same century, liturgical theatre was being incorporated in Spain through the writings of the clergy who, in concert with the aristocracy, wished to instruct the faithful in the precepts of the Christian faith. The Christian faith, in turn, was structurally and ideologically analogous to the political system of feudalism extant during the period. The first liturgical play in Spain is known as The Magi (Cortichs, 9–10).

Liturgical theatre, however, began to evolve as it came in contact with the folk. It was soon converted into what the Church fathers perceived to be a dangerous and subversive weapon. Thereafter, the prohibitions and bannings of the plays commenced. Leandro Fernández de Moratín reports that "abuses" in the religious plays began to be introduced as early as the twelfth century. He states: "This abuse lasted until Inocence III severely prohibited, at the beginning of the XIII [century], the clergy from participating as actors in such comedies" (Díaz and Ponga, 39). The Consul of Aranda, for its part, announced in 1473:

All of us present unanimously prohibit this type of corruption . . . and [prohibit] the representation and reenactment of such farces, plays, monstrous spectacles, disorderly fictions, as well as clumsy singing and illicit speech acts. We prohibit this in the metropolitan churches as well as in the cathedrals. (García Montero, 85; my translation)

Later, Phillip II prohibited the religious type of folk theater on June 11, 1596, by royal decree.

By 1766 the representation of all mystery plays was completely forbidden (Romero Salinas, 46). Spain's relatively undeveloped theatre in the medieval period is the result, in part, of these strictures and prohibitions. Thus, this is the first major instance in which we can link the evolution of the *pastorela* to two clashing political currents: the desire of the masses for sexual and political freedom of expression and the desire of the ruling classes for the conservation of the form and content of a genre they had introduced to the masses expressly for political and religious instruction.

Spain continued to prohibit religious theater up to the nineteenth century. Moratín reports that the bulletin directed to the clergy from the bishopric of León published a royal decree banning the production of liturgical plays thusly:

Influenced by the powerful reasons that have been posited by my Government Minister, I have come to decree the following:

ARTICLE 1:

From this day forward there shall not be allowed representations in the realm's theaters of any dramas from the so-called sacred or biblical repertoire, whose subject belongs to the mysteries of the Christian faith, or in which the characters come from the Holy Trinity or the Sacred Family.

ARTICLE 2:

All dispositions which have been made regarding these plays, be it from the Government Minister or from the Gracia y Justice, are herewith annulled.

ARTICLE 3:

The printing and circulation of religious [sacred] dramas or biblical ones can be authorized by the civil governing officials. [They should however] adhere strictly to the formalities prescribed in the printing laws given by the Palace on April 30, 1856. (Díaz and Ponga, 45–46; my translation)

The above edict was signed by the government minister Patricio de la Escosura on May 15, 1856.

Liturgical theatre arrived in Mexico with the Franciscan friars and the Jesuits in the sixteenth century (see Romero Salinas, 31–34). Again, the main objective of this theatre was to instruct the newly conquered subordinates of Spain in the Christian faith. In Mesoamerica, the goal was to introduce the Indians to the Catholic religion. As early as 1533, we find the enactment of the first European-based play in the American continent, entitled *Juicio final,* or *The Final Judgment* (ibid., 17–18). By the end of that same decade, seven plays had been brought to the stage.

The above plays were generally penned by the friars themselves and were religious in tone and subject matter. However, the plays soon began to evolve as the folk commenced to institute radical changes in the subject matter. Eschatalogical subjects, erotic imagery, sexual innuendos, and double entendres, as well as what Mikhail Bakhtin would categorize as humorous elements belonging to the lower bodily stratum, began to appear, to the delight of the masses (see Bakhtin). This, of course, did not sit well with church officials, and soon Fray Juan de Sumárraga, first bishop of Mexico, classified the mystery plays as "*poco honestas,*" meaning that they were sexually provocative. By 1540 he had prohibited their reenactment (ibid., 32). Fortunately for the development of the *pastorelas* in Mexico, the bishop died eight years later and the plays resurfaced on stage, to the delight of the pueblo.

The second major impact on the *pastorela*'s evolution and production came about when the Jesuits arrived in America in 1572. The Jesuits had had great success with theatrical productions in Europe, since they found the enactment of plays a powerful tool in reaching their teaching objectives. The word *pastorela* itself came into vogue, and the enactment of these plays spread to various states and countries. Since the Jesuits were not a particularly popular group, it was not long before both the plays and the Jesuits came under attack. Bishop Don Juan Palafox de Mendoza severely criticized the presentation of theatrical plays and exhorted the general public not to attend these functions, declaring that "the plays are a danger to virtue, incite sensuality, and are the tribunal of the devil" (ibid., 43; my translation).

The shepherds' plays received a near-mortal blow when the Jesuits are expelled in 1767. The plays began to be denounced, and were classified as "scandalous" (ibid., 37). But in spite of all the indictments against the plays and the Inquisition's prohibition against their enactment, they continued to live underground. In fact, the eschatological elements, together with the devils as protagonists, multiplied. Toward the end of the colonial period, José Joaquín Fernández de Lizardi decided to write a "clean" *pastorela* because the ones he had witnessed were not fit for decent ears. In the prologue to his play entitled *Pastorela en dos actos"* [*Shepherd's Play in Two Acts*] he expounds:

The most frequently enacted shepherds' plays have a devil as one of their main characters; and some of these plays not only have one devil but many devils, in fact, some have as many as seven devils.

This means that the best shepherds plays are bedeviled, full of violent improprieties, lacking in creativity and invention and as such should be excluded from all public theatres since they violate all the rules of good taste. (Fernández de Lizardi, 156; my translation)

However, Lizardi himself acknowledged that the audience took great delight and pleasure in these dramas, applauding all of their indecency and indecorum loudly and cheering lustily at the representations of those same improprieties.

The unstable political climate during the end of the colonial period and the beginning of the Wars of Independence, from 1810 to 1821, led to a resurgence of *pastorela* production. Since it had been the Spanish ruling classes and religious officials who had prohibited the enactment of shepherds' plays, the new revolutionary movements incorporated these dramas as a viable form through which they could criticize and attack Spanish officialdom. The ideological stance of the Independence movements supported freedom of expression and liberal democratic ideals. In fact, the newly independent United States was serving as the model for the formation of ideal republican nations. Thus, the *pastorelas* thrived in this revolutionary climate and evolved with the infusion of other theatrical currents that were extant during the period.

The nineteenth century crystalized three categories of *pastorela* production: (1) the traditional religious type of *pastorela*, (2) the mainstream "cultured" *pastorela*, and (3) *pastorelas* pertaining to the urban folklore genre. Lizardi's literary shepherds' play stimulated the production of other literary-type renditions written by various authors. The major theaters in Mexico City presented numerous *pastorela* productions, such as *The Sons of Bato and Bras or the Devil's Tricks* (1848), *The Devil's Leg* (1862), and *The Devil Preacher* (1888–89) (see San Martín).

The above three categories continue to be represented in the twentieth century. In Mexico City, the *pastorelas* pertaining to the urban-folklore category predominate. They are infused with sexually charged material, political satire, and social protest directed at government officials or economic conditions in Mexico. The plays are designed to entertain, but the social and political barbs are so strong that the writer and producer of the avant garde *pastorela Tapadeus*, Germán Dehesa, confided to me, in 1987, that he was constantly fearful the government would close down his play.

The shepherds' plays have experienced a long and productive life. The flexibility of their structure promotes evolution, since it is this flexibility that allows for the incorporation of material that is currently of interest to the general public. Much that is of interest to the masses is directly related to political and economic conditions. In a traditional religious genre, the folk have found an excellent vehicle through which they can speak their mind.

References

Bakhtin, Mikhail. *Rabelais and His World.* Bloomington: Indiana University Press, 1984.

Barrientos Joaquín Alvarez y Gutiérrez, Antonio Cea. *Actas de las jornadas sobre teatro popular en España.* Madrid: Consejo Superior de Investigaciones Científicas, 1987.

Campa, Arthur L. *Spanish Religious Folktheatre in the Spanish Southwest. University of New Mexico Bulletin,* Language Series, vol. 5, nos. 1 and 2. Albuquerque, 1934.

Carreter, Fernando Lázaro. *Teatro Medieval,* pp. 9–94. Madrid: Odres Nuevos, 1965.

Cole, M. R. *Los Pastores.* New York: Memoirs of the American Folk-Lore Society, vol. 9, 1907.

Cortichs, Estrella. *Teatro Medieval.* Mexico: Editorial Oasis, 1961.

Comunidad de Madrid Consejería de Cultura. *El auto religioso en España.* Madrid: Centro de Estudios y Actividades Culturales, 1991.

————. *Tradición y danza en España.* Madrid: Centro de Estudios y Actividades Culturales, 1992.

Díaz, Joaquín, and José Alonso Ponga. *Autos de navidad en León y Castilla.* León, España: Santiago García, Editor, 1983.

Donovan, Richard B. *The Liturgical Drama in Medieval Spain.* Toronto: Pontifical Institute of Medieval Studies, Studies and Texts 4, 1958.

Ducrue, Benno Iranciscus. *Ducrue's Account of the Expulsion of the Jesuits from Lower California (1767–1769).* St. Louis, Mo.: St. Louis University, 1967.

Engelkirk, John E. "Notes on the Repertoire of the New Mexican Spanish Folktheatre." *Southern Folklore Quarterly* 4 (1940): 227–37.

————. "The Source and Dating of New Mexican Spanish Folk Plays." *Western Folklore* 16 (1957): 232–55.

Fernández de Lizardi, José Joaquín. "Pastorela en dos actos." *Obras. II Teatro.* México: Centro de Estudios Literarios Universidad Nacional Autónoma de México, 1965.

Flores, Arturo C. *El teatro campesino de Luis Valdez.* Madrid: Editorial Pliegos, 1990.

Fulop-Miller, René. *The Power and Secret of the Jesuits.* N.Y.: Garden City Pub. Co., 1930.

García Montero, Luis. *El Teatro Medieval: Polémica de una Inexistencia.* Maracena, Granada: Editorial Don Quijote, 1984.

Gillmor, Frances. "*Los Pastores* Number: Folk Plays of Hispanic America—Forward." *Western Folklore* 16 (1957): 229–31.

Happé, Peter, ed.. *English Mystery Play*. New York: Penguin Books, 1984.

Kinghorn, A. M. *Medieval Drama*. London: Evans Bros., 1968.

Igo, John. *Los Pastores: An Annotated Bibliography with an Introduction*. San Antonio, Tex.: San Antonio College Library, 1967.

Kolve, V. A. *The Play Called Corpus Christi*. Stanford, Calif.: Stanford University Press, 1966.

————. *Los Pasotes (The Shepherds): An Old California Christmas Play*. Reproduced from the original manuscript at the Bancroft Library, with a foreword by Lindley Bynum, translation by María López de Louther. Hollywood: Homer H. Boelter, 1953.

Los Angeles Times, pt. 2, p. 5, Dec. 24, 1977.

————. pt. 1, p. 5, Dec. 19, 1985.

Lucero-White, Aurora, ed.. *Coloquio de los pastores*. Santa Fe: Santa Fe Press, 1940.

MacGregor-Villarreal, Mary. "Celebrating *Las Posadas* in Los Angeles." *Western Folklore* (1979): 71–105.

María y Campos, Armando de. *Pastorelas Mexicanas*. México: Editorial Diana, 1985.

Marie, Sister Joseph. *The Role of the Church and the Folk in the Development of the Early Drama in New Mexico*. Philadelphia: Ph.D. dissertation, University of Pennsylvania 1948.

Menéndez Pidal, R., ed.. *Auto de los reyes magos*. *Revista de Archivos, Bibliotecas y Museos* 4 (1900): 453–62.

Morner, Magnus, *The Expulsion of the Jesuits from Latin America*. New York: Alfred A. Knopf, 1965.

Múñoz Renedo, Carmen. *La representación de moros y cristianos de Zujar*. Madrid: Consejo Superior de Investigaciones Científicas, 1972.

Oinas, Felix J. *Folklore, Nationalism, and Politics*. Bloomington: Indiana University Folklore Institute, 1978.

Pearce, T. M. "The New Mexican Shepherds' Play." *Western Folklore* 15 (1956): 77–88.

Pradeau, Alberto Francisco. *La expulsion de los Jesuitas de las provincias de Sonora, Ostimuri y Sinaloa en 1767*. México: Antigua Librería Robredo de José Porrúa e Hijos, 1959.

Rael, Juan B. *The Sources and Diffusion of the Mexican Shepherds' Plays*. Guadalajara, Jalisco, México: Libreria La Joyita, 1965.

Robb, J. D. "The Music of *Los Pastores*." *Western Folklore* 16 (1957): 263–80.

Robe, Stanley L. *Coloquio de Los Pastores from Jalisco, México*. Los Angeles: University of California Folklore Studies, no. 4, University of California Press, 1954.

————. "The Relationship of *Los Pastores* to other Spanish-American Folk Drama." *Western Folklore* 16 (1957): 281–89.

Romero, R. A. *La Aurora del Nuevo Dia en los Campos de Belén*. México: Antonio Venegas Arroyo. Obra nacional de la Buena Prensa, A.C., 1985.

Romero Salinas, Joel. *La Pastorela Mexicana: orígen y evolución*. México: SEP Cultura Fondo Nacional Para el Fomento de las Artesanías, Fonart, 1984.

Rose, Martial. *The Wakefield Mystery Plays*. New York: W. W. Norton and Company, 1969.

San Martín, Beatrix (Vda. de María y Campos). *Pastorelas y Coloquios*. México: Editorial Diana, 1987.

Sturdevant, Winifred. *The Misterio de los reyes masgos: Its Position in the Development of the Medieval Legend of the Three Kings*. Baltimore: Johns Hopkins Studies in Romance Literature and Languages 10, 1927.

Thomas, R.G., ed.. *Ten Miracle Plays*. London: Edward Arnold, 1966.

Torres Marín, M. *Auto del nacimiento del Niño Dios en el portal de Belén*. Bilbao, España: Colección Mensaje, 1971.

Valdez, Luis. *La Pastorela: The Shepherd's Play*. Program Notes. San Juan Bautista, Calif.: El Teatro Campesino, 1989.

Woolf, R. *The English Mystery Plays*. London: Routledge, 1972.

5

Los Matachines de la Santa Cruz de la Ladrillera
Notes Toward a Socio-literary Analysis

Norma E. Cantú

Along with a number of religious celebrations connected with the major liturgical feast days, such as the *pastorela* at Christmas, the people of two barrios in Laredo, Texas, observe the feast of the Holy Cross on May 3 with a ceremony, *Los Matachines,* that has survived despite a move from the nearby Las Minas area and despite changes wrought through time. They refer to this celebration as *la fiesta.* Both the participants in the ceremony—the dancers, musicians, and elders—and the community where the ceremony survives cling tenaciously to a religio-cultural event that fulfills, at the same time, both individual and communal needs.

Tracing the historical origins of the *matachines,* in general, and of the group in the Ladrillera barrio in Laredo, specifically, one can see the cultural-religious trajectory that the fiesta has traveled. Analyzing the fiesta as a cultural text that represents the community's folk religious beliefs, one can see it as an example of cultural resistance and affirmation in a U.S.–Mexico border community.

A brief gloss of the etymological concerns associated with the word *matachin* reveals conflicting claims among scholars. It appears that the origin of the tradition is as problematic as assigning a definite etymology to the word *matachin.* We find that it appears in the dramatic tradition of the sixteenth century (*Diccionario de autoridades*). The *Velásquez Spanish and English Dictionary* says it is a dance performed by "grotesque figures" (449). Perhaps the entry in the *Diccionario de autoridades* says it best:

f.m. a man masquerading ridiculously with a mask and dressed in a tight-fitting costume from head to toe, made of multicolored alternating pieces constructed of: one-quarter yellow and another red. These figures form a dance

57

among four or six or eight of them which are called *Los Matachines,* and to the tune of a drumbeat they make different gestures and hit each other with a wooden toy sword and with bladders (balloons) full of air. Covarrubias gives it the etymology from the verb "to kill," because with the beating that they give each other it is as if they are going to kill each other. Latin: *mimus personatus* . . . Solis, *Loa for the Company.*

Hall traces the word to the Arabic *nutawajjihin,* to the Italian *mattacino,* and to the Spanish and French *matachin* (43). And still another scholar holds that there is a direct link between these European matachin dances and the cotswold Morris dance (Forrest, 13). Hewett describes another Amerindian matachin tradition that takes place during the fiesta in Santa Fe, where Cochiti Pueblo presents "Los matachines, a medieval mystery play" (203, 206). This particular performance is also claimed to be "a composite of the old miracle play and of original drama from Mexico" (Hurt, 18). Haggard refuses to engage in the etymological polemic and merely cites various origin stories (296–99). Robb concludes that the "Matachines dance and related American dances are of European origin" (89). In her work on the upper Rio Grande Valley dance rituals, Champé also traces the dance to Europe by way of Zacatecas, but she does not conclusively assign any etymological origin to the word *matachin* (1980–81, 38). De Huff, one of the few scholars who looks at pre-Columbian origins, claims that it is "an adaptation of an old Aztec satirical play" (14). Kirk cites letters and journals that "speak of matachines dances done for Christmas and for Corpus Christi" in San Antonio, Texas, at the San José Mission (32). She also believes that the term was brought to the Americas by Spanish missionaries, but "that the simple [dance] step was already part of the Native American religious ritual" (64).

The matachines tradition exists in a variety of forms in a geographical area that covers most of Mexico and the southwestern part of the United States. Matachines are found in other Texas towns, as far west as California, as well as in northern Mexico and in Yaqui and Mayo pueblos. In Picuris, New Mexico, it is a Christmas dance, a variant that keeps the image of the "viejo" with his whip (Parsons, 317). Matachines are also found along the U.S.–Mexican border. The Yaqui, who were forcibly dispersed by the Mexican government after 1886, retain their matachin dances (Spicer, 220). To escape the government's program, many fled to the north and into the southwestern part of the United States, bringing with them the Matachines, a men's sodality whose patroness is the Virgin of Guadalupe

(Spicer, 255). Their dances are "chiefly Indian in tradition" and European in choreography (Painter). They identify the Virgin Mary with various forms of the cross and with the traditional female supernatural called "Our Mother," as did the native residents of the Valley of Mexico. The Pascua Yaqui matachines often travel from pueblo to pueblo to dance wherever they are invited to celebrate. Similar to the Yaqui matachines are the Mayo, but unlike the Yaqui's sodality, which is exclusively male, and like the Laredo group, the Mayo allow young girls and women to participate.

Inheritors of the tradition by way of Mexico, the dancers in Laredo, Texas, combine both Spanish and Amerindian traditions. An analysis of the ceremony reveals a complex syncretic structure in which elements of the modern matachin dances (a syncresis themselves of the native Mexican and Spanish) and Mexican and U.S. icons are integrated to create a religious ceremony independent of the traditional church structure.

Because of geographical proximity and similarities in the celebration, it is easy to conjecture that the men and women Matachines in Laredo, who venerate the cross and the Virgin of Guadalupe with native dance steps and European choreography, dressed in modified native costumes, are related to the Yaqui or Mayo matachines. They could also be related to the San Miguel de Allende Conchero tradition that venerates the Holy Cross (Fernandez, 39–40). The Tarahumaras also have matachines who carry out the church fiesta dances, whose leader is called Monarca, and whose dances are but versions of old Spanish folk dances (Bennet, 301; Hawley, 35; Lea, 9). The evidence of influence in the matachines from the Coahuiltecan tribes who roamed the area as late as 1850 is limited to a far-fetched similarity of dress, for the Carrizo Indians wore a short *naguilla* and carried bows and arrows (Newcomb, 1). The matachines wear a more sophisticated *naguilla*, or skirt, decorated with *carrizo* (river cane), and sometimes carry stylized bows and arrows, characteristic of "matachines de la flecha." Other groups may dance "de la palma" or "de la pluma" and carry in their right hand either a feather or a fan made out of straw in the shape of a palm leaf.[1]

The Laredo group venerates the Holy Cross and has the Virgin of Guadalupe as patroness. The dance group of about fifty includes both men and women, who are led by an elder or *monarca* and dress in *naguillas* decorated with *carrizo;* it appears that they have incorporated into the ceremonies the language, including the name, and the dress from various Amerindian groups. However, any definite relationship is impossible to trace, and none of the informants knows of possible relationships. In the eighteenth-century, the entry in the *Diccionario de autoridades* does mention a yellow and red costume as well as a Hermit character in a Loa; therefore, it is possible that the idea of the matachines was taken back to the Spanish theater and the word given to a dramatic character who came from the indigenous dance-drama character.

The cross and the costumes used in the ceremony serve as the basis for the present analysis, for manifestations of the religious icons can be observed in both, and they attest to a cultural affirmation and a resistance to an en-croachment of on-border, or non-Mexican, culture.

To provide a sort of trellis upon which to hang our discussion, let us exam-ine the fiesta as it came to be in Laredo. As it now exists, the fiesta has changed from the time over fifty years ago when it came to Laredo, and yet it has preserved elements present in the ceremony since the turn of the cen-tury. This particular matachin tradition originated in Real de Catorce, a min-ing town near Matehuala and came with the miners' families to a mining community on the U.S. side of the Rio Grande, sometime around the turn of the century. The tradition, and the cross itself, later came with the people and their cross when the last of three coal mining towns upriver from Laredo was closed in 1936. The exodus from St. Tomas, Chanel, and Dolores began in the late thirties. Most of the displaced families moved to Laredo, about twenty miles southeast of the area now known as Las Minas, and settled in the west-ern part of the town of Laredo, Texas, around the brick factory where the ex-miners found jobs. The barrio became known as La Ladrillera, and here and in the adjacent Cantaranas the matachines live; the people from Las Minas built a chapel to house their Holy Cross in its own "terreno," its own place or land (Ortiz).

This explains how the celebration came to Laredo, but not how it came to be part of the tradition of the people. The elders give variant accounts of how the Matachines acquired their Holy Cross and their dances. In order to establish the fiesta entirely within the literary folk tradition, let us examine these narratives.

Sara Liendo, Florencio Ortiz, and Josefina Negrete came from Las Minas to Laredo with the cross; each tells a different story to explain how the matachines acquired the Holy Cross and how the dancing was first performed. In 1976, I interviewed Sara Liendo when she was eighty-seven and still in charge of "dressing" the cross and of keeping the "terreno" during the year. Liendo claimed that the people had always had the Holy Cross be-cause the "Ermitaño," or "El Viejo," a legendary figure from the *pastorela* came to the people at one time and helped them find the cross and taught them the dances; she had been told this story as a child. *La Malinche* is part of the story Liendo told. She, the *Malinche,* taught the people how to dance and how to make the costumes, and that is why women can dance with the men and why the women go to the river to cut the *carrizo* for the decorations. When Doña Sarita died in May 1989, her daughter-in-law, Carolina Liendo, inherited her position as the "keeper" of the cross.

Florencio Ortiz, who performs the duties of what in other groups is called the *monarca,* links the matachines with the legend of Sta. Elena—*la mujer perversa*—who is commanded to search for the "true cross" to atone for her sins.[2] After finding the two false crosses—that is, the two where the thieves were crucified next to Christ—she burns them. She continues her search and, finally, after digging a long time, finds it buried. She entrusts the "true cross" to the *Matachines* because she knows they "will venerate and honor it on the third of May, the feast day, the day of the Holy Cross" (Ortiz interview).[3]

Josefina Negrete, interviewed at age sixty-one in 1977, agrees that the *Matachines* must venerate the cross, but she doesn't know how they acquired it. According to Negrete, Moctezuma came to teach the people the dances, and they were to honor the Virgin of Guadalupe because she appeared to Juan Diego and wanted to be the mother of all Mexicans. She claims that this is what she was told as a child in Dolores (Negrete interview).

These three versions are representative of what most of the *Matachines* believe, but some of the younger dancers are unsure or unwilling to relate any such stories in the 1990s. They do, however, hold onto the tradition and are deeply devoted to the Holy Cross; some call themselves "soldiers of the Virgin" or "soldiers of the cross" (F. Ortiz and Castillo interviews).

The cross itself is the object of veneration, and Negrete claims that it is what keeps the people together, while regretfully explaining that not all of their traditions have stayed with them. The *matachines* made a vow and must keep their word; the cross is always with the people to remind them. "It is the cross we must carry," she says. The cross is owned communally, as is the *"terreno,"* and it is the people's responsibility to keep it. It serves as a structuring object, and it can be analyzed as such.

The cross serves as an allegory for the Church, not the priest's church but the people's; it must have a *"terreno,"* and the *matachines* are soldiers defending and honoring it and its territory. The cross is the object whereby the community is united as a Church. Vows are made to it to ensure health or the granting of favors. The commitment made on an individual level—be it in terms of dance, prayer, fasting, vigil, or service—is made in terms of sacrifice, individual sacrifice. The communal commitment is also made in terms of sacrifice. Sara Liendo vowed to "dress the cross every year until death" (interview). She inherited this honor when her predecessor died; but she had made the vow as a young woman, when she helped the old women prepare the cross for the ceremony. In like manner, some dancers have vowed to dance for a certain number of years or for life, usually to repay a "*promesa*" or as thanksgiving for an answered prayer.

The cross is a demanding charge; and the *Matachines* are the caretakers and defenders. Their leader, Florencio Ortiz, teaches the dancers their steps, repairs damaged *naguillas*, helps cut the river cane and prepare the *naguillas*, ensures that the food and other elements central to the fiesta are available, and, in general, keeps the group together. He has vowed lifelong service, and he is in charge of making decisions for the group as well as of leading the dancers during the ceremony. The matachines' commitment reinforces their individual vows, and the cross is a symbol for their "Church." There is a law and an interpreter, as it were, of the law, and the *matachines* are committed to upholding that law.

The cross serves as an object of structuring value, whereby the people by their vows and their participation in the ceremony have a "Church" that demands communal and individual commitment and assures the continuity of the tradition. The cross, on a personal level also serves as a metaphor for the human soul.

Topologically, the ceremony and the cross come together and participants atone for their sins, offer sacrifices, and honor or venerate the cross. The ceremony serves as a metaphor for the journey of the soul toward salvation. There is a procession after the preparation of the cross. The cross, taken from its usual place in the *terreno*, is set in an open area, where the dancers can honor it through their dance. Christ is present, as in medieval Christian iconology, "under the form and semblance of the cross" (Didion, 369), and the dancers share in His resurrection after traveling the road of suffering; the dances include *sones* that deal with death and suffering. In one such *son*—"El Viejo and La Malinche"—a drama is acted out. The dramatic presentation attests to the survival of *coloquios* and other religious folk dramatic traditions.

The cross is "dressed" in preparation for the ceremony by the elder, in this case a woman in charge of the *terreno*. Several women help her wrap the cross in colored sheets; the colors vary from year to year, but they are usually pastel colors. The cross covered with flowers over the sheets is reminiscent of Nahuatl iconography where, according to Laurette Séjourné, they are symbols for penitence and salvation (122). A white sheet is draped over the crossbar, clearly a symbol of the resurrection; once dressed in this manner, the cross is also like the tree of life or "flowering tree" in Tamoanchan, "the house of descent, place of birth, mystic west where gods and men originate" (Séjourné, 118). It is dangerous to assign a metaphorical explanation based on Nahuatl iconology, since there is no positive evidence linking the ceremony to Nahuatl culture; but the icons strongly suggest a relationship, and there are some *matachin* groups that do identify with pre-Columbian elements.[4] Nevertheless, the Christian iconography in terms of the cross, the sheet, and the procession place the cross, topologically, as a symbol for Christ's victory over death, a symbol for the dancers' victory over sin. The fact that the "flowering tree," or split tree, is also a symbol of regeneration in Nahuatl cosmology points to how thoroughly the *matachines* have syncretized the symbols of Christian and Nahuatl religious beliefs; or perhaps it points to an older inexplicable oneness of the two attempts at defining the human condition.

The *matachines* are the soldiers, the knights upholding the laws of the Church as represented by the cross, and they are also victors with Christ on an individual level as they travel the road to salvation. By being *matachines*, though, they also assure themselves a place in heaven as represented by the cross.

The cross is a promise of the reward that awaits a *matachin*, just as it is the "cross one must carry" (Negrete). Sta. Elena has fulfilled her penance, she has left the cross with the Matachines and has gone on to her reward. El Viejo, in one of the *sones*, is killed, and he likewise, after fulfilling his duty, goes to his reward. The cross remains a symbol for heavenly reward. It is, on an analogical level, the promise of eternal life: the warriors in Nahuatl culture were rewarded with an afterlife of service to Huitzilopochtli; the matachines are rewarded with eternal life with Christ (Negrete). On this level, the cross becomes the metaphor for salvation and eternal life.

The cross reappears as an icon emblazoned on the vests and *naguillas* of the ceremonial costumes. In some cases, it is the words "la Santa Cruz" (the Holy Cross) that are embroidered on the costume. The cross is at the center of the ceremony, and it is the object that offers the metaphor on several levels as it functions as a structuring religious correlative for the dancers and for the community at large.

Along with the analysis of the cross, we can also examine the costumes in terms of their function as part of the ceremony. The costumes also act as structuring items, giving the *matachines* a distinctive ceremonial dress replete with symbols, icons from both native and Christian traditions. According to the Ladrillera *matachines* themselves, the costumes show a great degree of degeneration, for there have been many changes that depart from the traditional way of constructing them. One such change which is not apparent, but which many older dancers hold to be of extreme importance, is the sound. As one informant put it, "the sound isn't right without the right *huaraches* (sandals), *sonajas,* or *carrizo*" (P. Ortiz). The sandals have given way to modern shoes: Florencio Ortiz's sons, for example, wear boots; most dancers don't carry the traditional gourd *sonaja,* but carry commercial *maracas* or even home-made *sonajas,* made by placing beans or grains of corn in a toilet-tank floater and painting it red and attaching a handle to it. The costume is now embroidered with beads and ready-made trim; and the *carrizo* is now cut indiscriminately. These transformations, in addition to the lack of adherence to the "right" colors, bothers the older dancers (F. Ortiz).

The one item that has not changed is the red *naguilla,* or skirt. All the dancers wear it; it is made of four lengths of red material, worn by both men and women. It is decorated with noisemakers made of four-inch pieces of river cane carefully cut, strung with flattened bottle caps or, more commonly now, with jingle bells; and it is usually embroidered with figures of Guadalupe, or with hearts, flowers, and crosses. These figures are also embroidered on the vests which, when worn, are either red, orange, or black. The dancers of the Ladrillera group no longer wear "coronas" although they still carry the stylized bows and arrows, as in the old days; "only a few still carry the things of the *matachines,*" says Florencio Ortiz, "much has been lost". The *naguilla* resembles the Coahuiltecan dress, as described by Newcomb, which included below-the-knee loin cloths, decorated with sea shells and twigs (1).

The costumes are important, and the changes are important, too. The fact that the people decorate the costumes with embroidered figures of the same icons observed in the dressing of the cross helps to establish the costumes as serving the same function as the cross. The construction of the costumes begins long before the ceremony, and often the dancers and those who make the costumes go as a group to cut the *carrizo* that will be used to decorate the *naguilla.* Groups of people will gather to sew the *naguillas* and to embroider the costumes (Martinez and C. Liendo interviews).

In the past, young boys were usually in charge of flattening the bottle caps for use as noisemakers on the *naguillas* and even on the arm and ankle bands. But, more recently, commercial jingle bells have replaced the bottle caps as noisemakers. The whole community joins in preparation for the ceremony.

Individuals are responsible for their own costumes and often use their names or initials as part of the embroidered decorations.

The ceremony is not a part of the formal church's liturgical celebration, and as with other Mexican celebrations of feast days, such as the Day of the Dead, the day of the Holy Cross is celebrated as a popular religious ceremony. The *matachines* fiesta functions for the people of the two barrios— La Ladrillera and Cantaranas—in terms of their lives and community. The cross remains an important part of life. Despite some pessimistic thoughts about the future of the ceremony voiced by some of the dancers, most of the participants agree that the *matachines* have made a vow and they must keep their word. They must "dance in honor of the Holy Cross and the Virgin of Guadalupe" (F. Ortiz). It is through such persistence that the dancers resist accommodation and simultaneously subvert hegemonic icons. Such subversion and accommodation can be seen in the recent Gulf War Cross, which was covered with yellow ribbons and decorated with red, white, and blue streamers; colors which reproduced the traditional *matachin* colors in the May 1991 celebration.

The *matachin* group that I have focused on for these preliminary notes lends itself to a socio-literary analysis because of its rich tradition. The origin narratives of the elders, the legends that inform the veneration of the cross and are most central to our discussion, the dance drama itself—all interpolate on the cultural "text" of the fiesta. A semiotic analysis serves us well, but to truly understand the function of the tradition as a unifying vehicle for the community, the cultural context as well as the socio-political role of the fiesta must be considered.

The working-class neighborhoods of Cantaranas and La Ladrillera have high unemployment rates and above-average high school dropout rates. Both lie literally on the proverbial "wrong side of the tracks" along the riverbanks of the Rio Grande. But their inhabitants do not live under the stigma of poverty, nor do they seem to be any worse off than most of the other inhabitants of a city of 126,000, whose dropout rates hovers around 50 percent and whose average annual income per household is well below the poverty level. But, unlike other recently settled barrios whose traditions are only now being established, these two have the *matachines,* the fiesta that affirms their identity, a self-defined and sometimes contradictory mestizo identity, perhaps a reflection of their "border" marginalized status in reference to U.S. hegemonic forces. Yet it is a strong and clear religious identity outside of the official church structure.

The *matachines* fiesta will survive as long as the needs of the community continue to be fulfilled by it. As one dancer expressed it, "mientras tenga aliento y pueda moverme, bailare, seguire bailando" [as long as I have breath and I can move I will dance, I will continue dancing]. And as Doña Sara Liendo defiantly proclaimed at the last fiesta she attended, "con o sin dinero, los matachines bailan" [with or without money, the matachines dance] (1988).

Notes

1. Frances Toor describes the Yaqui Matachin in this way (336–37).
2. There is a manuscript for a religious play in the Biblioteca Nacional in Madrid that tells almost the exact tale of how Sta. Elena found the cross.
3. The town of Caravaca in Spain also celebrates the day of the Holy Cross, but with different traditions. Several feast days in Mexico are celebrated with *Matachines*.
4. Another Laredo *matachin* group is called "Azteca" and its leader cites a Nahuatl origin for the tradition.

References

Aguado, Simon de. *Remedio de los Matachines*. Unpublished manuscript, Biblioteca Nacional, Madrid.

Bennet, W. C., and R. M. Zing. *The Tarahumaras*. Chicago: University of Chicago Press, 1935.

Baylock, Frank. "Indian Guide." *Albuquerque Tribune*, Dec. 11, 1952.

Bloom, Lansing B. "The Indian Ceremonies." *El Palacio* 15, no. 6 (Sept. 15, 1923), 96–97.

Castillo, Javier. Personal interview, July 5, 1987.

Champe, Flavia W. *The Matachines Dancers of the Upper Rio Grande: History Music, and Choreography*. Lincoln, Neb.: University of Nebraska Press, 1983.

———. "Origins of the Magical Matachines Dance." *El Palacio* 86, no. 4 (Winter 1980–81), 34–39.

De Huff, Elizabeth Willis. "December Indian Dances." *New Mexico* 10, no. 2 (November 1932), 14–15, 45–47.

Diccionario de autoridades (facsimile ed.) Madrid: Gredos, 1964. (Original, Madrid: Real Academia Española, Vda de Fco del Hierro, 1732.)

Didion, Adolphe N. *Christian Iconography: The History of Christian Art in the Middle Ages*, vol. 1. Translated by E. J. Millington. New York: Frederick Ungar Publishing Co., 1965. (Reprint of 1851 edition.)

Fernandez, Justino. *Danza de los concheros en San Miguel de Allende*. México: El Colegio de México, 1941.

Forrest, John. *Morris and Matachines: A Study in Comparative Choreography*. London: The English Folk Dance and Song Society, 1984.

Haggard, J. Villasona. "Matachines." *Theater Arts Monthly* 21, no. 4 (April 1937), 293–99.

Hall, Douglas Kent. "Los Matachines: Dancers Keep Old World Tradition Alive." *New Mexico Magazine* (December 1986), 42–47.

Hawley, Florence. "Dance of the Devil-Chasers." *New Mexico* 26, no. 9 (1948), 16, 35, 37, 39.

Hewett, Edgar L. "Plan for the Fiesta." *Art and Archeology* 18, nos. 5 and 6 (November-December 1924), 203–6.

Hurt, Amy Passmore. "New Mexico: Spanish Missions." *New Mexico* 10, no. 9 (September 1932), 7–9, 46–47.

Kirk Martha Ann. *Dancing with Creation: Mexican and Native American Dance in Christian Worship and Education.* Saratoga CA: Resource Publications, 1983.

Kloeppel, Richard J. *Los Matachines: A Dance Drama for San Lorenzo.* Bernalillo, N.M.: mimeographed, 1968.

Lea, Aurora (Lucero-White). "More About Matachines." *New Mexico Folklore Review* 11 (1963–64), 7–10.

Liendo, Sara. Personal Interview, Dec. 20, 1976.

————. Personal Interview, May 4, 1988.

Liendo, Carolina. Personal Interview, May 4, 1987.

Martinez, Alicia. Personal Interview, May 4, 1987.

Negrete, Josefina. Personal Interview, May 12, 1977.

Newcomb, W. W., Jr. *The Indians of Texas from Prehistory to Modern Times.* Austin, Tex.: University of Texas Press, 1969.

Ortiz, Florencio, Personal Interview, May 3, 1985.

Ortiz, Pedro. Personal Interview, May 3, 1982.

Painter, Muriel Thayer. *The Yaqui Easter Ceremony at Pascua.* Tucson: Tucson Chamber of Commerce, 1950.

Parsons, Elsie Clews. "Picuris, New Mexico." *American Anthropologist* 42, no. 2 (April-June 1939), 206–22.

Peña, Fernando. *Los Matachines: Memoirs.* Laredo, Tex.: Laredo Junior College Oral History Project, 1976.

Reagan, Albert B. "The 'Matachina' Dance." *Indiana Academy of Science Proceedings.* Austin: University of Texas General Library, 1904.

Robb, J. D. "The Matachines Dance—A Ritual Folk Dance." *Western Folklore* 20 (1961), 87–101.

Saavedra, Rafael M. "Los Matachines." *Avante,* México, D.F. (Aug. 15, 1935), 39–40.

Séjourné, Laurette. *Burning Water: Thought and Religion in Ancient Mexico.* London: Thames and Hudson, 1978.

Spicer, E. H. *Pascua: A Yaqui Village in Arizona.* Chicago: University of Chicago Press, 1940.

Tomlinson, Charles. *The Matachines: New Mexico.* Los Cerrillos, N.M.: San Marcos Press, 1968.

Toor, Frances. *A Treasury of Mexican Folkways.* New York: Crown Publishers, 1947.

Van Stone, Mary R. "The Matachina Dance," *El Palacio* 38, nos. 1–2 (Jan. 2–9, 1935), 10–12.

Velázquez de la Cadena, Mariano and Edward Gray and Juan L. Iribas. *Velázquez Spanish and English Dictionary, Newly Revised.* New York: Follett, 1964.

Part Two

Rituals of
Renewal and Return

6

El Santuario de Chimayo
A Syncretic Shrine in New Mexico

Ramón A. Gutiérrez*

On the western side of northern New Mexico's Sangre de Cristo Mountains, there sits a small village named Chimayo. Site of the most popular religious shrine in the United States, the Santuario de Chimayo for centuries has attracted pilgrims of every sort. Routinely, the pilgrims come to the Santuario's sacred earthen hole. Praying for miracles, blessings, and cures, they rejuvenate their bodies and spirits by drinking water from the stream that flows in front of the shrine. They bathe themselves with dirt from the shrine's miraculous earthen hole, at times mixing earth and water to form a mud plaster for their bodies. Legend holds that pilgrims have been traveling to Chimayo for at least six hundred years. They have come and continue to come for many reasons and motives, driven by different dreams and myths.

In 1990 and 1991, I visited the Santuario de Chimayo on four occasions, to study the range of religious behaviors displayed there. During each of these visits, timed specifically to observe the weekly and seasonal tempo of activities at the Santuario, I arrived at daybreak and stayed until dusk, observing who arrived, how much time pilgrims of various sorts spent there, and what behaviors they exhibited. When devotees spent more than a few minutes at the shrine, I interviewed those who were willing to talk. I asked about the legends of the shrine, the miracles that were said to have occurred there, and the specific motivations that had brought them to the

*I wish to thank the Cushwa Center for the Study of American Catholics at Notre Dame University for a fellowship that allowed me to write the results of this research.

Santuario on a specific day. Before reviewing some of the patterns of behavior I observed at the Santuario, let me first delineate the spaces that constitute the shrine complex, delving briefly into the history of each.

The symbolic center, and indeed the oldest spot in the shrine complex, is a small earthen hole, which measures about three feet in circumference and one to two feet in depth. Since pilgrims are always eating the dirt and taking small amounts for various religious purposes, the dimensions of the hole ebb; it is smallest right after the shrine's custodian has replenished it with new dirt. The hole itself is housed in a church complex that consists of three rooms: (1) the church nave with a main altar and sacristy (see A in Fig. 1); (2) a votive offering room, which runs parallel to and north of the church nave and is entered through the sacristy (see B in Fig. 1); and finally, (3) a small room that contains the sacred hole, entered through a small doorway at the eastern end of the votive offering room (see C in Fig. 1). Most of the religious behavior and touristic voyeurism that occurs at the Santuario on weekdays transpires in this church complex. In this essay, I will focus only on the history of this site. The extensive grounds surrounding the church complex become loci of religious and social activity primarily during Holy Week and Good Friday devotions, when the number of pilgrims at the Santuario can number as many as twenty thousand.[1] At such moments, the surrounding shrine grounds are utilized for open-air masses, rosaries, and picnic grounds—activities which are beyond the scope of this essay.

Cosmology and History

Archaeologists maintain that the modern village of Chimayo encompasses three older indigenous sites that date back to a period between approximately A.D. 110 and A.D. 1400. The Tewa-speaking Indians of the nearby pueblos of San Juan, San Ildefonso, and Nambé consider the ground on which the village of Chimayo now sits to be sacred earth. The Indians say that according to legend, at the beginning of time, the Twin War Gods, the sons of Father Sun, slew an enemy giant nearby. When this occurred, fire burst out of the earth at Chimayo, drying up the hot spring that once existed there and leaving only mud. The Tewa Indians continued to visit the spot because of its healing dirt, or *nam po'uare* (*nam*, "earth," *po'uare*, "blessed").[2]

Given the power of the earth here, the Tewa Indians made the place one of the focal points that demarcated their sacral topography. In Pueblo Indian thought, the natural world had many formations that were deemed particularly powerful points of entry into other cosmic levels. Lakes, ponds, springs,

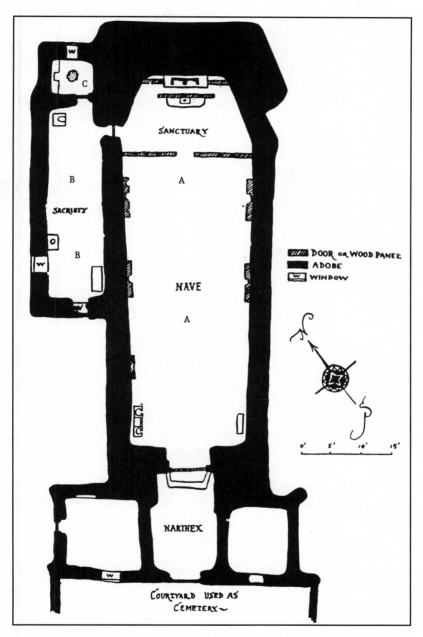

Figure 1   Santuario de Chimayo (After George Kubler, *The Religious Architecture of New Mexico*. Reprinted; UNM Press, 1990)

El Santuario de Chimayo

and sinkholes (known as *sipapus*) were potent nodes of entry into the un-
derworld, whence humans first emerged and to which they would return
after death. Mountain tops, particularly those surrounded by clouds, were
important sites of contact with the spirits that inhabited the sky. It was by
such cosmological rationale that the earthen hole at Chimayo (*Tsimajo'onwi*
in the Tewa language) became a pilgrimage site for the Pueblo Indians
who lived nearby.[3]

The Pueblo Indians maintain that *Tsimajo'onwi*'s transformation into a Christian shrine occurred when "the padres came and learned about the sipapu's
power... so they built a church." What occurred at Chimayo was a process
that was repeated hundreds of times throughout Spanish America. To con-
vert the Indians, Catholic priests frequently "baptized the local customs" by
building a church over native religious sites, hoping thereby to fuse architec-
tonically indigenous religious meanings and practices with those of the Christian faith.[4]

Throughout the seventeenth and eighteenth centuries, the Spanish
Christianization of Mexico's Indians proceeded, in part, through the creation
of such syncretic shrines. During the early nineteenth century, the shrine
constructed at Chimayo, which was devoted to the crucified Christ, Nuestro
Señor de Esquípulas, became the northernmost shrine in an extensive network of shrines that extended from New Mexico all the way south into
Central America. As one traveled from north to south along the Camino
Real, the royal road traversed by all personnel, commerce, and ideas between Santa Fe, New Mexico, and Mexico City, one passed through towns
that ostensibly had developed around pilgrimage sites. From north to south,
the most famous shrines were these: Nuestra Señora del Rayo in Parral,
Nuestro Señor de Mapimi in Cuencamé, Santo Niño de Atocha in Fresnillo,
Nuestra Señora de Patrocino in Zacatecas, Nuestra Señora de San Juan de
los Lagos in San Juan de los Lagos, Nuestra Señora de Zapopán in Guadalajara, Nuestra Señora de Talpa in Talpa, and Nuestra Señora de Guadalupe in
Mexico City. From Mexico City south, another network of shrines connected
the southern hinterlands of Central America with the religious center of the
Aztec empire in the Valley of Mexico.[5]

The Village of Chimayo: History

Spanish settlement of the Chimayo Valley came rather late in New Mexico's
colonial development. Though settlers had been in the Kingdom of New Mexico
since 1598, it was not until after the 1692 reconquest of the region, and the

defeat of the rebellious Pueblo Indians, that a hamlet named Plaza del Cerro was established near to what ultimately became Chimayo. The facts of the Plaza's foundation remain obscure. Mention of the Plaza del Cerro was made in documents dated 1714, but firm evidence of permanent Spanish settlement there does not really exist before the 1740s. Throughout the eighteenth century, the hamlet's residents eked out on existence through their agricultural endeavors and the production of woolen goods. The construction of a chapel at Chimayo, atop the indigenous *sipapu* and located just a few yards away from the Plaza del Cerro, was begun in 1813 and completed in 1816.[6]

Don Bernardo Abeyta, a wealthy resident of the area who traded the Chimayo Valley's products far and wide, personally commissioned the construction of the chapel that became known as the Santuario at Chimayo. Having personally traveled along the royal road that connected New Mexico with Mexico City, and noted how pilgrims flocked to the shrines along the route, thereby transforming these places into bustling commercial spots, one suspects that Don Bernardo hoped that by creating a shrine atop *Tsimajo'onwi*'s sacred hole, Chimayo would become a prosperous trading spot.[7] Such was the case. Quickly, the miracles attributed to the shrine attracted pilgrims. The pilgrims needed hospice and needed to be fed, and for these functions cottage industries emerged. As people moved to and fro, Chimayo's woolen and agricultural products began to circulate widely throughout northern New Spain. Prosperity for Chimayo's residents shortly followed.

How the chapel at Chimayo, New Mexico, came to be dedicated to Jesus Christ, Our Lord of Esquípulas, in honor of a shrine site in eastern Guatemala with a similar name, has been of great interest to historians over the decades. According to the most persuasive theory, that advanced by Stephen F. de Borhegyi, the cult of Our Lord of Esquípulas originated among the Chorti-speaking Maya Indians of eastern Guatemala around 1578, when Catholic missionaries constructed a chapel atop an ancient shrine site that had long been visited by the Indians for its miraculous earth and spring. The sacred earth here, when eaten, was alleged to have salubrious effects, and as the stories of the miracles and cures spread, so too did the devotees. During the seventeenth century, shrines devoted to the Christ of Esquípulas began to proliferate throughout southern Mexico. The first two, at Etla and Tlacolula in Oaxaca, reproduced two fundamental aspects of the Chorti shrine. Both new shrines were oriented around the practice of earth eating, and both had established a veneration to the crucified Christ. According to Borhegyi, by the end of the eighteenth century there were forty towns in Mexico, Guatemala, Honduras, El Salvador, Nicaragua, and Costa Rica that had shrines dedicated to the Christ of Esquípulas, all of which were associated with geophagy. The Santuario de Chimayo undoubtedly developed as an extension of this pattern.[8]

As early as 1805, it was evident that the devotion to Jesus Christ, the Lord of Esquípulas, had reached Chimayo. On March 5 of that year, an infant was christened Juan de Esquípula at El Potrero, the village next to Chimayo. Juan, coincidentally, was the son of Juana de Herrera and Mariano Abeyta, Bernardo Abeyta's brother. On March 14, 1813, the son of Bernardo Abeyta also was christened Tomás de Jesús de Esquípulas. From 1805 to 1820, the Esquípulas appellation was frequently used by the Abeyta clan as names for their own children and godchildren.[9] And when Bernardo Abeyta wrote Fray Sebastián Alvarez seeking permission to build a chapel at Chimayo on November 15, 1813, he stated that it was "to honor and venerate, with worthy worship Our Lord and Redeemer, in his Advocation of Esquípulas." Fray Sebastián Alvarez's cover letter, relaying Abeyta's request to the Vicar General, noted that an "image of Our Lord of Esquípulas," had been in Abeyta's possession for three years and that it was being housed and venerated in a small private chapel.[10] An episcopal permit was granted for the construction of the church at Chimayo on February 8, 1814. The building was completed sometime in 1816, and it soon became a frequently visited shrine.

Numerous legends that barely square with the known historical facts exist in New Mexico about how exactly the Santuario de Chimayo came into existence at its particular site. According to one of Bernardo Abeyta's grand-daughters, her grandfather constructed the shrine as a result of having encountered a cross during Lenten penitential rituals. One day, while in the hills near Potrero performing the Holy Week rituals of the Confraternity of Our Lord Jesus of Nazareth, or the Hermanos Penitentes, Don Bernardo discovered a bright light shining from a hole in the ground. He quickly dug at the spot and discovered a crucifix of Our Lord of Esquípulas. When the rest of the villagers saw the cross, they transported it to the parish church at nearby Santa Cruz, where it was placed on the main altar. But the very next morning, the crucifix had disappeared from its niche in the church and was discovered at the same hole where Bernardo Abeyta had found it. Again, the crucifix was transported back to the church, and again it miraculously returned to the original place where it had been discovered. This, obviously, was a significant sign. The cross wanted to be venerated at that spot. Bernardo Abeyta complied, commissioning the construction of an oratory for the cross, which became known as the Santuario de Chimayo.[11]

According to the legend recounted by Elizabeth Willis DeHuff in 1931,

Don Bernardo Abeyta selected the site for the Santuario as a result of a miraculous sign. One day, while the infirm Don Bernardo was sitting on the porch of his home, trying to recuperate his health, he looked out over his planted fields. "Then suddenly, down near the meandering acequia, there appeared to him the image of his Patron Saint, San Esquípula, beckoning to him. With great effort, the sick man threw off his blankets, arose and hobbled with difficulty in obedience to the summoning of the Saint; but before he could cross the ditch, the image of the Saint had vanished and Don Bernardo fell upon his knees on the spot where San Esquípula had stood. Immediately he was made well." To commemorate this blessing, Don Bernardo constructed a chapel atop the place where he had been cured.[12] Interesting as this legend is, it distorts some of the basic historical facts. There is no saint named San Esquípula; rather, the cult was a devotion to the crucified Christ, the Lord of Esquípulas. Later in this essay, I will try to explain why the Lord of Esquípulas might have been conflated in the popular imagination with an imaginary saint named San Esquípulas.

Benjamin M. Read reported in 1916 that the legend he had heard about the Santuario de Chimayo declared that it had been constructed soon after the 1837 Chimayo Rebellion, at the behest of the parish priest at Santa Cruz de la Cañada. Though the priest had admonished the residents to build a chapel, his pleas were ignored. But "one day the priest disappeared and the next morning, from a cottonwood that stood on the spot designated by the priest for a chapel, there protruded a foot. The people were so impressed with the miracle that they built the chapel and made it the most beautiful church in all of New Mexico."[13] Since the Santuario was evidently constructed by Bernardo Abeyta between 1813 and 1816, this legend too seems quite apocryphal.

As I noted above, the foundational legends of the Santuario de Chimayo are numerous. What they all tend to have in common is an association between the crucifix and the healing earth there. And, indeed, this was the principle reason the shrine became such a magnet in the early nineteenth century, just as New Mexico's missions were being secularized and many established parishes were being left without priests. To fill this void, many village locales in New Mexico established their own chapels, gathering together to create their own sense of religious community amid their sacred icons, which they placed on ground that they deemed to be sanctified.

Today, as one enters the room that contains the sacred earthen hole of the Santuario, one finds little in the room. It is a small room that is approximately seven feet by seven feet. Save for religious pictures of the Santo Niño, the crucified Christ, and the Virgin Mary, little else adorns the walls of this room. Against one wall is a table for votive candles, and given the small dimensions of the room, the heat these candles generate makes for a rather saunalike environment.

During one of my 1990 visits to the Santuario, I discovered two notes that had been attached to one of the walls inside the room with the sacred hole.[14] The longest note was carefully printed on poster board by a person named G. Mendoza from Las Cruces, New Mexico. It read:

I am blind, traveled many miles to Chimayo, a place I love, in its silence and peace I left this gift . . . a poem. If you are a stranger, if you are weary from the struggles in life, whether you have a handicap, whether you have a broken heart, follow the long mountain road, find a home in Chimayo. It's a small Spanish town settled many years ago by people with a friendly hand, their culture still lives today. They will tell stories about miracles in the land. Since 1813 Santuario is the key to all good. A church built as graceful as a flower swaying in a summer breeze, nested in a valley protected by wild berry trees. In the dusty road of Chimayo little children with brown faces smile, majestic mountain tops rule over the virgin land. When the day is done the sun falls asleep without regret. Sleeping in the twinkle of a starry, starrynight [sic]. Its that old country feeling in Chimayo I can't forget. In all the places in the world I have been, this must be heaven.

Next to this poem was a shorter note from María Rodriguez that simply said in Spanish, "Santo Niño, I beg that you grant my children and family good health and good luck."

Most pilgrims enter this room, take dirt from the hole, and quickly exit back into the votive offering room through which they entered. On the average, neither religious pilgrims nor tourists linger around the sacred hole because of the number of persons usually waiting to enter and because of the extreme heat in the room, in comparison to the coolness of the rest of the shrine complex.

Ex-voto Room

Pilgrims and tourists enter and exit the room with the Santuario's sacred hole through an adjacent oblong room that runs parallel to the church nave and which I will refer to here as the ex-voto room. The focal point of the ex-voto room is a statue of the Santo Niño de Atocha that sits in a wooden niche/grotto.

The ex-voto room is one of the original spaces of the shrine edifice that Don Bernardo Abeyta had constructed at Chimayo in 1816. But it was not until sometime in the 1850s that its current focal point, the statue of the Santo Niño de Atocha, was placed therein. Apparently, this was done due to economic rivalries that had developed in Chimayo as a result of the Santuario's success. As the number of pilgrims coming to the site grew, and profits from hospice and trade also increased exponentially, Severiano Medina, another Chimayo resident, decided to build his own chapel and pilgrimage site about twenty-five yards north of the Santuario. Medina's descendants maintain that he was suffering from severe rheumatism and got relief by praying to the Santo Niño. Having regained his health, Medina dedicated his chapel to the Santo Niño de Atocha, in honor of the shrine in Fresnillo, Zacatecas, Mexico. Hoping to capitalize on the lucrative business that accompanied shrines, Medina traveled to Fresnillo to buy a statue of the Santo Niño de Atocha, which he then installed in his chapel. This oratory, dedicated to the Santo Niño de Atocha, was completed sometime around 1860.[15]

As had been the case with the Santuario to Our Lord of Esquípulas, the Chimayo's shrine to the Santo Niño de Atocha began attracting numerous pilgrims. They were drawn by the stories of the miraculous nightly journeys of the Holy Child of Atocha, and of his enormous power to promote blessings and prosperity. Legend has it that the image of the Santo Niño came to reside in Severiano Medina's chapel as a result of a miracle. One day, a man and his daughter were driving their oxen to their fields when they heard a church bell ringing underground. The girl asked her father to dig out the bell. He did, but he also found a statue of the Santo Niño de Atocha underneath the bell. It was at this spot that the chapel to the Santo Niño was built. The figure of the Holy Child of Atocha was placed in a specially constructed grotto, dressed in elaborate clothing, and given a real pair of infant shoes. Chimayo's residents soon discovered that every morning the shoes on the Santo Niño were worn out, despite the fact that new ones were placed on him every day. "At the same time, sickness disappeared, the crops were abundant, the number of sheep multiplied, better markets were found for the Chimayo blankets woven in the homes, and the Chimayo's prospered wonderfully," explained Benjamin M. Read in 1916. "It was evident that the Christ child[16] each night went up and down the valley to bless its people and its households."[17]

Fearing that the Santuario, with its devotion to Christ, the Lord of Esquípulas, might dwindle in importance with the construction of a rival shrine to the Holy Child of Atocha, Carmen Chaves, the daughter of Bernardo

Abeyta and heir of the Santuario after his 1856 death, also bought a statue
of the Santo Niño de Atocha. This statue was placed in the ex-voto room so
that the Santuario de Chimayo could compete with the rival shrine down
the road. In the long run, the Santuario remained dominant as a shrine site,
boasting not only the crucified Christ of Esquípulas, the Santo Niño de
Atocha, but also miraculous images of St. James and St. Joseph, and the
miraculous earthen hole. In fact, I suspect that it was this conjunction of
various images with a particular sacred space that explains why many of
Chimayo's shrine legends refer to San Esquípulas, despite the fact that
there is no such saint. And this, too, may be the reason why many pilgrims
insist that the Santo Niño de Atocha's statue was initially discovered in the
shrine's earthen hole.

In contemporary times, despite the centrality of the statue of the Santo
Niño de Atocha and its grotto, what gains most attention in the ex-voto
room are the numerous votive offerings that have been left there by pilgrims.
Every wall space and every shelf space in the room is covered with religious
statues of various sizes, with equally varied pictures of Christ, the Virgin Mary,
the saints, and angels, with very personal missives and poems, as well as
canes, crutches, limb braces, and glasses. It is not uncommon for a person to
vow a pilgrimage to the Santuario if they recover rapidly from a broken bone,
surgery, or an illness. Thus, in the ex-voto room one finds, as I did in 1990,
twenty-five crutches, five canes, two leg braces, and two pairs of eyeglasses.
The room had over 170 religious pictures of various sizes, shapes, and quality
on the wall. There were eighteen pictures of the crucifixion, fifteen of Our
Lady of Guadalupe, fourteen of Our Lady of the Rosary, fourteen of the
Santo Niño, eleven of the face of Christ in agony, and a variety of pictures of
the Holy Family, the Last Supper, the Crown of Thorns, St. Stanislaus, St.
Teresa of Avila, St. Anthony, St. Martín de Porras, the Good Shepherd, and
Pope John XXIII.

The religious statuary that pilgrims had left as offerings was also immense,
numbering around 150. With the statuary, St. Jude was the most popular
icon, with nineteen statues of him in various sizes. The Sacred Heart of Jesus
was next in popularity, with sixteen statues. There were thirteen statues of St.
Joseph, thirteen of St. Anthony, eight of St. Martín de Porras, five of the Santo
Niño de Atocha, and a few of the Virgin of Guadalupe and Our Lady of
Sorrows.

Often, the pictures and statues that had been left in the room carried
personal inscriptions and missives. The note attached to a picture of the

Santo Niño read: "I thank you Lord for the good health I have been given by visiting your sanctuary, which you have given us"; it was signed Margarita de Fernandez. Juan Miranda attached his business card to a picture of the Good Shepherd, writing on the card, "Pray for Us." Jessica León Espinosa wrote on a picture of the Santo Niño: "Pray for Our Families. Thank You." A "Missing Person" poster of Manuel Espinosa described him as "39 years old, 5'8" tall, 150 lbs., Dark brown hair, light brown eyes, thick salt and pepper moustache, tatoos [sic] on right arm 'Jesus' and left arm 'Rose.' Last seen, Thursday October 30, 1986 at 1 p.m. in Española area." Attached to the poster was a small wallet-size devotional card with an image of St. Anthony, on which had been penned:

God. We pray to you O Lord that if you can return my lost father one day. We pray to you O Lord. Please protect him wherever he is and please keep him alive and well. Thank you. Amen.

On a picture of the Virgin of Guadalupe, Flora C. Romero left the following inscription:

Please Dear God help my boyfriend Robert Trejo get out of the mess he got into. Believe in him dear God. I no. I do. Help him be strong dear God. Help him face what's ahead, help him in anyway. Dear God, I don't care what the papers say or what people say. Dear God what matters is what I feel and what I see. Dear God, he's a wonderful person. Dear God I care for this person very much. Dear God, he's not capable of hurting anyone purposely. Dear God believe in him, help him, be with him [sic].

On a picture of Christ's Crown of Thorns, Mary, Paul, and John López had attached a slip of paper on which they had written:

Father God, in the name of Jesus we thank you for healing John our son. Thanks for bringing us together to worship you and thank you.

To a picture of Our Lady of Guadalupe, the Chacón family had attached the following note:

I have alway's have faith in Our Lady of Fatima, and all the saints there in El Santuario in Chimayo, this holy place. El Santuario has alway's made many miracles for our family. I know you are the saint that watches over the small children. Could you take care of my two boy's, keep them in good health and safe. Always remember to keep me and my wife and our two boys from any harm coming into us.

Attached to another picture of the Virgin of Guadalupe were four family photos and an inscription dated November 1986, which read:

We are donating this to El Santuario de Chimayo in loving memory of Eloisa Gabaldon Burke our beloved mother whom Our Lady of Guadalupe call to heaven on Her feast day December 12, 1985.

Numerous other notes, poems, and inscriptions were attached to the religious pictures in the ex-voto room. What they had in common, despite their variations, were pleas of divine supplication, seeking relief from an illness, help in securing work, assistance in locating missing persons and objects, and rest for departed brethren. At times, these ex-votos described the reason that a person had made a pilgrimage to the Santuario. Many times, the ex-votos were offerings of thanksgiving for a son's safe return from military service, for a healthy childbirth, for business success, and for a bumper crop and good rains.

Shrine Sanctuary

Chimayo's church was constructed in 1816 and followed the basic design and pattern of the "fortress church," which was introduced into the Kingdom of New Mexico by the Franciscan friars in 1610. Constructed of adobes, sun-baked mud bricks, the church is modeled along a single-aisle nave with a polygonal apse oriented toward the northwest. This orientation allowed the main altar to receive a flood of morning light from a transverse clerestory when the faithful usually congregated for Mass. The nave of the church is approximately four times as long as it is wide. Given the limited length of the vigas (wooden roof support beams) available in the surrounding mountains, the external width of Chimayo church is approximately thirty-three feet and about twenty feet internally, with a wall width of five feet. In length, the church is approximately eighty feet. The nave is about twenty feet high, the apse being higher, at about thirty feet. The only architectural embellishments in the nave are the painted floral decorations on the corbels that support the roof beams.[18]

Within the church nave, five wooden altar screens, known as *reredos* or *retablos,* adorn the church walls. There are two altar screens each on both sides of the church nave; the fifth one forms the backdrop for the main altar. The altar screens were built and painted by three local New Mexican artisans, José Aragón, Miguel Aragón, and a *santero* (saint maker) named Molleno, or the "Chili painter," in the late nineteenth century. Employing the standard spatial organization for such *retablos,* the *santeros* adorned each of the screens with familiar Franciscan iconography. Each *retablo* usually has at its top a figure of God the Father or the Blessed Trinity, flanked by the Virgin Mary and various apostles. Below these are images of St. Francis, the Franciscan Order's logo (the arms of Christ and St. Francis of Assisi crossed), and an assortment of Franciscan martyrs and saints. The focus of the main altar is the image of the crucified Christ, Lord of Esquípulas, which Don Bernardo Abeyta purchased and brought to Chimayo to serve as the founding image of the shrine.

If one studies the available historical photographs of the Santuario de Chimayo, little has changed in the internal nave and sanctuary since its construction in 1816. What has changed is the external facade. The original flat roof and elevated apse were covered over by a corrugated iron roof sometime around 1916. Wooden gables were added to the twin bell towers at the insistence of Bishop Jean Lamy in 1869, thus adding a medieval style to the church facade, previously characterized by its horizontal lines.[19]

Contemporary Pilgrims and Tourists, 1990–1991

On a routine spring or summer weekday, it is not unusual for from five to ten thousand persons to visit the Santuario de Chimayo; on Sundays, the number is even higher because of the parishioners who attend Mass here. The greatest number of visitors arrive in large tourist buses that stop at all of the "exotic" and "picturesque" spots that lie on the old mountain road that once was the only link between Santa Fe and Taos. Others come in rented cars, more leisurely ambling over the terrain of northern New Mexico. A small number of persons arrive on foot, by local transport, or in their own cars, having traveled the distance out of entirely religious motivations.

During the several weeks I spent at Chimayo, studying the history of the shrine and the behavior of its visitors, it was very clear that the ethnic group that most traveled to the shrine out of religious motivations were Hispanos. In the course of one hour, for example, I counted 218 Hispano pilgrims, 37 persons who appeared to be Anglo, and 10 Pueblo Indians, identified by their distinctive clothes and by the men's traditional pony-tail hairstyle.

The majority of tourists of various nationalities entered the shrine without any visible marks of reverence—they did not cross themselves with holy water on entering, they did not genuflect before entering the sacristy, and they did not touch or take any dirt from the sacred hole; and, instead, they entered dressed in short pants, armed with cameras, and speaking loudly throughout their visit. Thus, these tourists were quite easy to differentiate from religious pilgrims. Tourists entered the shrine and, on average, stayed about four minutes; the exception being one tourist who stayed eleven minutes.[20]

The religious pilgrims entered the shrine and immediately crossed themselves with holy water. They took a place in one of the church pews, kneeling there in prayer for anywhere from five minutes to two hours. Once their prayer behavior was complete, they genuflected before the main altar and proceeded to the room with the sacred hole. There, they knelt and took dirt. One Hispano man, carrying his two-year-old son, who was in a complete body cast, lowered the child into the hole and rubbed dirt on his cast. Several women in leg braces did likewise, rubbing dirt from the hole on their legs. After coming in contact with the sacred hole, pilgrims exited into the ex-voto room, and there they frequently spent ten to thirty minutes reading the votive offerings, praying, and lighting candles for the different saints represented there. Finally, when they existed the church complex, they spent several more hours by the stream that runs in front of the shrine, having a picnic or consuming food from the local concession stands.

On leaving the Santuario, the pilgrims attest that they have experienced great peace, renewal, and quite often, salubrious effects. "I have witnessed people on the verge of suicide, people depressed beyond what they can endure, suddenly changed. It is as if someone has become another person. . . . At the santuario people feel that God listens to them," notes Father Casimiro Roca, the resident priest at the Santuario since 1959.[21]

The Santuario de Chimayo renews, restores, and rejuvenates pilgrims tormented by the mental and physical pains, conflicts, and afflictions of modern industrial society. Since time immemorial, women and men of every faith have left their homes and normal surroundings, and as an act of penitence, they have traveled to a distant sacred place. There, by entering a particularly potent sacral topography marked by images, religious symbols, and offerings, they have nourished and restored themselves. Historically, this has been the function that the Santuario de Chimayo serves for its pilgrims, whatever their faith, whatever their woes.[22]

Notes

1. Father Casimiro Roca stated, in 1979, that the number of pilgrims at Chimayo were "10,000 to 12,000." Quoted in Scottie King, "Pilgrimage to a Hallowed Place: Good Friday at Chimayo," *New Mexico Magazine* 57, no. 3 (March 1979), 27.
2. The archaeological history of Chimayo is discussed in Stephen F. de Borhegyi, *El Santuario de Chimayo* (Santa Fe: Ancient City Press, 1956), 8. John Peabody

Harrington discusses the Tewa legends about Chimayo in "The Ethnogeography of the Tewa Indians," in the *Bureau of American Ethnology, Twenty-ninth Annual Report* (Washington, D.C., 1916), 341–42.

3. Ramón A. Gutiérrez, *When Jesus Came, the Corn Mothers Went Away: Marriage, Sexuality and Power in New Mexico, 1500–1846* (Stanford, Calif.: Stanford University Press, 1991), 5–34.

4. Victor and Edith Turner, *Image and Pilgrimage in Christian Culture: Anthropological Perspectives* (New York: Columbia University Press, 1978), 33.

5. N. Ross Crumrine and Alan Morinis, eds., *Pilgrimage in Latin America* (New York: Greenwood Press, 1991).

6. E. Boyd, *Historic Preservation: A Plan for New Mexico* (Santa Fe: New Mexico State Planning Office, 1971), 79–81, as quoted in Samuel Larcombe, "Plaza del Cerro, Chimayó, New Mexico: An Old Place Not Quite on the Highway," in *Hispanic Arts and Ethnohistory in the Southwest: New Papers in Honor of E. Boyd*, ed. Marta Weigle, Claudia Larcombe, and Samuel Larcombe (Santa Fe: Ancient City Press, 1983), 171–73.

7. Stanley F. Crocchiola maintains that one of the Franciscan friars stationed in the Santa Cruz Valley was responsible for the arrival of the cult to Christ of Esquípulas. He asserts this without any evidence. See his *El Potrero de Chimayo, New Mexico* (Nazareth, Tex.: Privately printed, 1969), p. 7.

8. Stephen F. de Borhegyi, "The Cult of Our Lord of Esquípulas in Middle America and New Mexico," *El Palacio* 61, no. 12 (December 1954), 387–401.

9. de Borhegyi, *El Santuario de Chimayo*, 11.

10. Ibid., 11.

11. Ibid., 17–18.

12. Elizabeth Willis DeHuff, "The Santuario de Chimayo," *New Mexico Magazine* (June 1931), 16–17.

13. Legend reported by a Mr. Walter, as quoted in Benjamin M. Read, "El Santuario de Chimayo," *El Palacio* 3, no. 4 (August 1916), 82.

14. Because of the great number of items left at the Santuario by pilgrims, the shrine's custodian regularly removes the accumulation. Thus, the items can change from day to day.

15. David Roybal, "Legends Abound about Chimayo's 'Other' Church," *The Santa Fe New Mexican*, March 18, 1979, B-3.

16. Read is wrong in calling the Santo Niño of Atocha the Christ Child. The Holy Child of Atocha was a child who provisioned imprisoned Christians during the Moorish occupation of Spain. On this point and on the history of the Santo Niño de Atocha, see Alexander M. Frankfurter, "A Gathering of Children: Holy Infants and the Cult of El Santo Niño de Atocha," *El Palacio* 94, no. 1 (Summer/Fall 1988), 31–39; Yvonne Lange, "Santo Niño de Atocha: A Mexican Cult Is Transplanted to Spain," *El Palacio* 84, no. 4 (Winter 1978), 2–8. See also Elizabeth Kay, *Chimayo Valley Traditions* (Santa Fe: Ancient City Press, 1987).

17. Legend reported by a Mr. Walter, as quoted in Read, "El Santuario de Chimayo," 82.

18. Bainbridge Bunting, *Early Architecture in New Mexico* (Albuquerque: University of New Mexico Press, 1976), 55–59; and *Of Earth and Timbers Made: New Mexico Architecture* (Albuquerque: University of New Mexico Press, 1974), 73.
19. Bunting, *Of Earth and Timbers Made,* 73.
20. For two days, I followed at a distance every tenth person, noting their behavior from the moment they entered the shrine until they left.
21. Joseph Dispenza, "Hallowed Ground: Spiritual Paths Lead to New Mexico," *New Mexico Magazine* 65, no. 3 (March 1987), 46–55; quote on 49.
22. On the social and psychological functions of pilgrimage, see Turner, *Image and Pilgrimage in Christian Culture.*

References

Bunting, Bainbridge. *Early Architecture in New Mexico.* Albuquerque: University of New Mexico Press, 1976.

————. *Of Earth and Timbers Made: New Mexico Architecture.* Albuquerque: University of New Mexico Press, 1974.

Crocchiola, Stanley F. *El Potrero de Chimayo, New Mexico.* Nazareth, Tex.: Privately printed, 1969.

Crumrine, N. Ross, and Alan Morinis, eds. *Pilgrimage in Latin America.* New York: Greenwood Press, 1991.

de Borhegyi, Stephen F. "The Cult of Our Lord of Esquípulas in Middle America and New Mexico." *El Palacio* 61, no. 12 (December 1954), 387–401.

————. *El Santuario de Chimayo.* Santa Fe: Ancient City Press, 1956.

Dispenza, Joseph. "Hallowed Ground: Spiritual Paths Lead to New Mexico." *New Mexico Magazine* 65, no. 3 (March 1987), 46–55.

Frankfurter, Alexander M. "A Gathering of Children: Holy Infants and the Cult of El Santo Niño de Atocha." *El Palacio* 94, no. 1 (Summer/Fall 1988), 31–39.

Gutiérrez, Ramón A. *When Jesus Came, the Corn Mothers Went Away: Marriage, Sexuality and Power in New Mexico, 1500–1846.* Stanford, Calif.: Stanford University Press, 1991.

Harrington, John Peabody. "The Ethnogeography of the Tewa Indians." *Bureau of American Ethnology, Twenty-ninth Annual Report,* Washington, D.C., 1916.

Kay, Elizabeth. *Chimayo Valley Traditions.* Santa Fe: Ancient City Press, 1987.

King, Scottie. "Pilgrimage to a Hallowed Place: Good Friday at Chimayo." *New Mexico Magazine* 57, no. 3 (March 1979), 27.

Lange, Yvonne. "Santo Niño de Atocha: A Mexican Cult Is Transplanted to Spain." *El Palacio* 84, no. 4 (Winter 1978), 2–8.

Read, Benjamin M. "El Santuario de Chimayo." *El Palacio* 3, no. 4 (August 1916), 82–84.

Roybal, David. "Legends Abound about Chimayo's 'Other' Church." *The Santa Fe New Mexican,* March 18, 1979, B-3.

Turner, Victor and Edith. *Image and Pilgrimage in Christian Culture: Anthropological Perspectives.* New York: Columbia University Press, 1978.

Weigle, Marta, Claudia Larcombe, and Samuel Larcombe, eds. *Hispanic Arts and Ethnohistory in the Southwest: New Papers in Honor of E. Boyd.* Santa Fe: Ancient City Press, 1983.

Willis DeHuff, Elizabeth. "The Santuario de Chimayo." *New Mexico Magazine* (June 1931), 16–17.

7

"First You Feed Them, Then You Clothe Them, Then You Save Them"[1]
The Hungry and Homeless and the Sunday Feast at a Pentecostal Storefront Church in East Harlem

Anna Lou Dehavenon

A number of anthropologists have studied the role of ritual practices in the ecology of human groups (Harris, 1974; Moore; Piddocke; Rappaport). This approach is used here to observe and analyze the role of a Sunday feast in the efforts of a small, storefront, Pentecostal church, in a predominantly low-income African-American and Puerto Rican neighborhood in New York City, to feed and nurture the homeless.

Introduction: the Place and the People

The "Glorious Church without a Spot or a Wrinkle"[2] Pentecostal Church is located in the East Harlem block where, since 1971, I have conducted research and observed the processes of landlord abandonment and public disinvestment in housing that culminated in the city's low-income housing crisis and the homelessness of the 1980s and 1990s. These processes included the conjunction of (1) rent-control laws first enacted during World War II, and (2) the high rates of inflation that escalated the costs of heating fuel after the 1974 oil embargo, while decreasing the purchasing power of the rent money paid by the state for families on public assistance. As a result of these two factors, thousands of landlords stopped paying taxes and making the necessary repairs on the buildings that they no longer found profitable. Many eventually abandoned or set fire to their properties in order to collect the insurance.[3]

Furthermore, by the mid-1970s the city was on the verge of bankruptcy and therefore unable (or lacking the political will) to maintain most of the hundreds of buildings it inherited through landlord tax default as low-income housing. As time passed, the city razed many of them because they were public hazards or to make way for future redevelopment.

In the block where the church stands, these processes resulted in the destruction, after 1973, of eighteen of the structures that had formerly stood on the block's forty-one building lots. Soon these eighteen empty lots were strewn with garbage and other trash, and by 1989 only six of the buildings still standing were occupied. Among the buildings still erect were an abandoned elementary school and six tenements that new owners had bought recently from the city to renovate as condominiums and to sell at prices far higher than the previous tenants could pay. The loss of habitable, low-income housing after 1970 resulted in a decrease of at least 80 percent in the block's population. Nevertheless, the ethnic and class diversity of East Harlem was still represented by the people who continued to live there. Most identified themselves as African American or Puerto Rican, but there were also Hispanics and a few Asians, Africans, and whites. Furthermore, the young professionals who were beginning to move into the condominiums added to a class mix that included marginally employed, low-income families as well as those on public assistance and a number of "street" or homeless people.

The church rents the small, storefront space of one of the occupied tenements, where it has performed all of its rituals and missionizing activities since 1978. While the rent has increased fourfold, the landlord has not yet repaired the two large windows facing the street, the toilet, or the two electrical outlets, all of which have been broken for some time.

Historically, Pentecostalism is one of the fundamentalist Protestant religions that grew out of a movement beginning in the early twentieth century in the United States, and emphasized a perfectionist doctrine of holiness. Among its practices are baptism by the Holy Ghost, religious excitement accompanied by possession trance, glossolalia or "speaking in tongues," faith healing, and a belief in the impending second coming of Christ. Bourguinon (55) describes traditional, lower-class, Pentecostalism as follows:

There is . . . a positive side of possession belief in Christianity, namely the idea of being "filled" with the Holy Spirit. It is based . . . on the account of the Pentecost (Acts 2) when according to the text the Holy Ghost descended on the apostles and bestowed on them the gift of tongues. That is, they preached to a multitude in languages they themselves did not know. . . . Pentecostal cults are religions of salvation, with dramatic conversions, spiritual healing, group participation in ritual, singing and music, sometimes dancing, but generally a broad range of motor behavior. . . . It is a characteristically

American phenomenon; it developed among both black and white poor, in relatively isolated rural areas.

Bourguinon argues that the needs satisfied through these ritual practices relate specifically to the "healing of physical illness in societies where medical care is inadequate and where the stresses of life lead to a number of psychosomatic disorders."

The leading participants in the Glorious Church's activities (and especially the pastor, Mother Christine Hall)[4] define the church's goal as "saving souls for the Lord." I focus here on how the Sunday ritual, and the preparation and consumption of the feast that follows it, contributes to the realization of this goal while shielding the participants from some of the extreme effects of the poverty that exists in New York City today.

Participation in the Ritual Directly Observed[5]

On Sunday May 7, 1989, the ritual week began as usual at 10:00 A.M. with Sunday school and Bible reading for both children and adults. The principal ritual service, which followed at 11:00 A.M. did not conclude until 3:30 P.M. Seventy people attended all (or some part) of the service, during which the final preparations for the feast were being carried out behind the curtain partition that separates the miniscule kitchen from the sanctuary.

The church members and other regular participants seated in the sanctuary included all ages. Twenty-two younger children were equally divided by gender; of seven adolescents, four were girls and three were boys. During the ritual, one of the adolescent girls played the organ, while two of the boys and one of the girls took turns at the drums. Also present were the eight older women who are known as the "saints" or "mothers" of the church, and the three older men who are either elders or deacons. Seated down front and up on the podium were the pastor, Mother Hall, the assistant pastor, Elder Patrick Lee, and Elder John Pickett. Included among thirty-three remaining participants were several men who had come from the large city homeless shelter for men, which is fifteen minutes away by foot.

Throughout the ritual, a line of eighty more people was forming on the sidewalk outside the church. They gathered and waited for the feast, which was to be served after the conclusion of the ritual. Most of them were young, African-American and Hispanic men who, because of the limited space inside the church, could enter only in shifts of fifteen. Figure 2 shows the church's physical layout.

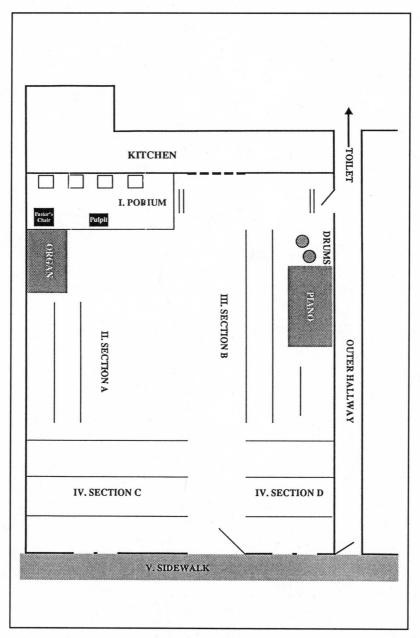

Figure 2   Physical Layout of the Glorious Church without a Spot or Wrinkle

The status of each participant is hierarchically defined by degree of holiness and authority, role in the ritual, age, and the space occupied. Figure 3 shows the status hierarchy.

I. Seated in Front on the Podium:

Pastor, Assistant Pastor, and Male Elder

II. Seated in Front below the Podium:

Female Saints, Male Deacon, and Children

III. Seated in Back:

All Other Adult Participants

IV. Standing on the Sidewalk outside the Church:

Homeless People Waiting to Eat

Figure 3

The pastor's chair was placed strategically to the immediate left of the pulpit and just above the organ. From there, she was able to monitor and direct all activity inside and outside the church: microphone in hand, she showed the ushers where to seat each person who entered, directed the order of the ritual, reprimanded the children as needed, and commanded the "army" of homeless men she had saved and "enlisted in the Lord's work." When the first cash offering did not yield enough money, it was she who decided when to call for a second. To sing or deliver "the message," she stood up at the pulpit.

At the very end of the ritual, she walked down the two steps from the podium to the parterre and turned left to enter the kitchen, to briefly oversee the progress of the feast. A few minutes later, she returned and slowly proceeded down the aisle while greeting those seated on either side. When she came to the door, she went outside and greeted each person standing in line.

During the ritual, the assistant pastor and the male elder sat with the pastor on the podium. Unlike the pastor, they were seated behind the pulpit, from where they were only visible to the other participants when they stood up. These two men's principal responsibilities included giving their personal testimonies of how they had been saved, delivering the message when the pastor asked them to, annointing those who came forward to give themselves to the Lord, and collecting and counting the offering.[6] They also fulfilled any other request the pastor made of them. Since they both drive cars, they were to transport to the church the food that some of the members prepared in their homes. However, neither of the elders prepared or served any of the foods for the feast.

The saints were seated in Section A in Figure 7.1, immediately below the podium, next to the organ, and next to the entrance to the kitchen, where one of them went in and out to help cook while still participating in the ritual. The saints supervised the younger children seated directly opposite them in Section B, and ministered to both the spiritual and the physical needs of those who were being saved. The adolescents sat with the younger children, or (if they performed) at one of the musical instruments. All the children participated in the entire ritual, and after a few hours, the younger ones fell fast asleep, leaning back in their chairs with their mouths open.

The other church members and the visitors were seated in Sections C and D further back and on either side of the aisle. During the ritual, each participant who had already been saved was expected to "testify," or give their own description of how this had come about and how it had changed their lives. All those who had not yet been "saved" were expected to "give themselves to the Lord" before the ritual was over and to comply with all of the pastor's other requests as well. The men were to remove their hats before coming into the church, and when one of them apparently forgot, she sharply reprimanded him.

Participation in the Feast Directly Observed

The preparations for the feast had begun the previous Friday, when, at 5:00 A.M., the pastor drove her car from her apartment in a large public housing project near the church in East Harlem to the wholesale food market in the Bronx. There, she personally chose and paid for the fresh fruit and vegetables for the feast, which were purchased off the trucks that had brought them from New Jersey and other, more southern states. All week long, she had watched the newspapers for the "buys of the week" on groceries and on chicken, for which she tries not to pay more than thirty-eight cents a pound. On this Friday, her next stop was the Manhattan supermarket that advertised the lowest prices that week. After finally purchasing all of the ingredients for the feast, she transported some back to the church and some to the apartments of certain of the church members who were to cook at home.

The food preparation, which began Saturday morning at the church, would not be over until after the feast was served. It stopped for the night at 10:00 P.M., only to resume the next morning and continue throughout the Sunday ritual. There were four cooks at the church: two of the saints and two of the homeless men who had been saved and had joined "Mother's Army." Halfway through the ritual, in full view of all the participants and in succession, the assistant pastor and one of the elders carried eight large platters of food down the aisle, past the altar, and into the kitchen. For some time now, cooking aromas wafting over the curtained partition had become more and more tantalizing. Only after the ritual had ended, and Mother Hall had greeted everyone both inside and outside the church, did she regain her seat on the podium and indicate to the soldiers that the serving of the feast should begin.

Three of the adolescent girls had already gone around the corner immediately after the ritual to spend their own pocket money on their favorite small snacks. The pastor's first concern was for the small children who, by now, had been sitting for six hours. She asked the soldiers to "feed my children first. They have been here the longest." But before anyone could do this, she asked the children to "give up your chairs to those who came to eat." The children moved quickly to the steps that lead to the podium, the outer hallway, and the toilet. These passageways (and the one to the kitchen) were soon so constricted that the slightest misstep would have led to a spilled tray of food or beverages. The children sat and waited to be fed.

While both the soldiers and the saints cooked, only the soldiers served food. First, one of them placed a small, white cloth-covered table on the podium to receive the generously served platters of "Mother's food." She blessed this food and then served her own plate. In order, this consisted of rice, collard greens and ham, macaroni and cheese, cornbread, lettuce and tomato, and roast chicken. (Also included on the menu that day were fried chicken, pigs' feet, and rice and beans.)[7] Next, the pastor tasted each of these foods and then motioned to the assistant pastor, the elder, and me (those sitting at her table) to serve ourselves. This accomplished, the soldier who had carried the platters from the kitchen carefully covered each one with paper towels.

One of the soldiers placed a second small, white cloth-covered table on the parterre just below the pulpit. Three colorfully frosted cakes, which had been cooked in members' homes, were then put on display there. One of the saints, Mother Smith, brought a chair to the table, sat down on it, and began slicing the cakes. She first asked those seated at Mother Hall's table which one they wanted to try, and then she cut and handed them a plate with the slice of their choice. By contrast (and in full view of everyone), she would later cut much smaller slices of all three cakes and place them on top of each generously served plate that would be handed from a tray four at a time to each of the other participants. In like fashion, while those at the pastor's table were asked to choose between orange juice, ice tea, or ice water served in glasses, the other participants were handed Koolaid already served in a plastic cup. Only those at her table enjoyed the other niceties of hot sauce and a bottled salad dressing, and only they could take what they wanted and serve themselves.

Meanwhile, the pastor monitored the food on all the other plates. Before the soldiers handed out a single plate of food, they brought a tray of four for her to inspect. She tasted each item of food, one by one. If something was not to her liking, she called out in a loud voice to those behind the partition, asking them what else they had and telling them to increase the portion of a given food, or to add or eliminate another.

Finally, she asked those who had attended Sunday school to raise their hands, and she indicated that they be served first. Then she asked those who had attended the ritual to show their hands, and she told the soldiers to serve them next. When one of the soldiers apparently made a mistake as to whether or not one of his shelter mates had attended the ritual, she and the other participants all corrected him immediately and admonished the pretender to attend the ritual the next week in order to be among those to eat first.

As soon as those served first had finished eating, the ushers led them outside, to make room for those on the line who had been handed one of fifteen numbers earlier. They came in and sat down. After all of the seats were taken, Brother Bill (one of the soldiers the pastor had already saved) began recounting how he had been saved "sitting right here on this chair" and how he had "given up his stem for the Lord."[8] He concluded by asking them to do what he had done; but when only one of them came forward to the podium, the pastor rose up out of her chair to stand at the pulpit and tell them "not to be shy but stand up and give yourselves to the Lord who made you and not yourselves." She added that for her they were "all stars, all beautiful and all of the Lord's own heart." After each one sang or spoke their own testimony, she asked them all to stand up and answer this question: "Do you believe that Jesus died on the cross for your sins?" Only when each one had responded "Yes" did she raise her arms and proclaim, "According to my Bible, you are saved!" Next, she commanded them to kneel down right where they were and pray. Only after they had all finished and returned to their seats did the soldiers begin to hand them the plates of food. This process was repeated fifteen at a time until all those who waited on line had heard Brother Bob's testimony, had given their own, and had been saved and fed.

One of the soldiers came to tell the pastor that there were several people on the line who wanted to come in to speak with her. She granted each of these requests, and as each person entered she motioned them to come toward her. She listened attentively to whatever they had to tell her. Those whom she knew often spoke about their families and asked her to help in specific ways. She also listened carefully to those she did not already know and advised them concerning the personal problems they described to her. She always ended these tête-à-tête with the same admonition: "I know you came for the physical food, but I have spiritual food for you. Come see me during the week."

Throughout the ritual and then serving of the feast, Mother Hall had also maintained a watchful eye for those whom she recognized as being in special need of her help or of salvation. These she called to her, serving them personally from the food from her table, and offering them second helpings of the food she thought had particularly pleased them. She pointedly directed this "favoritism" to those whose testimonies had particularly moved her, or to those to whom her attention was somehow otherwise drawn. She asked each one if they didn't think that the church's food was like their mother's. She told them that she needed them for her army, "because I am building a great church and want to take you along with me." She ended by asking each one to come see her during the week, while pointing out the formerly homeless men she had already clothed, found jobs and housing for, and helped rejoin their families.

Discussion

An analysis of the feast can be made on three levels. On an emic level, which represents the perspective of the participants (Harris, 1983; Headland, Pike and Harris), it is a gift to those who consume it in Mauss's sense of the term, for example, as a total social phenomenon in which religious, economic, aesthetic, and moral values combine, and which he describes as follows:

Une partie considérable de notre morale et de notre vie elle-même
stationne toujours dans cette même atmosphère du don, de l'obligation
et de la liberté mêlés (258). . . . Les distributions de la nourriture sont
des indemnités pour travaux, pour rites accomplis. . . . Au fond, de même
que ces dons ne sont pas libres, ils ne sont pas réellement désintéressés.
Ce sont déjà des contre-prestations pour la plupart et faites même en
vue non seulement de payer des services et des choses, mais aussi de
maintenir une alliance profitable et qui ne peut même être refusée. (268)
[An important part of our ethical behavior, and of life itself, is situated in
this . . . mingled atmosphere of the gift, obligation, and freedom. . . .
[Thus], the distribution of food may serve as compensation for work, for
rituals accomplished. . . . Fundamentally, just as these gifts are not free,
they are not disinterested. They are for the most part counter loans
made not only with the idea of paying for services and things, but also to
maintain a profitable alliance which cannot be refused.][9]

The gift of the feast (both the receiving and the consuming of it) depends
upon the men waiting long hours and on participation in the ritual. The
pastor's expectations weigh on them heavily, as do those of all the others
who are already saved. These expectations can only be fulfilled when each
person on the line testifies and gives her/himself to the Lord to have their
soul saved.

Furthermore, receiving gifts other than the feast depends on joining
Mother's Army and taking responsibility for such tasks as cooking, serving the feast, cleaning the church, being a security lookout, running er-
rands, singing, playing an instrument, coming to services during the week,
and (above all) giving up an addiction. This participation can bring one
clean clothes, regular meals, and a spiritual and physical home in the
church; for example, four men who had previously stood on the line,
had been saved, and had participated in the feast were living in the church
in 1989. In this way, ritual binds the structure of the groups, as shown by
Levi-Strauss.

From another emic perspective, the feast's role in the church's mission of
saving souls is analyzed as the literalization of a mythic construct in which
the meal is a concrete gift that has the power to heal.[10] From this perspective, the association of Jesus as the multiplier of loaves and fishes, the bread
of life, and the savior with the gift of a meal is an attempt at social engineering, since the testimonies of most of those who are saved recount the breaking
of a drug or alcohol addiction through spiritual rebirth. The role of the

pastor as a holy woman and a stern but nurturing "Mother" reinforces this association.

Generally, addicts who try to control their addiction in the United States today have three therapeutic options: (1) participation in a program that has a religious base and a mythic construct, (2) participation in Alcoholic or Narcotics Anonymous meetings and a medical program that does not have an overt religious orientation, or (3) to be on one's own. Those who testify and are saved at the church have chosen the first option, or a combination of the first and second. These testimonies are a dialogue between personal interior being, scriptural text, and the physical experiences of addiction, hunger, and homelessness. Each one represents an individual search for connecting points between numinous mythical structures, self, and a restructuring of daily life sustained by ritual.

On the etic level of the observer's perspective (Harris, 1983), the socio-economic conditions in New York City since 1980 (Dehavenon, 1990, 1991), the prevention of addiction and of participation in the drug trade, and the feeding and sheltering of the hungry and homeless have become a massive public/private effort. As Mother Hall says, she first opened her church to the hungry and homeless five years ago in response to the mayor's appeal to the churches and synagogues to help out. Throughout the 1980s, the city experienced a worsening housing crisis due to the conditions already discussed above. Furthermore, because of the high rates of unemployment among marginal workers and the low level of public assistance or "welfare" grants, the drug trade was the principal economic opportunity for many young people. Often, this resulted in the addiction, homelessness, and family dismemberment that correlate with the current cocaine epidemic.

The homeless people who participate in the church's ritual and Sunday feast are among the thousands the city now shelters in large barrack-style quarters, where five hundred or more sleep in the same room without privacy or security. Many of them do not have a regular income, and most suffer from chronic medical problems, including tuberculosis, hypertension, diabetes, AIDS, and alcohol and drug addiction. These conditions are often untreated.

The other people who live in (or frequent) the church's block, and many of those who participate in its rituals, also experience these conditions. While the owners of two of the renovated condominiums have sent the pastor important cash contributions and asked her to stop feeding the homeless so they can sell their apartments, she adamantly refuses. She says she will not quit or move until she finds a larger church.[11]

Conclusion

Rappaport argues that most functionalist theories of religious behavior are based on the assumption of an empirical independence between the ritual and the world external to the congregation that practices it (Durkheim; Malinowski; Radcliffe-Brown; Rappaport, 1). From a functionalist perspective, ritual performances serve primarily to suppress personal anxiety, dispel fear, and provide a sense of security to those who feel helpless and unable to control their own lives. By contrast, Rappaport's work shows how ritual can systematically mediate critical relationships between groups and their physical and social environments. Levi-Strauss employs this idea to show how social structure is displayed in the reciprocal giving of food and gifts. Similarly, this study shows how the ritual and the feast in a small storefront church in a poor, urban neighborhood serve as the physical-psychological point of reentry into a social structure with a set of social behaviors that offer some of society's most vulnerable members a culturally relevant opportunity to break addictions, rebuild their lives with family and community, and feed, clothe, and shelter themselves rather than continuing to rely on the state—or going entirely without.

Notes

1. Mother Christine Hall, the pastor of the church.
2. The pastor and the assistant pastor renamed themselves and the church for the writing of this study.
3. Personal communication during the 1970s and 1980s from the women religious or nuns who participate in the research of the Action Research Project on Hunger, Homelessness and Family Health in East Harlem.
4. The pastor is referred to, in different contexts, as "The Pastor," "Pastor Hall," "Mother Hall," or simply "Mother," with the latter most frequently used during the serving and consumption of the feast.
5. The data in this study were collected through the etic or direct observation of verbal and nonverbal behavior, not through asking questions of the informants.
6. The cash offering is collected in three baskets: "One for the Pastor," "One for the Church," and "One for the Mission."
7. This menu consists of foods referred to as "soul food" in the African-American culture; however, these foods are also representative of the low-income rural diet in the southern United States generally.
8. "Stem" is one of the words that crack-cocaine addicts use to refer to the pipe in which they smoke it.
9. Translation by this author.
10. I thank Father Frank Durkee for his help in developing this level of the analysis.
11. Returning to New York City on Tuesday, July 21, 1992, I found messages on my

answering machine from three different members of the congregation, inform-
ing me that "Mother had passed the day before at 8:30 in the morning." She
died of a heart attack after having undergone open heart surgery in September
1991. Members of the church are now discussing how to continue "Mother's
ministry to the hungry and homeless."

References

Bourguinon, Erika. *Possession.* Prospect Heights, Ill.: Waveland Press, 1991.

Dehavenon, Anna Lou. "Charles Dickens Meets Franz Kafka: The Maladministration
of New York City's Public Assistance Programs." *New York University Review of Law
and Social Change* 17, no. 2 1990.

———. *No Room At the Inn: An Interim Report with Recommendations on Homeless
Families with Children Requesting Shelter at New York City's Emergency Assistance
Units in 1991.* New York: Action Research Project on Hunger, Homelessness and
Family Health, 1991.

Durkheim, Emile. *Les Formes elementaires de la vie religieuse.* Paris: Alcan, 1912.

Harris, Marvin. *Cows, Pigs, Wars and Witches: The Riddles of Culture.* New York: Ran-
dom House, 1974.

———. *Cultural Anthropology.* New York: Harper and Row, 1983.

Headland, Thomas, Kenneth L. Pike, and Marvin Harris. "Emics and Etics: The In-
sider/Outsider Debate." *Frontiers of Anthropology,* vol. 7. Newbury Park: Sage
Publications, 1990.

Levi-Strauss, Claude. *Structural Anthropology.* Garden City, N.Y.: Doubleday Anchor
Books, 1967.

Malinowski, Bronislaw. *Magic, Science and Religion and Other Essays.* Boston: Beacon
Press, 1948.

Mauss, Marcel. *Sociologie et anthropologie.* Paris: Presses Universitaires, 1968.

Moore, Omar K. "Divination—A New Perspective." In *Environment and Cultural
Behavior,* ed. Andrew P. Vayda. Garden City, NY: Natural History Press, 1969.

Piddocke, Stuart. "Potlatch System of the Southern Kwakiutl: A New Perspective." In *Environment and Cultural Behavior,* ed. Andrew P. Vayda. Garden City,
N.Y.: Natural History Press, 1969.

Radcliffe-Brown, A. R. *Religion and Society. Structure and Function in Primitive Society.*
Glencoe, N.Y.: Free Press.

Rappaport, Roy A. *Pigs for the Ancestors: Ritual in the Ecology of a New Guinea People.*
New Haven: Yale University Press, 1984.

8

The Celebration of Life in New Orleans Jazz Funerals

Sybil Kein

Just a closer walk with Thee,
Grant it, Jesus if you please.
Daily walking close to Thee;
Let it be, Dear Lord, let it be.

When this weary life is o're,
Time for me will be no more;
Lead me, lead me, lead me o're,
To that shore, lead me to that shore.

This religious song, "Just A Closer Walk," gives us a clue to the essence of the New Orleans jazz funeral. That essence is the continuation of the African/West Indian religious heritage of New Orleans African Americans blended with elements of European Christianity. In the first verse of the song, one finds a reference to the Christian concept of Jesus as a God to appeal to in time of need; and in the last verse, the reference to "that shore" may be interpreted as meaning not the Christian heaven, but Africa, or Guinea, as was implicit in the slaves' usual concept of afterlife. "As has been frequently noted," Raboteau declares, "African slaves of the new world were convinced that death would free them to return to Africa" (32). The cultural memory, though filtered by time and fused with Christianity, is still connected to Africa as a root source, and that cultural source, then, continues as a part of this African-American community's heritage. Since many New Orleans African Americans descended from slaves from the West Indies as well as from Africa, it is reasonable to assume that West Indian cultural sources also played a significant role in the development of the New Orleans African-

American heritage. Indeed, studies have been done that prove the close kinship between these two groups in the areas of music, language, and the celebration of Carnival, as well as in certain rites of passage. This study will show the importance of African and West Indian religious ritual in the development of the New Orleans jazz funeral. It will be suggested also that these patterns are blended with the adopted rituals of European Christianity.

One of the remembered African cultural patterns associated with burial ritual is the formation of social organizations that assure their members a proper burial according to religious and cultural dictates. According to Buerkle and Barker, in *Bourbon Street Black* (188), these societies were the models for the benevolent societies that incorporated the use of brass bands in New Orleans. Similarly, Vlahos, who studied African ceremonial life, notes: "Besides the large associations, there are burial societies whose members are sworn to attend one another's funerals and mourn long and loud. There are musical groups whose members concern themselves with ceremony" (218–20). Early eighteenth-century accounts of slave burials in the United States include the addition of singing and playing instruments as well as large processions to accompany the dead to the graveyard (Epstein, 27; Raboteau, 31). The custom is again cited in the nineteenth century:

Writing in 1790, Beckford stated that the . . . principal festivals of the slaves are at their burials. . . . Their bodies lie in state, an assemblage of slaves from the neighborhood appear. . . . When the body is carried to the grave, they accompany the procession with a song; and when the earth is scattered over it, they send forth a shrill and noisy howl. . . . After this ceremony . . . the affected tear is soon dried . . . the instruments resound, the dancers are prepared; the day sets in cheerfulness and the night resounds with the chorus. (Emery, 42)

Similar to Beckford's account, a citation of New Orleans slave-burial customs show that singing and procession followed the slave to his grave. Harry Walker, in his thesis on black benevolent societies in New Orleans, gives a description of a slave funeral: "It was a common thing for masters to permit slaves to attend funerals. Following the funeral service in the church, they formed a column, and singing mournful dirges followed the corpse to the graveyard" (35). Walker also cites the earliest organization for self-help in New Orleans as the Perseverance Benevolent and Mutual Aid Association, founded in 1783. From the above information on slave societies, it is reasonable to assume that slave funerals in New Orleans accompanied with music did appear quite early, before the nineteenth century. Also, New Orleans has had a long history of parading. "Governor Miro, in 1787, thought it proper to entertain thirty-six Choctaw and Chicksaw chiefs with a parade. From then on opportunities for a parade were readily found" (Kmen, 202). However, the already cited founding of the first mutual-aid society, with its funeral tradition from Africa, precedes this date of Miro's parade for the Native Americans. Segregation prevailed in religious ritual as well as in other areas of social life; no doubt this African-oriented burial custom of procession, although contiguous with the military oriented tradition of parading, developed as a separate cultural entity within the African-American community. It is no wonder, then, that in 1819, the funeral parades that "struck" visitor Benjamin Latrobe were African American. Latrobe describes two such funerals, both of them Negro burials. In one, he estimated that there were at least two hundred people in the procession, with "all the women and many of the men . . . dressed in pure white" (Kmen, 205). (White, of course, is the African color for mourning.) Whatever the use of the procession and the music of bands in American funerals of this early period, the intent and purpose surely were not the same as with those in the African-American community.

The parades and band music of early white funerals rather expressed the military idea of pomp and display, as in the funeral of a Colonel Macarty in 1808 (Kmen, 205). It was from the African tradition of African-American benevolent and social clubs that the funeral procession and its use of band music began in the New Orleans African-American community. African roots, as opposed to military ones, were expressed.

It was not until after the Civil War that the use of brass bands became connected with the growth of these social clubs. As they blossomed to promote the political advancement of blacks during Reconstruction, these clubs became one medium through which black street bands were born. Shafer, in his *Brass Bands and New Orleans Jazz*, notes the connection between these clubs and the emerging jazz funerals:

Benevolent or burial associations that New Orleans blacks joined offered burial insurance, as well as other forms of assistance and social coherence. But their final obligation was to sponsor a decent, decorous burial for their dues paying members. Part of this burial contract included at the request of the member and his family, music for the funeral cortege. (66)

By the period of Reconstruction in Louisiana (1865–77), a brass-band tradition was firmly rooted in the black community. This twin growth of social-aid societies and the brass-band tradition connected with funeral rites gave birth to a rather unique form of celebration.

The religious idea of the meaning of death, as a time of rebirth and not as the end of life, is another African cultural pattern still present in the jazz funerals. The idea of returning to Africa, as expressed in the song already mentioned, is based on a "firm religious belief in reincarnation" (Raboteau, 32). Therefore, a funeral is less a cause for sadness than an occasion for celebration. One will be reborn in another life. Related to death and rebirth is the belief that ancestors are the link between the creator and mankind, equal to and in addition to other gods.

Another African religious link comes from the West African religion of ancestor worship, which was creolized in the West Indies as voodoo. The significance of this religious consciousness on New Orleans African Americans has often been neglected. However, there is a long and persistent history of voodoo practices in New Orleans. Numerous accounts of slave gatherings acknowledge voodoo-related rituals. Louisiana's earliest historian, Le Page du Pratz, cites these gatherings, as do many witnesses to the dancing in Place Congo and other locations during the eighteenth and nineteenth centuries. This religion is very much alive both in the West Indies and in New Orleans. The remembered link of the African and West Indian religious funeral ritual is also apparent in the dances of the "second liners," or African-American community members who follow the brass band in the jazz funerals. Expanding the African processional tradition, the jazz funeral parade includes the funeral dances of the West Indian voodoo religion, chiefly the banda, a sexually motivated dance used to symbolize the act of rebirth. Katherine Dunham has given a precise description of the dance, as she observed it in Haiti:

Halfway between the sacred and the secular . . . the highly sexual form of most of the movements undoubtedly has to do with the stimulus to procreate new life to replace death. . . . The banda is officially a funeral dance and may be private and ceremonial . . . or free, secular, and public. (10)

The banda is also found in Trinidad and Tobago, where it is known as the bongo and is "danced in honor of the dead. This dance originates in West Africa where death is not mourned. . . . It is believed that the deceased must be provided with the necessary conditions for a happy passage beyond" (Ahye, 93). A description of this funeral dance shows that it is almost identical to the dances seen at jazz funerals. Along the parade route of a jazz funeral, and very spontaneously, a group of "second liners" will form a circle around two of their members. Other "second liners" crowd around them. If the two dancers are male and female, the movements of the two become highly sexual, and they are encouraged by those in the close circle around them, who are singing (one of the songs is a repetition of the line: "Aint got no drawers on"), shouting remarks, and handclapping to the rhythm of the song being played by the band. If two males are inside the circle, the dance they do becomes highly competitive, though still sexual. These male dancers sometimes mimic each other's steps, or add twirls, which are usually low to the ground, and leaps, which end in poses of rebellious strength; and sometimes they end with what is called "doin' the dog" or "doin' the alligator," featuring a prone position of the body on the ground, a copulation with the earth. This compares almost exactly with a description of the bongo by Molly Ahye:

Musicians and singers form a large circle, outside of which the onlookers who actually participate by joining the singing and spurring on the dancers sometimes have to be pushed back when they close in on the dancers in their enthusiasm. At times on impulse, one of them . . . will jostle through the crowd to challenge one of the dancers of the moment. Full encouragement is given to him by all. . . . Two dancers, usually males, jump into the circle and move energetically, mirroring each other in competitive spirit, each trying to outdo the other. (93)

The "second liners" in a jazz funeral do not need costumes, but as with the bongo dancers of Trinidad and Tobago, "they make adjustments to what they may be wearing at the time. They sometimes roll their trousers up for freedom of movement and add scarves (handkerchiefs for second liners) around their necks and headbands which serve to absorb perspiration" (Ahye, 94). Ahye also mentions the bongo croisee or the crossed bongo, which "maintains a clipped crossing of the feet and legs with variations. Movements of stamping, jumping and turning encourage many variations and improvizations, but the emphasis is on the constant crossing of the feet, whatever the design" (94). This bongo croisee is also kept intact by the participants in the jazz funerals. "The Banda is . . . a funeral dance, its sexually suggestive hip-thrusting movements showing that life emerges from death" (Nunley and Bettelheim, 154). Dunham has observed that "the dance complex has fortunately resisted strongly the impact of European culture, and today the same dance forms and patterns of rhythm recorded more than two centuries ago can be observed in the islands of the Caribbean" (Dunham, xx). This can also be said of the dances by the participants in the jazz funerals, untouched by the faddish or popular dances of blacks in the United States. This is surely the continuation of African memory, albeit unconscious.

Although the pattern of the traditional jazz funeral has changed due to urban expansion, the route to the grave site is largely reflective of the voodoo funeral procession. "The Voodoo procession ... moves swiftly ... the route is not direct. The cortege goes down one path, then moves back along another ..." (Gilfond, 36). This same pattern of movement is used by participants in jazz funerals. Sometimes, "a grand marshal" makes his turn "unexpectedly, and the second line is swept along on the beat without noticing that the procession has sneaked away around the corner. The second line runs to catch up ... " (Shafer, 85; Zander, 8–10). This zigzag method of parading has roots in African customs (Nunley and Bettelheim, 20). There are many other examples of this pattern of parading connected with African and West Indian festivals.

Explicit also is the connection between African ritual dress and the dress of the parade leaders of jazz funerals, as is shown in a description of the ceremony in Dahomey of the sacrifice of a bull to Heviosse, the thunder god (listed by Rigaud as "Heviozo," a voodoo god):

The two chief fetishers wore a white cotton cap, red and yellow sashes across their chest, and round their waist a pagne which fell to their feet ... and the two chief priests had huge sacred umbrellas to shelter them. These umbrellas have a flat top and a panelled fringe; they are made of white cotton and the panels have designs in black cloth applique'd [sic] on them; one was decorated with ships, the other with rams. (Gorer, 156)

In the jazz funeral we see the use of the sashes, the loincloth, here short-ened to an apron, and the large umbrellas, often decorated with sequins, maribou, flowers, fringe, and a white dove (a Christian symbol by way of Egypt) on top. We also find the use of sashes and banners in certain voo-doo rituals in Haiti; and the above-mentioned Dahomean god is found in the Haitian voodoo pantheon (Metraux, 28).

Despite the acculturation process, then, African religious rituals and be-liefs are kept. The white color of mourning from Africa is seen here in the use of white shirts, gloves, plumes, and aprons by parade leaders. The raising of the coffin three times is an African custom, although it is thought to represent the Catholic theological virtues of faith, hope, and charity by some participants (Bannock). The manner of parading, the use of the voodoo funeral dance, and the joyful spirit of the jazz funerals all connect to the African roots. Other African rituals, such as the burial of favorite objects with the dead, were lost. The merging of Catholicism and American Protestantism is reflected in the use of the "dove of peace" (Barker) on the shoulder of the grand marshal and on the top of umbrellas. The black color on some of the uniforms indicates the Christian color for mourning. There is also a preference for traditional Protestant hymns to be played by the band. An 1819 description of an African-American funeral in New Orleans includes elements of this acculturation as well as the African customs and rituals (Zander, 33).

A similar European Christian processional pattern is found in some of the Irish funerals in New Orleans, but without the element of joy of celebration. However, in the jazz funeral, other Christian burial rites are performed at the various churches, at the funeral home, and at the grave site. And since many people who have jazz funerals are members of social-pleasure clubs and Freemasonry organizations, the rituals of these clubs are added to other rites. In addition to the dances already mentioned, one finds the African-American strut dance of the cakewalk (Tinker, 119) and the African-Creole "boutucots" dance used by the second liners.

The ritual celebration of the jazz funeral is perhaps unique to New Orleans and can be traced to its African and West Indian roots. If it managed to integrate elements of European Christianity, it is still informed with African beliefs and practices, with African performing styles—in burial ceremonies and societies, processional tradition, band music and ceremonial dances—and with a spirit of resistance to European presence and domination. As such, it establishes strong ties with Africa, mostly Dahomey, but also with other communities in the diaspora, Haiti, Jamaica, Tobago, Trinidad, and Brazil. This African-American celebration is a unique example of the process of creolization that took place in some parts of the United States, blending cultures from the Old World, Africa, and Europe with those from the New World, the West Indies, and the Americas.

References

Ahye, Molly. *Golden Heritage: The Dance in Trinidad and Tobago.* Petite Valley, Trinidad and Tobago: Heritage Culture Limited, 1978.

Bannock, Larry. Interview, Apr. 22, 1989.

Barker, Danny. Interview, July 2, 1989.

Buerkle, Jack V., and Danny Barker. *Bourbon Street Black.* New York: Oxford University Press, 1973.

Dunham, Katherine. *Dances of Haiti*. Los Angeles: Center for Afro-American Studies, University of California, 1983.

Emery, Lynne Fauley. *Black Dance from 1619 to Today*, 2d, rev. ed. Pennington: Princeton Book Company, 1988.

Epstein, Dena J. *Sinful Tunes and Spirituals: Black Folk Music to the Civil War*. Urbana: University of Illinois Press, 1977.

Gilfond, Henry. *Voodoo: Its Origins and Practices*. New York: Franklin Watts, 1976.

Gorer, Geoffrey. *Africa Dances*. London: John Lehmann, 1949.

Kmen, Henry A. *Music in New Orleans*. Baton Rouge: Louisiana State University Press, 1966.

Metraux, Alfred. *Voodoo in Haiti*. New York: Schocken Books, 1972.

Nunley, John, and Judith Bettelheim. *Caribbean Festival Arts*. Seattle: University of Washington Press, 1988.

Raboteau, Albert J. *Slave Religion*. New York: Oxford University Press, 1978.

Rigaud, Milo. *Secrets of Voodoo*. New York: Pocket Books, 1971.

Schafer, William J. *Brass Bands and New Orleans Jazz*. Baton Rouge: Louisiana State University Press, 1977.

Tallant, Robert. *Voodoo in New Orleans*. New York: Collier Books, 1971.

Tinker, Frances and Edward. *Old New Orleans: Mardi Gras Masks—The Nineties*. New York: Appleton, 1931.

Vlahos, Olivia. *African Beginnings*. New York: Viking Press, 1968.

Walker, Harry Joseph. "Negro Benevolent Societies in New Orleans: A Study of their Structure, Function and Membership." Ph.D. dissertation, Fisk University, June 1937.

Zander, Marjorie Thomas. "The Brass Band Funeral and Related Negro Burial Customs." Master's thesis, University of North Carolina, Chapel Hill, 1962.

———. "Creole Culture's Food, Music, A Way of Life." New Orleans *States Item*, Apr. 21, 1970.

Part Three

Celebrations and the
Creation of Identities

9

Celebrating Rizal Day
The Emergence of a Filipino Tradition
in Twentieth-Century Chicago

Roland L. Guyotte and Barbara M. Posadas

José Rizal (1861–1896) is the Philippines' national hero. A martyr executed by a Spanish firing squad at the onset of the movement for national independence, Rizal has since been memorialized in numerous ways—his name the password for a secret society and eventually a Philippine province named after him, his statue the decoration of countless town plazas and a central monument in Manila, his memory enshrined in folklore as a faith healer and canonized in several religious cults. In the 1950s, legislation made his two novels required reading for all Filipino college students. His long poem "Ultima Adios," composed on the eve of his death, has long been a classic of Filipino elocutionists. Since 1898, the anniversary of Rizal's death, December 30, has been a national holiday in the Philippines, commemorated at home and abroad. This essay explores the significance of Rizal Day as an overseas celebration in the United States, in the various meanings it has taken on over the years. As with many "invented traditions," one can find within Rizal Day observances illustrations of ambiguities and contrasts characteristic of times of intensive change.[1]

The development of the Rizal Day holiday is, in many ways, bound up with the complex relationship between the Philippines and the United States. Although Rizal lived and died before the United States annexed the Philippines, and although the Rizal Day holiday was proclaimed by Filipinos before the United States seized the islands in the wake of the Spanish-American War, the development of the holiday in both the Philippines and the United States was greatly influenced by the contact between the two cultures. Filipinos made much of the distinctive qualities of their national hero during the

American colonial period (1898–1946) as a means of showing their worthiness and readiness for independence. American leaders from Theodore Roosevelt and William Howard Taft, the islands' first American governor general, onward promoted the celebration of José Rizal as a means of offering a model toward which Filipinos might strive under American "tutelage" toward eventual autonomy. At times, the bond between Rizal, the Americans, and Filipino colonial elites became so strong that more radical nationalists suggested that different national heroes might be more appropriate to a nation seeking to define itself as different from the United States. Yet Rizal and Rizal Day persisted.

In the United States, the celebration of Rizal Day became bound up in the fate of the overseas Filipino student community. Filipinos came to the United States during the American colonial period primarily in two categories, as laborers and as students, although in some places, particularly in Chicago, the boundaries between the two often were not hard and fast. Both sets of Filipinos initially shared one characteristic: they intended their stay to be temporary. Laborers were recruited on contract to Hawaii, or they migrated on their own to the agricultural and fishery regions of California and the Pacific Northwest. Students flocked to the academic centers of the United States, which during the early twentieth century generally meant the Northeast and the industrial Midwest. Members of both communities expected to do well in America, the laborers to earn money to improve their lot at home and the students to earn degrees that would win them favored places on a ladder of mobility after they returned. In substantial ways, both groups found disappointment rather than fulfillment. Neither expected the racism or indifference that they found among Americans.

Rizal Day developed in the United States as a means to national identity. Led by students during the 1910s and 1920s, Rizal Day celebrations provided a source of identity across class lines for Filipinos in the United States. The exercises honoring Rizal reminded sojourners of the land back home and supplied a tangible representation of national pride overseas. Of equal importance, in the colonial years, Rizal Day provided a formal channel of Filipino communication to Americans, a means of Filipinos massing themselves to constitute a visible and respectable entity in American society. As time passed and, for some of the Filipinos, migration turned into immigration, Rizal Day's significance altered subtly in the direction of an American ethnic festival, a means of display now characterized more by a Filipino adaptation of the embodiments of American popular culture than of the politics of the independence movement.

The origins of Rizal Day in the Philippines, with parallel Filipino and American connections, provide a backdrop for the emergence of the celebration of the holiday in the United States. Although Rizal's polymathic qualifications as ophthalmic surgeon, novelist, sculptor, poet, and linguist attested to Filipinos' pride in a hero of broad, largely European cultural achievements, his importance to the Philippines during his lifetime lay in his ability to focus national and international attention on the particulars of Spanish misrule. That he did so from a Westernized nineteenth-century liberal perspective only heightened Rizal's appeal overseas. A reformer more than a revolutionary, Rizal was able to communicate to both Filipino elites and masses. Honoring Rizal as hero and martyr began at the moment of his death, and the Philippine republic proclaimed at Malolos in 1898 formally established Rizal Day in one of its first acts. Filipino revolutionaries, whose methods if not whose cause Rizal opposed during his lifetime, embraced Rizal the martyr. Middle-class Filipinos eagerly identified Rizal as a symbol of multitalented accomplishments to which other Filipinos could aspire. Veneration of Rizal survived both the Philippine revolution against Spain and the bloody war with the United States.

During the first years of American rule, both Theodore Roosevelt and William Howard Taft sought to use José Rizal for their own purposes, primarily as a token of the "policy of attraction," whereby Filipinos might be wooed away from revolution with vague promises of eventual independence after an extended period of American rule. Even as American soldiers massacred Filipinos and the governing Philippine Commission banned the display of the Philippine flag, American leaders invoked Rizal as an exemplar of moderation. Defending U.S. policy in a speech at Fargo, North Dakota, on April 7, 1903, President Roosevelt conceded "occasional instances of wrongdoing" by American troops, yet declared: "Remember always that in the Philippines the American government has tried and is trying to carry out exactly what the greatest genius and most revered patriot ever known in the Philippine Islands—José Rizal—steadfastly advocated." Roosevelt cited a document, composed during Rizal's imprisonment by the Spaniards, in which Rizal urged "study and civic virtue" rather than rebellion. In a like vein, according to historian Theodore Friend, Taft, "with other American colonial officials and conservative Filipinos, chose [Rizal] as a model hero over other contestants—Aguinaldo too militant, Bonifacio too radical, Mabini unregenerate."

The American colonial government approved and encouraged the exhuma-
tion of Rizal's remains and their reburial in 1912 at a national monument in
the Luneta Park of downtown Manila, the site of the Bagumbayan field where
Rizal met his death. This enterprise was cynically characterized by Katherine
Mayo, a journalist who wrote a highly controversial, frequently inaccurate,
and thoroughly insensitive survey of the islands during the 1920s. For her,
Rizal Day was

a holiday invented by Mr. Taft during his governor-generalcy, as an effort
to create public spirit among the Christian Filipinos . . . that if a national
hero could be given them, a much needed ideal might, in time grow up
around that name. No Filipino was thus known to the people. Mr. Taft . . .
decided, therefore to pick out José Rizal . . . and, by a deliberate publicity
campaign, artificially to create him the Filipino hero. This was accordingly
done.[2]

Whatever motives the colonial administrators may have had, they could
claim no monopoly on Rizal. Throughout the American period in the Philippines, Rizal Day took on the varied meanings each group wished to give it,
and, for the most part, celebrations of Rizal Day pointed away from Taft's
ideal of "tutelage" and toward independence. As Reynaldo Ileto has shown,
speeches at Rizal Day commemorations in the Philippines, given in the Tagalog language known by many Filipinos rather than in the English language
promoted in the educational system by the Americans, contained far more
forceful independence rhetoric than Taft favored. Newspaper accounts of
Rizal Day celebrations periodically record the presence of militants, occasionally carrying arms, as accepted participants in the observances. As
a nationalist holiday, Rizal Day in the Philippines expressed the ambiguities about colonial status that characterized the first generation of the
American presence there.[3]

Rizal Day was thus an established, if "new," tradition when Filipino students brought it to the United States in the early 1900s. Sending young
Filipinos to college in the United States was an important part of American
colonial policy in the first years of the century. American teachers who
arrived in Philippine communities almost as soon as American soldiers left
them extolled the values of "democratic" education in the United States.
Wealthy Filipinos eager to make favorable arrangements with their new
colonial masters financed their sons' schooling on the mainland. Starting in
1903, the Philippine government sponsored several hundred *pensionado* students in America, requiring them to work an equivalent period for the insu-

lar government as teachers or civil servants following their return. After the relatively successful experiences of the early students of the 1900s and 1910s, still more Filipino young men (only about 5 per cent of these migrants were women) flocked to the United States during the 1920s, many of them hoping to work their way through college without parental or scholarship support. Until the Great Depression of 1929 and the immigration restriction provisions of the Tydings-McDuffie Act of 1934, which prepared the way for Philippine independence, the Filipino student population supplied leadership to the modest Filipino communities in American cities.[4]

The first Filipino students, those of the *pensionado* generation, saw themselves not only as temporary residents acquiring an education but self-consciously as ambassadors of their country eager to demonstrate its worthiness as well as their own. Some, indeed, were offspring of leaders of the Philippine *Federalista* party, whose platform favored statehood for the islands. They could claim a special identification with José Rizal, himself a Filipino foreign student in the Madrid, Paris, and Heidelberg of the last century and an advocate of model behavior for his countrymen. In the Chicago area, there is evidence of a Rizal Day commemorative program at the University of Chicago as early as December 30, 1905, whose participants included Filipino students from the universities of Wisconsin, Indiana, Illinois, and Notre Dame. Further downstate, where he was one of fewer than a half-dozen Filipino students at the Western Illinois Normal School, Camilo Osias, a *pensionado* and later a prominent educator and politician in the Philippines, recalled his oratorical triumphs among Americans, which won him a paid lecture tour in the summer of 1908. In performance, he delivered from memory speeches by Lincoln, Patrick Henry, Daniel Webster, and Robert Ingersoll and, he added, "I used to recite Rizal's poems such as Maria Clara's song and several stanzas of his 'Ultima Adios.'"[5]

If for Osias the life and works of Rizal served as a means to practice his talents among Americans in fairly congenial settings, other Filipinos believed that their country's relations with the United States required more urgent action. Many Filipinos found a persistent, unexpected racism in the United States, not only in the southern states that they had been warned to avoid. A particularly egregious early example occurred during the St. Louis World's Fair of 1904. Educated Filipinos who attended or worked at the fair were shocked. Packaged as typical, the Philippine village, featuring scantily clad mountain Filipinos, a small minority in the population of the islands, attracted much attention and left a long-lasting image of the primitive, tribal

Filipino that nationalists felt they had to combat for decades. This negative image of the Filipino came also as a personal affront to the diligent students, who, in the early 1900s, were themselves mostly from prosperous, sometimes Hispanicized families. The figure of Rizal, who spoke six European languages, corresponded with international scholars from several disciplines, and won distinction as surgeon and poet alike, seemed a much more appropriate symbol of the students' identity and an increasingly important counterbalance to American tendencies to regard the islands as a nation of tribes and savages. In this spirit, following the 1905 Rizal Day celebration in Chicago, the assembled students vowed to hold an annual Filipino Students Convention each summer. As they declared, "We are in a strange land. It is, therefore, necessary and desirable that those who are near to each other should gather at least once a year. Every one of us can remember the unspeakable joy which he experienced in mixing with a crowd of his fellow-countrymen in this strange land. We must unite our forces to solve the problem of how we can show the American people that we are not a savage or barbarian or semi-civilized race."[6]

Although the racism the students confronted was far less severe than that faced by the agricultural workers in California and Washington and by the cannery workers in Alaska, as time passed indifference also caused considerable worry, especially given the twists and turns of American colonial policy toward the islands. What at the turn of the century had seemed to be, depending on one's point of view, either a noble venture or a sacrifice of the American republic to desires for empire had become by the 1910s a matter of much diminished significance. The soldiers had returned to the United States, and increasingly fewer civilians went to the Philippines as teachers or administrators after the Wilson administration began its policy of "Filipinization." Filipino students in America discovered the phenomenon that scholars later termed "the forgotten Philippines," a persistent disinterest in the islands as a colony or a ward coupled with a dilatory approach to independence.

Carlos P. Romulo, sent in the late 1910s on a scholarship to Columbia, complained about being mistaken for a Chinese and vowed to do something about it: "I had left a country I knew was as beautiful and vital as any in the world, and I had traveled in China, Japan, and Canada to the United States, to be greeted like an arrival from Mars." As Romulo put it, "To begin any sort of crusade one must find a flag to wave and to follow. I found an emblem in Rizal Day," he said, comparing it to "Washington's birthday in America."

Romulo learned that "groups of Filipinos living in New York and Brooklyn" had each planned separate celebrations, so he brought them together on the university campus for a "major ceremony" in December 1918. "Once organized," he said, "we were a cross section of Philippine life. We were students, professional men, laborers, waiters and entertainers. In Manila we would have had little in common. In New York we had Rizal." The resultant celebration—"a big success"—featured "American and Filipino notables" on the platform and "Filipino singers and dancers on the program." The highlight, Romulo remembered, was "the popular star Nemesio Ratia and his dramatic rendition of Henley's 'Invictus,'" in the presence of Columbia's president Nicholas Murray Butler and other notables.[7]

Romulo's account of the New York celebration captures several elements that continued to characterize Rizal Day activities during the 1920s, the time of the largest and most energetic student communities. The celebration, at least in form, emphasized solemnity, with patriotic addresses, musical selections, and dramatic readings—including, but not confined to, Rizal's works. The proceedings were conducted in English, the adopted language of the students. Americans were invited, and ordinarily at least one featured address was delivered by an American, often the most distinguished person who could be recruited to the task. Rizal Day thus proclaimed harmony between Filipinos and Americans, even as it looked forward to a future of independence. The celebration also emphasized the theme of "unity," reflecting Filipino nationalists' concern, in America, about the propensity of Philippine society to fragment into factions based on region, language loyalty, personal ambition, or social class. On this last point, Romulo's observation about the *seemingly* classless character of the Filipino-American celebration contrasted with the rigid stratification of the homeland.

For the thousands of Filipino students in the United States during the 1920s, Rizal Day became an annual fete recorded in short-lived community newspapers and national student publications. Each year, articles and photographs documented the growing numbers of Filipinos in the United States and the expansion of commemorative activities across America. In college towns, the celebration continued as a campus event. In the larger cities, Filipinos held Rizal Day observances at major downtown hotels. In Chicago, where the population defining itself as "student" was, in fact, working and grew to a noticeable presence during the decade, collegiate organizations combining to sponsor Rizal Day programs included the Filipino Circle of the tuition-free Crane Junior College, where Filipinos supported themselves as busboys, postal workers, and barbers in order to attend its evening classes, as well as student groups from the Second City's more prestigious institutions, the University of Chicago and Northwestern University, where Filipinos generally enjoyed family or government financial sponsorship. But because most Chicago Filipinos were increasingly students in name only and socialized less through campus affiliation than through club membership based on provincial or work-related ties, organizational sponsorship of Rizal Day festivities became as diverse as the community itself. The 1924 celebration, held in the YMCA banquet hall, reflected the comparatively small Filipino population in Chicago before the late 1920s. While several Filipinos brought American women to the banquet, most did not. Several of those honored by seating at the head table were American.

Within a few years, circumstances changed. By the late 1920s, Chicago Filipinos observed Rizal Day in splendid settings. Photographs reveal that a majority of the Filipinos attended in black tie. An elaborate dinner preceded the program on December 30, 1926: celebrants drank a "Luzonese cocktail," and nibbled "Visayanese celery" and "Mindanaoese olives," thereby representing all three island regions of the Philippines. The main course, accompanied by a "Rizalina Salad," commemorated Rizal's birthplace with a "Milk-fed Chicken a la Calamba" and his residence of enforced exile with "Dapitan Peas Paysanne." "Josephine Cakes," in honor of the martyr's common-law wife, Josephine Bracken, and "Coffee Manilense" concluded the menu. Notables present included the postmaster of the Chicago post office, where many Filipinos worked, and the president of Crane Junior College, where many Filipinos studied. The program included examples of "Typical Filipino Dance" and, as always, a dramatic recitation of the "Ultima Adios," doubtless in Charles Derbyshire's English translation as "My Last Farewell." An oratorical contest winner gave his address, "Rizal and the Age in which He Lived," and the program ended with the singing of the Philippine and American anthems.[8] Two years later, in 1928, the banquet and program at the LaSalle Hotel on New Year's Day featured the presentation of a bust of Rizal to the Newberry Library by Francisco Alayu, president of the Rizal Club of Chicago; a speech of acceptance by the library's representative, George B. Utley; the distribution of prizes to winners of the oratorical and declamatory contests by Dean G. R. Moon of the University of Chicago; the prize winner's recitations; several vocal and piano solos; musical selections played by the Filipino Intercollegiate String Orchestra; and an address from former Chicago mayor William Dever.[9]

By the end of the decade, Rizal Day had evolved almost imperceptibly from the solemn occasion of the *pensionado* era to a festive one more typical of the Roaring Twenties. It is doubtful that the content of the speeches themselves changed. Rizal was invoked as a hero who promoted self-development, morality, excellence, nationality, and unity. Americans and Filipinos alike recognized Rizal's accomplishments and honored his memory. But the occasion itself changed, as some Filipinos noted ruefully, from a feast of civil religion to a society ball.

As young Filipino supporters scurried to secure votes for their favorite candidates, the fixation on an annual Rizal Day queen contest seemed, to some, to rob the commemoration of the Philippine martyr of both dignity and meaning. In December 1929, just weeks after the onset of the Great Depression, Dominador S. Olegario wrote home in disgust, to the *Philippines Free Press,* to protest that year's observance of Rizal Day in Chicago:

The celebration was not only unique, but a decidedly unpatriotic one. . . . the celebration should have been conducted in such a manner as to inspire respect for the Filipinos in the eyes of Americans rather than invite ridicule and perhaps even contempt.[10]

The choice of an American girl, Dorothy Reyes, the stepdaughter of a Filipino, when there were "at least 10 Filipino girls, each of whom was willing to become Rizal day queen," was "an insult to our respected sweethearts, sisters, and above all, our dear mothers."[11]

The 1930 gala in Chicago, held "at the spacious Sherman Hotel ball room," was described as the "Annual Memorial Banquet." In the journalistic idiom of a newspaper society column, "the Banquet was attended by prominent Filipinos in Chicago and vicinity and their friends." Once again, according to the correspondent of the *Filipino Student Bulletin,* "the main feature of the program was the presentation of the Queen for the Rizal Day."[12] But, at least in 1930, Chicagoans probably redeemed themselves in the eyes of the folks at home by choosing Eleuteria Mangibin from the La Unión Province as their Rizal Day queen. Three American contestants had been relegated to places behind Miss Mangibin and two other Filipinas.[13] Chicago-based Filipino journalist Luis S. Quianio wrote approvingly:

This city of 5000 islanders, center of Filipino intellegenzia [*sic*] in the United States, did not forget her [the Filipina woman] at the eleventh hour. . . . Nationalism has become a watch word and they must solidify to uphold the dignity of their race.[14]

Two years later, coronation of a Jewish queen, Pearl I, survived scrutiny, undoubtedly because Pearl was the daughter of short, chunky Ida Nasberg, who had long "mothered" young Filipinos in the near West Side neighborhood where she and her husband ran a dry-cleaning business. Chicken soup could silence even the most ardent nationalist![15]

As Filipino Americans institutionalized themselves through the creation of numerous regional, religious, fraternal, and mutual-assistance associations, the idealized unity of Rizal Day also shattered into conspicuous fragmentation. In 1932, at least three Rizal Day celebrations took place concurrently in Chicago, illustrating the segmentation of the city's Filipinos. At two of them, the banquet, dance, and queen contest followed the emergent pattern, yet reflected a split among sponsoring organizations, with the proximate cause being the length of the speaker's table and the number of organization representatives allowed to sit there. At least one longtime American friend of Filipino students complained that "Americans have often observed to me, how do the Filipinos expect to become a unified independent nation when they exhibit such a poor example of unity among themselves." A Chicago Filipino declared bluntly that "such a divided commemoration program . . . clearly justified the mistaken [belief] . . . that we are a people of different tribes." It was as if nothing had happened since the World's Fair of 1904. The rival Chicago organizations, at this time, were mostly clubs representing different Philippine provinces—Balagtas Club, Pampangan Circle, Big Visayans, Zambalenios—or whose names indicate the transition from student community to immigrant community—Married Couples, Filipino Postal Club, Filipino American Legion Post 509. A third celebration, conducted by the Filipino Gibbons Club, an organization of Catholic students, self-consciously tried to retain the original solemn tone with speeches, readings, and the laying of a wreath at the bust of Rizal in Chicago's Newberry Library. Yet at the end of the American period in the Philippines, more Chicago Filipinos participated in Rizal Day as a secular celebration of Americanized ethnicity—with tuxedos, evening gowns, banquet, dance band, and queen—rather than as a solemn commemoration of the hero and martyr.[16] That not all Filipinos shared in the spirit of the changed character of Rizal Day is evident in an editorial published a few years later:

While we realize the difficulty in presenting a program that will meet with the approval of all organizations, not to say of all the members of the same, nevertheless, it should be in keeping with the spirit and true significance of the day. It is a commemoration day and should be devoted to the exultation of the high principles and ideas of Dr. José Rizal and not to the jollification of the observants.[17]

In Chicago, as elsewhere, the status of Rizal Day served as a barometer of the cohesiveness and the concerns of the local Filipino community. As the prospect of independence for the Philippines approached during the 1930s, Filipino communities in America lost an element of the original impetus for their annual celebration: no longer need one impress the Americans with Filipino worthiness for self-rule. Yet racism persisted: American willingness to grant independence was accompanied by a willingness to be rid of Filipinos. West Coast states had passed anti-miscegenation laws, and even in Chicago Filipinos faced racially based challenges to their employment at the post office or on the railways with the Pullman Company. Restriction of immigration was likely to be a part of any independence legislation. Midwestern Filipinos, like their counterparts on the West Coast, scrambled to help each other during the ravages of the Great Depression. Amid these hard times, Rizal Day flourished, even as Filipino-American unity faltered.

By the 1940s, most of Chicago's Filipinos had made the transition from a student community to an immigrant community. Numbering only a few thousand—perhaps half the size of the city's Filipino population of the late 1920s—Filipinos living in Chicago during World War II had settled into patterns of work and family life that were more typically "American." A short-lived publication of this era, the *Philippine Quarterly,* featured notices of Filipino club life, bowling and golf leagues, and a "teen tattler" column, which recorded the doings of some of the old-timers' offspring. Yet Rizal Day remained at the heart of the community's sense of itself, as writers and editorialists annually commented on Rizal's life, periodically reprinted "My Last Farewell," summarized speeches delivered at Rizal Day gatherings, and—after some community members returned to the Philippines at the end of World War II—described the commemorative ceremonies as they took place in the homeland. Because Rizal Day was the one event that seemed to bind the scattered Filipinos together, as well as the one predictable means for local clubs to raise funds, some hoped that Rizal Day would promote unity within the community, and even pay for a clubhouse as a center for organizational life. As in the 1930s, however, Chicago's fete also recorded the dimensions of community conflict.[18]

From the middle 1940s on, Chicago's Rizal celebrations included prominent Filipinos as primary speakers. Carlos P. Romulo, now a general and resident commissioner in Washington, D.C., gave the 1945 address, and in the first years after independence in 1946, Philippine consuls, ambassadors, cabinet ministers, and UN delegates occupied the head table, sometimes evoking the spirit of Rizal to seek assistance toward rebuilding their war-torn land. For the representatives from the Philippines, Chicago's Rizal Day remained primarily an occasion for nationalism, as Minister Emilio Abello reminded his audience on January 2, 1949. Alluding to Rizal's reading in "Anglo-Saxon history and American politics" and his trip to the United States "to observe the American people and be imbued with their ideas and their ideals," Abello's message included a sharply worded moral about the meaning of Rizal's life in the era of postwar decolonization: "His accomplishments, notwithstanding his color, proved to all the detractors of all colored peoples that there was no race destined by God to be superior over other races and that the Filipino was not inferior to any other."[19]

At the same time, Chicago Filipinos lamented local disunity. Though the recent commemoration had been blessedly free of competing celebrations, editor Felisberto R. Villar complained, in 1949, about the lack of "TEAM WORK" in "the management of the whole affair." As Villar observed, banquet tables "allotted to twenty or more organizations," which, according to prearranged plan, were "supposed to be near the speakers' table," were, instead, "placed at the farthest end of the dining room." The editor found fault with the march of the royal court, the failure to invite the priest who frequently gave the invocation, and the bad manners of several at the speaker's table, who "sat leisurely and in any position they felt most comfortable . . . and conversed with one another while the program was going on, especially when Minister Abello was delivering his address." The old-timer concluded angrily, "The shortcomings of the last Rizal Day cannot be repeated in the years to come. We are no longer young people."[20]

Philippine immigration to the United States slowed greatly following the independence legislation of 1934, the dislocations of World War II, and the establishment of the Philippine republic in 1946. Not until after favorable U.S. immigration legislation once more opened the gates in 1965 did Chicago's Filipino American community grow substantially. A generation or more separated the young Filipinos of the 1920s and 1930s, now the old-timers, from the post-1965 immigrants. The latter group included far more credentialed professionals, women and men alike, and families. For most adults, the educational process was completed in the Philippines, where in recent decades, even among educated Filipinos, English has been displaced by Tagalog as the national language. The commemoration of José Rizal since the 1960s has served as a tentative link between these two waves of Filipino immigrants in America, who have interacted somewhat more gingerly elsewhere.

The form of Rizal Day observances has usually followed the pattern set in the 1930s. Featured non-Filipino speakers have included prominent Chicagoans linked to the ethnic community by the ties of occupation, religion, and politics. Since the establishment of a consulate in Chicago shortly after independence, the Philippine consul has always appeared. More recently, in acknowledgment of the Chicago Filipino community's growing size and potential power, the annual program has often featured greetings from Chicago mayors, from Richard J. Daley to Richard M. Daley, and from Philippine presidents as diverse as Ferdinand Marcos and Corazón Aquino. While provincial clubs have continued to cosponsor Rizal Day activities, primary responsibility for Rizal Day has usually devolved upon the Filipino American Community Council (F.A.C.C.), formed in 1965 as an umbrella group for the city's Filipino organizations "to perpetuate the useful, social, historical and cultural heritage of the Filipino American people toward enriching the nation's cultural pluralism . . ."[21] The queen contest has remained a central component of the yearly celebration and a reminder of the persistence of Philippine regionalism. The Rizal Day queen's court, rather than the menu, can now routinely represent the various Philippine regions; Miss Visayas, Miss Mindanao, Miss Luzon, and the queen herself are uniformly the daughters of Filipino immigrant families, rather than the American girlfriends of yesteryear.

Since 1974, the setting for some of the Rizal Day celebrations and other encounters between the generations has been the aging, and until 1989 heavily mortgaged, Dr. José Rizal Memorial Center, itself the culmination of a long quest by leaders of the old-timers' group who sometimes employed the Rizal Day queen contest as a fund-raising opportunity. In 1976, the F.A.C.C. broke with tradition to relocate Rizal Day to the Rizal Center. In their joint "Foreword" to the program, Eduardo G. Fernandez and Romeo C. Gatan called the step "one bold move that attempts to shy away from plush, ostentatious and expensive settings of previous Rizal Day celebrations." Why the change? Filipinos need not worry about the sanctity of the holiday—"we are part of a now established tradition"—but the community ought to "renew the unifying bonds that tie us together as a distinctly rich and richly distinct ethnic community in these parts of the Midwest." That might best be done in the Rizal Center, "its limitations and modest facilities notwithstanding." "Still another reason," Fernandez and Gatan wrote, was "our desire to prove our maturity by going back to basics by living within our means," "to publicly manifest our support for the on-going, very trying efforts towards the eventual ownership of this Center—to ensure that Dr. José Rizal's name is here to stay."[22] Rizal's name would indeed survive, emblazoned on the front of the Center and linked to the Center's numerous self-improvement activities, including language classes in Filipino and Spanish, folk-dance classes, and study groups for those seeking to pass Illinois state licensing examinations in various fields. The Center's mortgage was finally retired and ceremoniously burned in August 1989, but the Rizal Day gala was once again held in the splendor of a hotel ballroom by 1979.

Yet celebrating Rizal has not remained immune to change. A stronger cultural nationalism and a growing self-consciousness of Filipino American ethnicity altered the observances honoring Rizal. In recent years, Rizal Day has become a bond between the Philippines and the Chicago Filipino-American community, in which the colonial relationship between the islands and the United States has almost disappeared. The Chicago chapter of the Knights of Rizal, a ritualistic fraternal organization first founded in Chicago in 1906,[23] was reestablished in Chicago in August 1977, eight months after Sir Quirico Evangelista, KGOR, attended the first Rizal Day at the Center and "was touched by the . . . festivities outside his native Philippines."[24] Old-timer Francisco (Frank) Alayu, who had presented the Rizal bust to the Newberry Library at the Rizal Day banquet in 1928, became the chapter's first commander. "The membership grew from then on and they started commemorating *in a fitting manner* [emphasis ours] the nativity and martyrdom of our foremost national hero, Dr. José Mercado Rizal."[25] The Knights of Rizal hold a dinner and "programme" at the Dr. José Rizal Memorial Center on December 30, the exact anniversary of Rizal's death, which is reminiscent of the solemnity of the student efforts of the first decades of the century.[26] In June 1989, in conjunction with the 128th anniversary of José Rizal's birth in 1861, the Knights, along with the Ladies of Rizal and the Youth of Rizal, conducted a two-day "North America and Canada Chapters Regional Meeting," whose highlight was likely the Miss Maria Clara USA 1989 Banquet and Pageant.[27] The Knight's "queen," Maria Clara of Rizal's *El Filibusterismo,* "the ideal Filipino woman . . . beautiful, sincere, loving, faithful, humble, and obedient,"[28] celebrated the same qualities as had Eleuteria Mangibin almost a half-century earlier.

A subsequent commemorative activity can serve as a coda to this story of Rizal Day in Chicago. In late August of 1989, a Philippine Patriots Week program took place at the Rizal Center and was attended by about 150 persons—men, women, and children, most being casually attired. A proclamation from Chicago's mayor officially designated the week as a city observance. Speakers offered capsule biographical sketches of about a dozen Philippine heroes, Rizal among them, including some gunned down during the Marcos era. Several speakers prefaced their statements to indicate that they had chosen a particular patriot because "he came from my province." Two speakers delivered their remarks entirely in Tagalog. Singled out among all others, however, was the assassinated Senator Benigno S. Aquino: several eulogists compared him to José Rizal. Toward the end of the program, a soloist gave a forceful vocal rendition of Rizal's "Ultima Adios," singing the verses twice, once in Spanish and once in Tagalog, but not at all in English. No Anglo Americans appeared on the program, although half a dozen were present in the audience. The ceremony concluded with emotional, arm-linked singing of "Ang Bayan Ko," a nationalist anthem identified with recent struggles in the Philippines.

Thus, today, as they construct and reconstruct the varied segments of their community in Chicago, Filipino Americans endow Rizal's memory with multiple layers of meaning on separate festive occasions, even as the observance of Rizal Day continues to be the symbolic culmination of each annual calendar. In making Rizal the focus of a fraternal network extending across the Pacific, the Knights of Rizal have reinvigorated the bonds of nationalism. In numbering Rizal as one of a proud pantheon, the promoters of Philippine Patriots Week have restored the political spirit of the early years of the century and have tapped a passion now absent from the older celebration. Still, Rizal Day remains, transformed from a political occasion to a cultural celebration, as a genuine tradition and as a link among the generations.

Notes

1. The literature on Rizal is immense. A standard recent biography is Austin Coates, *Rizal: Philippine Nationalist and Martyr* (Hong Kong: Oxford University Press, 1968). On Rizal's significance to all sectors of Philippine society, see Reynaldo C. Ileto, "Rizal and the Underside of Philippine History," in *Moral Order and the Question of Change: Essays in Southeast Asian Thought* ed. D. K. Wyatt and A. B. Woodside (New Haven: Yale University Southeast Asia Studies, 1982). For comparative and theoretical perspectives, see Eric Hobsbawm and Terence Ranger, eds., *The Invention of Tradition* (Cambridge: Cambridge University Press, 1983); Werner Sollors, ed., *The Invention of Ethnicity* (New York: Oxford University Press, 1989); and Benedict Anderson, *Imagined Communities: Reflections on the Origin and Spread of Nationalism,* rev. ed. (London: Verso, 1991).

2. "The Philippine Islands and the Army," Fargo, N.D., Apr. 7, 1903, Theodore Roosevelt Papers, Library of Congress, Series 5B, vols. 6–11, reel 425. Theodore Friend, *Between Two Empires: The Ordeal of the Philippines, 1929–1946* (New Haven: Yale University Press, 1965), 15. Katherine Mayo, *The Isles of Fear: The Truth about the Philippines* (New York: Harcourt, Brace and Co., 1925), 313.

3. "Solemnity marks Rizal Day Celebration," *Philippines Free Press*, Jan. 4, 1936, 37, records the presence of Sakdal rebels at a Manila ceremony late in the American period. For varied uses made of Rizal's memory, see Reynaldo C. Ileto, "Orators and the Crowd: Philippine Independence Politics, 1910–1914," in *Reappraising an Empire: New Perspectives on Philippine-American History*, ed. Peter W. Stanley (Cambridge: Harvard University Press, 1984), esp. 92–95. See, also, Peter W. Stanley, *A Nation in the Making: The Philippines and the United States* (Cambridge: Harvard University Press, 1974).

4. A fuller treatment of the Filipino student experience, with Chicago as the focus of the inquiry, is in Barbara M. Posadas and Roland L. Guyotte, "Aspiration and Reality: Occupational and Educational Choice among Filipino Migrants to Chicago, 1900–1935," *Illinois Historical Journal* 85 (Summer 1992), 89–104, and in Posadas and Guyotte, "Unintentional Immigrants: Chicago's Filipino Foreign Students Become Settlers, 1900–1941," *Journal of American Ethnic History* 9 (Spring 1990), 26–48.

5. "Circular of a Proposed Convention in Chicago," *Filipino Students Magazine* (July 1906), 28. Camilo Osias, *The Story of a Long Career of Varied Tasks* (Quezon City: Manlapaz Publishing Co., 1971), 98. Osias later, during the colonial period, authored textbooks, for the Philippines public schools, in which Rizal figured. He also wrote a biography of Rizal, and translated his works into English and Ilocano.

6. "Igorrotes in the Shows," *The Filipino Students' Magazine* (July 1906), 2–3. The best account of the World's Fair episode is Robert Rydell, *All The World's a Fair: Visions of Empire at American International Expositions, 1876–1916* (Chicago: University of Chicago Press, 1984), 154–83. "Circular of a Proposed Convention," 28.

7. Carlos P. Romulo, *I Walked With Heroes* (New York: Holt, Rinehart and Winston, 1961), 144–45. Years later, Romulo would be the featured speaker at the 1945 Rizal Day ceremonies in Chicago, not long before he was elected president of the United Nations General Assembly.

8. The account is in *Philippine Republic* 4, no. 2 (March 1927), 10.

9. "Banquet and Program Given by the Filipino Community of Chicago in Commemoration of the Thirty-first Anniversary of the Death of Dr. José Rizal, Philippine Patriot and National Hero, to be Held in the Grand Ball Room of the La Salle Hotel, January 1st, 1928, Sunday at 6:30 P.M."

10. Dominador S. Olegario, "Filipino in Chicago Objects to Rizal Day Celebration There, American Girl Named Queen," *Philippines Free Press*, Feb. 8, 1930, 36.

11. Ibid. See, also, Luis S. Quianio, "Coconut Politics in Chicago," *Philippines Free Press*, May 3, 1930, 4, 64. During these years, Filipinos who, in the absence of Filipinas in the United States, frequented taxi dance halls and consorted with American women were regularly denounced in Philippine periodicals. See Bar-

bara M. Posadas, "Crossed Boundaries in Interracial Chicago: Philipino American Families since 1925," *Amerasia Journal* 8 (Fall 1981), 31–52.

12. "Rizal Day: Here and There," *Filipino Student Bulletin*, 8 (February 1931), 6.

13. Luis S. Quianio, "Filipina Wins in Chicago," *Philippines Free Press*, Feb. 21, 1931, 26.

14. Luis S. Quianio, "Chicago Elects Her Queen," *Filipino Nation*, Jan. 1931, 37.

15. Luis S. Quianio, "A Mother to Them All," *Graphic*, June 23, 1933, 10–11, 53, 60.

16. Luis S. Quianio, "Rizal Day Celebration Splits Chicago Pinoys," *Philippine Graphic*, Feb. 23, 1933, 18–19; R. B. Ronquillo, "Chicago Filipinos Honor Rizal," Ibid., Feb. 15, 1934, 6. See, also, Posadas and Guyotte, "Unintentional Immigrants."

17. "Rizal Day Commemoration," *The Filipino Student* 13 (December 1934), 4.

18. Antonio D. Andres, "What Chicago Filipinos Need Most Is a Clubhouse, *Philippine Quarterly* (Spring 1949), 28–29.

19. "Speech Delivered by Minister Emilio Abello before the Members of the Filipino Community on the Occasion of the 'Rizal Day' Celebration on January 2, 1949," *Philippine Quarterly* 8 (Winter 1949), 13, 14.

20. "We Simply Cannot Have Unity of Action," *Philippine Quarterly* 8 (Winter 1949), 26–27.

21. "1979 Rizal Day Coronation and Ball, Saturday, December 29, 1979, Conrad Hilton Hotel, Chicago, Illinois, under Auspices of the Filipino-American Council of Chicago, Inc."

22. "Filipino American Council of Chicago, 1976 Rizal Day Celebration: Cocktails, Dinner, Coronation, Dance; Rizal Center, New Year's Day, 1977, 6:30 P.M., 1332 W. Irving Park Rd., Chicago, Illinois 60613.

23. "Chicago Boys Active," *The Filipino Students' Magazine* (December 1906), 21, reported the establishment and listed the officers of both a "North Chicago Branch" and a "South Chicago Branch" of the Knights of Rizal.

24. Eliodore Faypon, "History of the Chicago Knights of Rizal," in "Order of the Knights of Rizal and its Auxiliary North America and Canada Chapters Regional Meeting, June 17–18, 1989, Chicago, Illinois, Dr. José Rizal Memorial Center, 1332 W. Irving Park Road, Chicago, Illinois."

25. Ibid.

26. See, for example, "Order of the Knights of Rizal, Chicago Chapter, Filipino-American Community Commemoration of the 90th Anniversary of the Martyrdom of Dr. José P. Rizal, 6:00 P.M., Tuesday, December 30, 1986, Rizal Center, 1332 West Irving Park Road, Chicago" and "Order of the Knights of Rizal, Chicago Chapter and Its Auxiliary, in Commemoration of the 92nd Death Anniversary of Dr. José P. Rizal, Rizal Day 1988, Installation of Officers, Literary and Musical Program, Friday, December 30, 1988, 7:00 P.M., Dr. José Rizal Memorial Center, 1332 W. Irving Park Road, Chicago, Illinois."

27. "Maria Clara USA 1989 Banquet and Final Selection," in "Order of the Knights of Rizal . . . , June 17–18, 1989, . . . "

28. "José Rizal and Leonor Rivera . . . ," in "Order of the Knights of Rizal, . . . December 30, 1988, . . . "

10

Harvest Celebrations in the Rural South and the Challenge of Mass Culture, 1865–1920*

Ted Ownby

Studying how societies celebrate the harvest can be a useful way to examine the relationship between traditional forms of cultural life and a larger
mass culture. This essay concentrates on white families in the American
South and argues that their encounter with mass culture in the early twentieth century brought out and intensified tensions that had long been present
in southern culture. This is not the place to debate whether white southerners
should be considered an ethnic group. A number of scholars, most notably
George Tindall and John Shelton Reed, have argued that southern whites
constitute an ethnic group in the sense that they feel and have long felt
distinct and alienated from a dominant American culture.[1] Analyzing the
intersection of local traditions and national institutions, this essay traces the
transition from local forms of celebration, such as corn shuckings, cotton
pickings, fodder pullings, hog killings and log rollings, to county fairs—
harvest celebrations organized by state governments and influenced by
national mass culture.

Southern whites in the nineteenth century lived in an awkward balance
between two conflicting forces: Evangelical Protestantism and the combat-
ive, masculine side of what some scholars have called southern honor. Evangelicalism was centered in both the church and the home, it was upheld by

---

*Portions of this article are based on material from chapters 5 and 9 of Ted Ownby,
Subduing Satan: Recreation, Religion, and Manhood in the Rural South, 1865–1920
Chapel Hill: University of North Carolina Press, 1990. Reprinted by permission.

129

women more than by men, and it stressed piety, self-control, harmony among individuals, and the special purity of white women. The aggressive side of southern honor was centered wherever men gathered, and it stressed competition, physical ability, and the frequent need to prove oneself to one's peers.[2]

Some elements of the traditional celebrations mirrored and supported the conventional distinction between the proper roles for the sexes, but other elements allowed some release from those conventions. Men turned shucking corn and picking cotton and pulling fodder—that is, stripping the leaves off corn plants still in the field—into contests, some between individuals and some between teams. Southerners, in their reminiscences, stressed the intensity of competition and the public significance of winning. One said men pursued the competitions "in good earnest, each side vying to beat the other." Another spoke of "endurance tests," in which "betting was heavy and high, quickness and aptness were pitted against strength and endurance."[3] Turning group work into a race reflected the men's desire to assert their wills over nature as well as over each other.

Other forms of group work likewise allowed men to express their self-assertiveness and their mastery over nature. Clearing ground and rolling logs were strenuous group activities that emphasized strength and the ability to conquer nature. One southerner referred to clearing land as "a real man's job," and another showed how log rollings allowed opportunities for the conquest and some that were crucial to male culture. When two men were lifting a particularly large log, he said, "sometimes the stronger man on the end of the lifting stick could pull the one down who was on the other end. To be pulled down in such a fashion was an embarrassment, and considered as a reflection on a man's muscle power."[4]

A final arena for physical achievement in group work was the winter hog killing. In this, as in rolling logs and clearing ground, men showed their power over nature, this time in a dramatically gory process from which parents usually shielded children, especially girls, at least from the bloodiest moments.[5]

While the men raced through contests and performed feats of strength, women generally sewed quilts and cooked the meals, and it is significant that they pursued both activities inside the home. Cooking a big meal was, of course, a domestic, motherly activity, and the fact that women cooked as a group showed how the harmony of domestic activities contrasted with the competition of those of men. A more vivid illustration of the domestic side of the work sharing was quilting. This was a cooperative enterprise requiring considerable discipline, thus reflecting the peace and harmony that Evangelicals valued in their family lives. Seated around quilting frames prepared in advance, the women created lasting items that would be used by a family for decades. The quilts themselves often symbolized both family unity and Christianity and, sometimes, the connections between the two. Pieces of clothing that belonged to different members of a family were woven into many of the quilts, thus tying images of family members together into a single unit. The names of some of the patterns of the quilts, such as Grandmother's Flower Garden and Grandmother's Pride, reflected a desire to keep family memories alive for generations. The popular Wedding Ring and Double Wedding Ring patterns celebrated those symbols of a lasting marriage. Many other quilts drew their names and patterns from Christian sources. More commonly, women worked together to sew the Star of Bethlehem, the Star of the East, the Tree of Life, the Tree of Paradise, Rose of Sharon, and the Crown of Thorns.[6]

With these separate activities, the work sharings mirrored and even celebrated the conventional division between domestic and masculine culture, with the men outside the home in competition, the women in the home performing domestic responsibilities. What is more interesting are the ways in which work sharings allowed an important release from two closely related themes in the culture of white southerners—the Evangelical stress on the purity of women, and the division between men and women in recreation. The harvest celebration provided rare settings in which activities usually forbidden were not acceptable. The first was the ritual of shaking a cat, which occurred at the end of a quilting. According to a woman who grew up in Arkansas in the 1870s, "each girl would take hold of the quilt—at corners, sides or ends, to accommodate everyone present—and began shaking it for dear life. Someone would pitch a cat into the center of the quilt, there was great glee in seeing which girl it ran closest to—that girl would certainly get married first".[7] At some events only the single women had the privilege of shaking the cat, but the practice always indicated forthcoming marriage. In the second ritual, women and girls joined the men near the end of a corn shucking for a practice that involved a red ear of corn. The men who discovered a red ear got to kiss the women of their choice. Sometimes, couples sat together around long tables. Sometimes, men stored up their red ears for a giddy series of kisses at the end; sometimes, planners of the events determined who would sit next to whom and kept seating and reseating the participants.[8] The unifying point was that finding this special ear of corn allowed a form of liberty that young men and women rarely experienced in public. We can better understand the meanings that these rituals held for southern farm families by seeing them together. First, a group of women engaged in a ceremony that used a cat to indicate which of the younger women would be the next to marry. Then all of them hurried down to the corn shucking for one of the few—if not the only—public displays of premarital physical contact, displays in which the entire group participated.

Why a cat? Why would cats be particularly telling objects to indicate forthcoming marriage? Some evidence suggests the connection. We know that men used metaphors about cats to refer to female sexuality. A young man in Louisiana, for example, said in 1874 that a former girlfriend "gave her pussy" to her new husband. On the female side, in 1866 a nineteen-year-old woman in Alabama wrote in her diary: "I'm getting to be such an Old Maid that I actually touched a cat the other day. And I was never known to do such a thing before; for of all the things in the world, I think a cat the last."[9] To clarify that curious statement, we need to look at the place of cats in southern households. First, cats were, more than any other animals, associated with the home and with women. While dogs and horses often accompanied men on sporting excursions far from the home, cats spent most of their time in or near the house and, simply for that reason, symbolized a closeness to women rather than to men. The mating practices of cats may be relevant as well. Unlike other animals around the house—dogs, horses, cows—cats did not normally mate in public view. Their mating was a secret affair, hidden except for an occasional howl in the night. This seeming shyness, or even disinterest, in mating should be interpreted in relation to the air of haughty self-control and self-assurance that almost everyone sees in cats. Cats, simply because of their bearing and facial expressions, seem to know more than we do. To toss a cat into any chaotic situation, such as a quilt being shaken by a roomful of laughing women, was to enjoy watching a loss of composure. A woman in Tennessee recalled that the shaken cat was "astonished" and "bewildered."[10] That such a loss of composure should indicate a forthcoming wedding, and that the entire ceremony should precede a giddy kissing custom, suggests that shaking the cat was an acceptable public acknowledgment of the emotional intensity and, quite possibly, the pleasure of youthful sexual experience.

The meaning of such festivities becomes more clear when we consider them in light of other harvest celebrations. After successfully gathering a crop, most agricultural societies can put aside their worries about survival for at least a short time, and their practical concerns become secondary to the pursuit of more immediate pleasures. Crop celebrations often allow a release from the norms of daily behavior, particularly in relationships between the sexes. Harvest celebrations throughout the world support folklorist Roger D. Abrahams's claim that "in our agrarian past, there was a common-sense connection made between the fruitfulness of the earth and human sexuality."[11] It might be an overstatement to characterize the southern customs as fertility rituals in the tradition of other, more dramatic harvest celebrations. White southern farm families did not overtly make the connection between sexual potency and the fertility of the soil; a kiss on the cheek cannot be considered a tribute to the regenerative power of the soil. But it was about the closest they ever came to it, serving as one of the rare moments when the community allowed a release from Evangelical values and showed an acceptance of youthful sexuality.

In the rural South, the fact that the purity of white women—a concept so central to southern culture—could be put aside even at a moment as important as the harvest shows the ability of rural culture to use ritual to balance and relieve the tensions within it. In *The Ritual Process,* Victor Turner argued that societies tend to move from structure, defined as the everyday world with all of its clear and not so clear hierarchies, through a liminal phase outside the norms of everyday standards, to communitas, in which distinctions are temporarily forgotten, and then back to structure. Turner thus described social life as a process, in which the tensions within societies can find periodic relief in brief, ritualized experiences of communitas.[12] Rural southerners lost that ability in the twentieth century.

In the late nineteenth and early twentieth centuries, the work-sharing celebrations fell one after another to the commercialization of agriculture and the technological innovations that accompanied it. They lingered on, and some continue today, but they continued with little of their former significance. New machines gradually made fodder pullings and corn shuckings obsolete, and the rise of the South's lumber industry made log rollings unnecessary. Even more important was the decline of self-sufficient family farming, which decreased the significance that corn and hogs had long had in the southern economy.[13]

The new harvest celebration in the early twentieth century was the county fair. Fairs were not new to the South; a few wealthy men in agricultural societies had tried since the late antebellum period to use fairs to spread the word of scientific farming beyond their relatively small circle. But they only grew enough to reach into local communities in the early twentieth century when state governments began to sponsor the events, working through state departments of agriculture and new agricultural colleges. Evidence of the growth of the events shows in North Carolina, where the efforts of the state department of agriculture increased the state's number of fairs from 30 in 1914 to 251 just four years later.[14]

The question here is what the fairs meant for the traditional relationships between Evangelical and masculine culture and between men and women. One element of the fairs—the agricultural and domestic contests—continued the division between the sexes. The contests and exhibits had clear areas for men's and women's activities, with men and boys presenting for judges samples of their best crops and best livestock, and women presenting canned goods, sewed goods, and even the quilts that were so important in the traditional work-sharing events. The new element in the contests was the presence of judges, who were appointed by the departments of agriculture and who hoped to bring modern scientific techniques to men on the farm and to women in the home. Organizers of the fairs tried to preserve the moral purity of the events either by sponsoring separate events for blacks or by scheduling one day a week when blacks could attend and whites would know to stay away. Organizers of one fair in Alabama, in 1915, made clear in their advertisements that "the white and colored will not compete with each other."[15]

The cultural ideal that the exhibits and contests offered to women was a cleaned-up, modernized version of the domestic ideal that had long been so central to southern culture. Fair speakers—both female and male—glorified the religious values of home life just as fully as preachers always had. They told women how to do their household jobs in ways that would allow them more time to extend the influence of the domestic virtues that both women and men associated with motherhood. Through contests and exhibits, the fairs tried to teach women how to make the home healthier and their work easier. And they tried to teach modern versions of domestic virtues to girls, giving prizes to members of so-called canning clubs for the quantity and quality of their canned tomatoes. Thus the fairs' goals for women were to reinforce and improve on traditional notions about the virtues of home life.

For men, however, the goals of science and organized progress, carried out under the careful direction of state agencies, did not reinforce tradi-tional masculine values. The contests and exhibits for men criticized their traditional reliance on the power of muscles and sheer physical force, at-tempting to substitute, instead, the ideal of the thoughtful, scientific farmer. Again, fair planners tried to work through the young, giving prizes to boys in corn clubs and pig clubs not only for their products but also for showing an understanding of the latest agricultural techniques. They asked them to keep daily journals recording their step-by-step progress. Agricultural experts evaluated samples of crops and livestock with long, detailed checklists of the thirty-two different features of the hogs or thirty-seven different features of the horses. In the contests and exhibits, the fairs were trying to replace the old male virtues that emphasized the physical strength necessary to force a living out of the soil with newer scientific and professional virtues that em-phasized mind over muscle. Thus, while the fairs attempted to reinforce tra-ditional values for women, they were attempting to soften old notions of masculine honor.[16]

Of course, there was another part of the fairs, a part that allowed a release from everyday life just as fully as the rituals of the cat shaking and the red ear of corn. That was the midway, and through the midway the fairs took into the rural South a suspiciously immoral form of modern culture. Pro-moters of the fairs found that midway amusements were necessary to at-tract large crowds, and they promised a dramatic suspension of everyday reality. The East Alabama Fair offered in 1915, for example, "Thrilling Free Shows or Free Acts. Among the 10 Big Shows on the Midway, you may enjoy the Dog and Pony Shows, Goat Circus, of Educated Goats; the Motor Drome, 10-in-one-Circus, Plantation Shows, the great Ferris Wheel, the su-perb Merry-Go-Round; and the Jitney Swings."[17] Most county fairs had smaller midways, and many promised balloon ascensions, airplane exhibits, or tight-rope acts. All rides and shows mocked nature, either by placing the fairgoers in unusual physical situations—on ferris wheels, for example—or by display-ing the latest, seemingly miraculous technological innovations, such as air-planes, or common animals with extraordinary abilities.

Unlike the traditional work-sharing events, many southerners worried about the immorality of the midway amusements. Fair companies claimed that their midways were morally respectable and even uplifting, but the more they made those claims the more obvious it is that they were never successful in cleaning them up. Many midways offered games and even horse races that involved gambling, and the sheer novelty and physical charac-

ter of many amusements offended fairgoers who enjoyed the moral respectability of the agricultural and household exhibits. Fair advertisements frequently
stressed, as one said in North Carolina in 1916, "This year every one may
rest assured that the entertainment will be absolutely clean and high class."
But despite this optimism, concern about the midways was still evident in
1929, when the Association of Georgia Fairs stated hopefully that "the un-
desirable type of carnival is gradually being weeded out and the higher-class
carnivals, with no gambling devices, and clean amusement features, are being
brought into the state."[18] In the midway shows, the fairs were bringing to
the rural South the supposed decadence of national mass entertainment.
Ministers condemned the events and churches were quick to warn their
members against the temptations of fairs, bringing disciplinary charges against
men who wagered, as one said, "on them wheels of fortune."[19]

The fairs provide some insight into the changes that twentieth-century
institutions were bringing to rural southern culture. The work sharings of
the nineteenth century had both mirrored the traditional distinction between male and female culture and also allowed courtship customs that
were thoroughly respectable releases from conventional notions of proper
behavior. Having long roots in southern culture, those customs bore no
stain of immorality. In Victor Turner's language, they allowed people to move
from structure to communitas and back with relative ease and with no
moral reservations. But the escape from Evangelical sensibilities offered by
midway amusements at the fairs always carried a strong hint of sinful self-
indulgence. When southerners, particularly southern white men and boys,
enjoyed themselves at such events, they did so under the disapproving eye
of the Evangelical community. The sense of communitas offered by the fairs
was no longer acceptable to those who set the South's moral standards.

Can we reconcile this change from an acceptable release in the cat-
shaking with the fact that the central experiences at the fairs were, for many,
pointedly moralistic? In fact, some parts of the fairs celebrated a heightened
form of Evangelicalism through their goals of the improved homemaker and
the quietly thoughtful farmer. The change in the meanings of harvest celebrations must be considered in light of the larger changes in rural life. Until
late in the nineteenth century, few organized urban institutions affected the
daily lives of most southern farmers. But the agents of change—the increasing significance of a national market and the decline of self-sufficient farming,
improvements in technology and transportation, and the growth of important inland cities—brought farmers in much more frequent contact with

cosmopolitan cultural institutions. Better roads, even the rural mail, and, eventually, such innovations as motion pictures and the radio brought rural southerners into a large cultural world.

As long as popular recreation retained its decidedly local character, southern Evangelicals could tolerate a substantial degree of deviation from conventional moral standards. The best evidence of this is that Evangelicals did not make serious efforts to pass laws against what they considered sinful activities until the late 1800s. But modern, urban-based institutions that began to penetrate the rural South in the late nineteenth century threatened the tenuous acceptance of certain forms of sinfulness, particularly male sinfulness. The checks that communities had posed on undesired behavior weakened as southerners learned to enjoy new forms of recreation totally outside the influence of home and church. Thus, the late nineteenth and early twentieth centuries saw such developments as intensified attempts to use the government to enforce Evangelical notions of morality, most obviously through prohibition. The fairs exemplified both of the paths that southern rural culture were taking under the influence of urban culture, with new opportunities for excitement outside the boundaries of traditional morality, but also with new efforts to purify society along the lines of Evangelical morality.

Too often we tend to deal with the mass culture's effects on local cultures either by describing how mass institutions did away with important features of local culture or by describing how local groups proudly found strength in preserving their traditions. In this case, mass culture brought out and intensified tensions that had long been central in the lives of white southerners, and it made it much more difficult to balance those tensions.

Notes

1. George Brown Tindall, *The Ethnic Southerners* (Baton Rouge: Louisiana State University Press, 1976); John Shelton Reed, *One South: An Ethnic Approach to Regional Culture* (Baton Rouge: Louisiana State University Press, 1982).

2. See Bertram Wyatt-Brown, *Southern Honor: Ethics and Behavior in the Old South* (New York: Oxford University Press, 1982); Edward Ayers, *Vengeance and Justice: Crime and Punishment in the Nineteenth-Century American South* (New York: Oxford University Press, 1984); Donald G. Matthews, *Religion in the Old South* (Chicago: University of Chicago Press, 1977); W. J. Cash, *The Mind of the South* (New York: Knopf, 1941); Ted Ownby, *Subduing Satan: Recreation, Religion, and Manhood in the Rural South, 1865–1920* (Chapel Hill: University of North Carolina Press, 1990).

3. Wiley C. Hamrick, *Life Values in the New South* (Gaffney, S.C.: Observer Printing House, 1931), 37; Martha Mizell Puckett, *Snow White Sands* (Douglass, Ga.: South Georgia College, 1975), 28–29.

4. J. Harold Stephens, *Echoes of a Passing Era (Down Memories Lane)* (Orlando, Fla.: Daniels Publishers, 1971), 8.

5. See Belinda Jelliffe, *For Dear Life* (New York: Charles Scribner's Sons, 1936), 19; Elijah L. Shettles, *Recollections of a Long Life* (Nashville, Tenn.: Blue and Gray Press, 1973), 15.

6. On the popularity of quilting, see Hamrick, *Life Values*, 72; Ruth Gates McBroom, *An Orange County Childhood* (n.p.: Betsy Holloway, 1983), 30. On the quilts, see Suzanne Yabsley, *Texas Quilts, Texas Women* (College Station, Tex.: Texas A and M University Press, 1984); Bets Ramsey and Merikay Waldvogel, *The Quilts of Tennessee: Images of Domestic Life Prior to 1930* (Nashville, Tenn.: Rutledge Hill Press, 1986); Arkansas Quilter's Guild, *Arkansas Quilts: Arkansas Warmth* (Paducah, Ky.: Arkansas Quilter's Society, 1987); Jonathan Holstein and John Finley, *Kentucky Quilts 1800–1900: The Kentucky Quilt Project* (New York: Pantheon, 1983).

7. Hattie M. Drummond, *Hoot Owls and Orchids* (San Antonio, Tex.: Naylor Company, 1956), 37. See also Lila May Pamplin, *The Scamps of Bucksnort: Memories of a Nineteenth-Century Childhood in Rural Tennessee* (New York: Exposition Press, 1962), 67.

8. See C. Waldo Cox, *Hoot Owls, Honeysuckle and Hallelujah* (New York: Vantage Press, 1966), 129–30; Pamplin, *Scamps of Bucksnort,* 68; J. M. Eleazar, *A Dutch Fork Farm Boy* (Columbia: University of South Carolina Press, 1952), 122.

9. Silas F. Talbert to N. M. Hale, Keachi, L.A., Apr. 24, 1874, Benson Family Papers, Louisiana State University; Jennie Samuel to Edward H. Samuel, Tuscaloosa, Ala., May 24, 1866, Caroline Virginia Samuel Letters, Louisiana and Lower Mississippi Valley Collections, Louisiana State University Libraries, Baton Rouge. For an interpretation of the meanings that cats carried in French culture, see Robert Darnton, *The Great Cat Massacre and Other Episodes in French Cultural History* (New York: Basic Books, 1984), 89–96.

10. Pamplin, *Scamps of Bucksnort,* 67.

11. Roger D. Abrahams, "The Language of Festivals: Celebrating the Economy," in *Celebration: Studies in Festivity and Ritual,* ed. Victor Turner (Washington, D.C.: Smithsonian Institution Press, 1982), 163.

12. Victor W. Turner, *The Ritual Process: Structure and Anti-Structure* (Chicago: Aldine Publishing Co., 1969).

13. For descriptions of the decline of the events, see Eleazar, *Dutch Fork Farm Boy,* 121; Hamrick, *Life Values,* 70; Caroline S. Coleman, *Five Petticoats on Sunday* (Greenville, S.C.: Hiott Press, 1962), 55; J. L. Herring, *Saturday Night Sketches: Stories of an Old Wiregrass Georgia* (Boston: Gorham Press, 1918); John Quincy Wolf, *Life in the Leatherwoods* (Memphis, Tenn.: Memphis State University Press, 1974), 116. On new machinery, see *Southern Cultivator,* December 1891, p. 608; *Southern Cultivator,* August 1891, p. 383; *Progressive Farmer,* Aug. 9, 1906, p. 5; David O. Nourse, "Corn Husker and Fodder Cutter," *Virginia Agricultural and Mechanical College Agricultural Experiment Station Bulletin* 33 (October 1893);

C. J. Zintheo, "Corn Harvesting Machinery," *USDA Office of Experiment Stations Bulletin* 173 (1907). On the decline of self-sufficient farming, see Steven Hahn, *The Roots of Southern Populism: Yeoman Farmers and the Transformation of the Georgia Upcountry, 1850–1890* (New York: Oxford University Press, 1983), 245–51; Forrest McDonald and Grady McWhiney, "The South from Self-Sufficiency to Peonage: An Interpretation," *American Historical Review* (December 1980); Gavin Wright, *Old South, New South: Revolutions in the Southern Economy since the Civil War* (New York: Basic Books, 1986), 34–39.

14. S. G. Rubinow, "Some Results of Fair Work in North Carolina," *North Carolina Agricultural Extension Service Circular* no. 94 (1919), 3. See also Roy V. Scott, *The Reluctant Farmer: The Rise of Agricultural Extension to 1914* (Urbana: University of Illinois Press, 1970).

15. Premium List, Chilton County Fair, Clanton, Ala. (1915), 29.

16. Information on the activities of the fairs comes from a vast collection of county-fair programs housed at the National Agricultural Library, Beltsville, Md.

17. Catalog and Premium List, East Alabama Fair, Alexander City, Ala., 1915.

18. Premium List, Rutherford County Fair, Rutherford County, N.C., 1916; Official Premium List, Middle Georgia Fair, Milledgeville, Ga. (1929), p. 113.

19. Longfield Baptist Church Minutes, Anderson County, Tenn. (1900), Southern Baptist Library and Archive, Nashville, Tenn. See also First Baptist Church, Summitt, Miss., Records, May 1890, Mississippi Department of Archives and History; Sam Jones, *Sam Jones' Revival Sermons* (New York: Fleming H. Revell, 1912), 141; Rufus B. Spain, *At Ease in Zion: Social History of Southern Baptists, 1865–1900* (Nashville, Tenn.: Vanderbilt University Press, 1967), 155.

11

Imagining Culture
New York City's Village Halloween Parade

Jack Kugelmass

On Halloween night in 1973, Ralph Lee, a theater director and puppet maker, assembled 150 friends and fellow artists to dance through the streets of Greenwich Village wearing masks and holding giant puppets. In doing so, Lee began a tradition that would quickly gain momentum, attracting by the 1980s some tens of thousands of participants and well over a half-million spectators. What began as an artists' and a countercultural event is now so ensconced within the festival life of the city that the *New York Times* has called the parade "the best entertainment the people of this city ever gave the people of this city" (Oct. 31, 1983) while the *Village Voice* (Nov. 6, 1984), in describing the parade, wrote that it "must be the largest theatrical event staged publicly in New York. It's certainly the best." Indeed, given the increasing presence of international television and film crews—French, Japanese, Yugoslavian, to name just a few—the Village Halloween parade is no longer, as the *Daily News* suggested in 1984, "on the verge of becoming a major, major tourist event as an east coast version of the Mardi Gras" (Oct. 25, 1984). It already is.

Until 1987 much of the parade's appeal stemmed from the work of Ralph Lee, who early on placed his personal stamp on the parade by designing giant articulating puppets such as three-masted pirate ships with rats scurrying off its decks; a giant articulating snake whose head could reach down to kiss a child spectator; or sweeper hags on stilts at the head of the parade, whose job was to cleanse the city of evil spirits. As the crowds grew, an increasing number of professional designers and talented lay people used the event to showcase their work: giant roach motels, malfunctioning subway cars, human pizza slices, and a vast assortment of drag-queen costumes found their way into the parade, much to the delight of almost all who came to watch.

Despite the event's popularity, not everyone is happy with it. A small number of residents of Greenwich Village, fearing the possibility of mass violence and vandalism, resent the annual insertion into their neighborhood of hundreds of thousands of people, and they have tried unsuccessfully to ban the event. Most residents hold very different views, and they oppose any rerouting that might prevent them from watching the parade from an apartment window or fire escape. Even the police support the parade. They consider the event one of the most peaceful in the city, and they attribute to it the annual drop in crime on Halloween. Most critics are less opposed to the event than they lament the changes that success has forced upon it. Since the event is open to all who wish to participate, drag queens and gay designers used the event to publicize themselves, their handiwork, and their life-style, making the parade less the children's celebration that some people felt it had once been under Lee's direction. Many resent the change en route. In its early years, the parade wound its way through the narrow brownstone sidestreets of Greenwich Village. As it grew in size, barricades had to be installed, separating participants from spectators just to allow the parade to move forward. And in order to accommodate the size of the crowd, increasingly the route was changed to large boulevards. The event is now a mass spectacle rather than the intimate street theater it had been in its first few years, and those familiar with the earlier version lament the change.

Still, the vast majority of New Yorkers remain quite pleased with the parade, considering it more than any other public event a unique statement about the city and its culture. And there is good reason for them to feel that way since the parade differs considerably from other New York spectacles, such as the highly commercial and nonparticipatory Macy's parade, the repetitive and narrowly political St. Patrick's Day parade, and the Caribbean Carnival, which is both culturally and geographically isolated from most New Yorkers because of its ethnic base and Brooklyn location. The Halloween parade remains an unofficial event that eschews the use of a reviewing stand and has no dignitaries or celebrities at its head; funded in a limited way by public and private grants, it is organized from the street, with minimal scripting from the organizing committee. The parade is open to anyone who wants to join it, and most participants do not even bother to register in advance but simply show up as the parade begins to assemble. Such openness not only contributes to its character as a people's event, but also to the parade's ability each year to purvey the unexpected; it is very closely connected to a specific neighborhood—Greenwich Village—once associated with New York's bohemian subcultures, and even now associated with the commercial artists and gay community whose personal stamp is so evident in the quality of the costumes that appear in the parade. Despite the recent changes, particularly the need to extend the parade uptown into the twenties in order to accommodate and disperse the large number of spectators, its route remains largely within Greenwich Village. By contrast, most New York parades do not occur on home turf, but march up Fifth Avenue. Moreover, the sense of being in a special place is all the greater given the appeal of Halloween to gay people generally and the fact that parallel to the parade is a "promenade" of drag queens who strut along Christopher Street—the center of New York's gay community—and work the crowds into the early hours of the morning. Although the promenade is a separate event from the parade (it began as a specifically gay event), once the parade is over, tens of thousands of spectators—gay and straight alike—head to Christopher Street, hoping to get a closer look at some of the more outrageous costumes. The promenade gives the Halloween celebration a festive quality somewhat less ephemeral than a parade, more participatory and enduring, and because of it, New York feels more like New Orleans at Mardi Gras than the capital of corporate America.

Despite the parade's success and the relatively small number of critics, by the mid-1980s Ralph Lee had become one of those dissatisfied with the event. In 1987, he resigned as its organizer and withdrew the giant puppets that, until then, had been the parade's centerpieces. Elsewhere, I have described the impact of Lee's resignation and the efforts—now quite successful—on the part of his successor, Jeanne Fleming, to reinvigorate the event (Kugelmass, 1991, 1992). In this essay, I would like to focus on only two individuals: the parade's creator, Ralph Lee, and a participant named Fred. My purpose in doing so is to illustrate the significance of the Halloween celebration as a vehicle for communicating "New Age" ideas about time and the cosmos into the life of a contemporary metropolis. By focusing on a creator and a participant, I hope to illustrate the fact that an event is not just a text scripted by its creator, but something actively read by participants and, in that way, assimilated and transformed. Moreover, what will become apparent after reading the interviews is that despite what many critics of the parade's recent incarnation see as the gulf between Lee's intention and the appropriation of the event by drag queens, the material presented here suggests that, to the contrary, there exists a striking commonality of intentions and worldview between the event's creator and some of its most outrageous participants.

Lee had invited me to see a play he was directing at La Mamma's experimental theater in New York City's East Village. The piece was based on an Eskimo myth. It was graphic and dreamlike, incorporating some of his giant puppets. I was curious about the connection between the piece and the parade.

R. L.: "Basically the kind of theater I am interested in is the kind of celebratory theater. In the theater pieces the visual images turn people on to a different way than they do in a parade, for instance. When it's in a parade it's like a surprise creature being amongst everybody and people really get excited about that. People will get excited about the size, the scope of that. I think I begin to understand a little bit more the power of masks, because masks really are magic. Because you are looking at an inanimate object and you can swear that the thing is alive. And so there is this funny thing happening there. It's very uncanny. You know it's not alive, but it is expressing life in a very potent fashion. I think that's why people—at least in our kind of culture—find them compelling. In other cultures they have to do very specifically with cosmology and the spirit world and so forth. For us that connection is not as clear. Nonetheless, there is a connection there. And people are just surprised, delighted, amazed by seeing this thing that is alive, that is something that you wouldn't expect to be alive at all.

"I often feel like a mask is like a child in a way and really oftentimes the effort is the effort of giving birth. I once had this exhibit. It is a big kind of retrospective up at the Graduate Center at Forty-second Street—that big open mall there. And all my stuff that I made for many years was up there. And I was up there one day looking at it and this guy came through, this black guy. And I was talking to him and he found out that I made these and he said: 'Man, you got voodoo in you.' I was very tickled by that. It's nice to think that you have a kind of shamanistic role to some degree, but I don't know. It does fulfill that role to some degree, but I haven't gone through the kind of rigorous kind of training that a traditional shaman goes through. I mean I have gone through my own kind of training, which is just years of experience more than anything else."

J. K.: "You have experienced curing people?"

R. L.: "It's a flattering thought. I mean, I suppose. I like to think that I do change people's lives a little bit. Because that's the purpose of all of this. It really is. It's the purpose of doing the parade—it's to somehow help people make connections. In the parade to make connections with forces in nature or spirits that they might have forgotten about and bring them back to people's lives, to make people aware of certain kinds of potentials that might be there. When the parade is good, it clears the air, it sends fresh air through the streets. The collective energy of everybody out there is what shakes it up. Perhaps my creations have helped guide people in one direction or another. Most of the spirits, even if they are kind of ferocious and terrifying, they are relatively benign spirits. By and large, the people who are working the figures are positive people. Because the parade was allowed to grow gradually, whatever kind of positive quality was there to start with has managed to continue to prevail. It charges people up, it warms their insides, energies are allowed to flow between people. The mask in that situation gives people permission to play with each other and assume roles that allow them to give vent to things that they may be holding back. The obvious example is the gay people. For them to be able to be out there in the street doing their dream persona is pretty fantastic. Not just them, but if somebody wants to be Ronald Reagan to the *nth* degree, he can do it, he can act that out or be Nixon or be some witch or guru or whatever you want to be. I don't think people are aware of what they are doing a lot of the time or what they are revealing about themselves. The choices they make as to what their disguises are going to be are heavy duty choices.

"We've always had a wonderful relationship with the police. I always think of the police as coming from a different neck of the woods than I come from in terms of that mental set. To be sitting there working with the cops, planning out this parade, realizing that they personally dig the parade, are incredibly fond of the parade and care about it—I find tremendous satisfaction in it. The parade gives them a chance to play a little bit, to relax a little bit, to appear to people as something less than Gestapo. It's great to set that up, to have my great Floosie to go over and embrace a cop. I've seen some police with Dracula teeth. They occasionally sneak in something like that. If they're on duty, they couldn't get away with it."

J. K.: "How critical is the neighborhood in setting the stage?"

R. L.: "It used to be essential at some point that it was part of the West Village, but I don't think it is anymore. The narrow streets, the fact that the buildings and windows are close to the street, so that you can have masks in the windows and they can relate to the people in the streets. It has a kind of a small town or Old World feeling about it, a lot of these streets, given the fact that it's almost like an ancient ritual that we are reenacting, all the environment could help with that in a big way and you can't get that on a major avenue. To some degree, the people who participate made it be a West Village parade. In the old days there used to be a lot of Village people participating. Families from the Village, artists, performers, people like that who live in the Village used to participate in it. I have always felt that there were more artistic types living in the Village than in other parts of the city. Maybe that's just a statistic that was true in the twenties. The reputation of bohemianism still is present in the Village. The Village thinks of itself that way, as being a place for free spirits, much more than other parts of the city. Although, statistically, I believe there are as many musicians who live on the Upper West Side as in the Village. The Village reflects the feel of the people who live there more than other parts of the city can. You get more idiosyncratic buildings, more old quirky buildings that are sagging on one end. It's less true than it used to be, but it's still somewhat the case. There are trees on the streets in the Village. Halloween has a lot to do with nature and the changing seasons and the fact that there are all those bare branches at that point is a great backdrop to Halloween. You see a figure against those branches, you can imagine yourself in the countryside. We also bring a truckload of swamp grass in from New Jersey, which we hand out to people. That gives them a connection with the season. We usually give them out toward the beginning. I can't remember if it was as effective this year as some years. Some years you'd get someone really good, who performs the function of handing the stuff out. We have it in a cart and they hand it out. You got to have someone who is aggressive to do this. I would be busily getting the parade ready and then all of a sudden I'd look out and there is this sea of swamp grass out there. All this dancing and waving a block long. I'd look up a street and I'd see all that stuff just waving around. It really does my heart good."

J. K.: "It must give you a tremendous sense of power to have that kind of impact on a city."

R. L.: "The parade is funny in that respect. It has always been so vast. I would go out there in the street when the parade was happening and I'd be so dumbfounded that in some way or other I was responsible for this thing. It's mindboggling to see 250,000 people in the street and they are hopping up and down and somehow you've made them all hop. Not that it's only me who's done it, but without me they wouldn't be there. That's really bizarre. It really tickles me. It's a wonderful thing. It's kind of terrifying, too. There are times when I've been in the parade by myself and I lose my personality. It's partly just sheer exhaustion. There is nobody around that I know that I can talk to. I just have to get out of it. I have to go to the end of the parade. It's too overwhelming.

"When I was a kid, seeing as how I did have interest in the theater, I always fantasized coming to New York and living here. I feel like it's nice to be accepted. Do you need this much to really feel you are accepted? But in a strange way, maybe I do. But it certainly gives me a good feeling to know that it has triggered something in so many people. When I was growing up, I was the person that nobody really understood. I was this oddball character. Yet there have been moments in my life when I have been pleasantly surprised to realize that that was a wrong assumption on my part; that I was really connecting with people and that people were really happy that I was around and who were happy that I was doing what I was doing and that they could respond to what I was doing and see some value in it."

J. K.: "Do you think the parade will lose something by your departure?"

R. L.: "One reason why for me to disappear might be a good thing, because then other people would be forced to pick up the pieces. I've been curious to what degree the parade is responsible for the real revival of Halloween in general in the city and also it seems that there is much more interest in Carnival, in Mardi Gras, than there used to be. People are dressing up for that. That usually happens at parties rather than in the streets. It seems like there are many more masquerade parties or I just haven't been aware of it."

J. K.: "Will the story that you set in motion change now that you are no longer directing the event?"

R. L.: "I never felt there was *one* story in the parade. There are certain characters that inhabit certain spaces for certain reasons. There may be a story there, but it has never been stated. I think people make their own stories out of it, they certainly establish their own relationships. I don't know how elaborate any of the plots are."

I have chosen the following from among dozens of interviews because it speaks directly to Lee's last comment. Lee generated a stage for a celebration. Although he suggested a certain plot to the performance, he provided only a sketchy scenario, not a script.[1] In constructing costumes and assuming personae, participants create largely through performance their own some-times very elaborate scripts. The following is from my notes during and after the 1987 parade.

I don't know him by name yet, but I spot Fred dressed as a fairy god-mother in a white gown, silver crown, and a large wand with a tinsel ball at the end. He is casting magic spells on a row of Japanese tourists who, in turn, are shooting him with their cameras. He doesn't pay much attention to me, I suppose, because I'm busy with a note pad rather than a camera, so I cannot exchange stardom for a spell. Feeling somewhat slighted, I approach him and ask for one. He looks strange up close with his stubby complexion. But he's friendly and in response to my request he casts the spell. "Do I get a wish?" I ask. "Yes. Anything your heart desires." "I want your phone num-ber." "My phone number?" "Yes. You see I'm an anthropologist and I'm doing research on the Halloween parade. I'd like to talk to you." Two weeks later we're sitting at the Bagel And, a fast-food restaurant on Christopher Street. Fred isn't dumb. I knew that when I called him to confirm our appointment. Before hanging up, he tells me to look for someone in red glasses and brown curly hair. I, of course, would have looked for a man dressed as a fairy godmother. Fred spots me even before I recognize him. Out of costume he is a tall, slender, good-looking man, about forty. I learn that he is a playwright and lives in a still not gentrified block in the East Village. Fred has been involved with the parade either as a spectator or a participant for the past ten years.

Fred: "This year there seemed to be a lot more observers than partici-pants. But even so I must say I was touched by the crowd. I was going up to people with all their facades and defences and 98 percent of the people just melted. There were three black kids, very, very angry teenagers. I went up to them, and with my wand I went bonk, bonk, bonk, and they melted. One guy came as a ghoul. I bonked him on the head and nothing happened. I did it again and he just stood there. He wouldn't give me an inch. He was just stubbornly staring me down. So I said, 'Oh, come on.' And I bonked him. And he melted. A Korean woman came up to me and said, 'What does it mean when you bonk them on the head?' I said, 'It means you get your wish, darling!' 'Oh,' she said, 'do me, do me.'

"Then another woman dressed as a frog hurled herself at my feet and she said, 'Make me into a prince!' I kept going like this [Fred motions with his outstretched arm as if he were waving a wand] but it didn't work so I figured I would try it again. I thought, 'Maybe if she wanted to be a princess it might have worked. It's too complicated, I can't deal with it. It's two wishes. I could do it. But I thought she needed to live with it a little longer. Also I thought it was touching, there would be a group of friends and they would say, 'Oh, get him. He really needs it.' I could tell that this person was really hurting. Whether it was for personal breakup or heartbreak or physical situation. And they come up to me with such earnestness. Like, you know, 'Make this better!' And it was a very rewarding thing to hit them with the wand. It seemed to cheer them up anyway. People have this innate reverence for the power of this mythological figure. And I guess that was what I was thinking of. It was really the power of goodness that captivated me about it and also instructed me. I had no idea that I would get such a response going out as some embodiment of mercy and goodness. It was really very gratifying. A friend of mine who was with me and is very spiritual, kept saying, 'Fred, you're really healing people. I even had a fantasy of going to midtown dressed as the good fairy. I may even do it. I think there's a magic in Halloween that allows people to suspend things and allow certain fantasies and let their own wishes come true. So I don't know if that would work on a Tuesday afternoon in the middle of 'reality.'"

J. K.: "But it does work on Halloween?"

Fred: "It certainly did. I was just impressed with the power of goodness. I guess that Halloween is a custom we have. On a certain day we feel this. On a certain day we feel that. We're patriotic on the Fourth of July. We feel a certain sense of renewal around Easter in the Christian world. On the other hand, I'm also into astrology. And Halloween is in Scorpio. And it has to do with the sense of death and renewal, too, which is the sign of Scorpio. And the Christians have taken that up and made it All Saints Day. Before that is when the dead people rise from the grave. It's sort of the dark side of it. So that's I think where the ancient roots are from. And so it's both sides. The dark side on Halloween and the light side on All Saints Day which is both sides of Scorpio in a sense. But I felt like I wanted to be a good figure on that night. It's funny but I guess it's just like that out of darkness does come light. Maybe that's mixing up a lot of symbols but it seems like out of negativity is a lot of potential for good. And I just felt like my costume was a lot more successful than the people who were trying to be scary. I felt like there was a magnetism and a magic coming from me."

J. K.: "Why did you choose this particular costume?"

Fred: "It came to me. I just said I wanted to be the good fairy. It just came to me. It was like a gift. I think that's creativity. I also used to be in children's theater. So I have access to the fairy tales and I also had access to those costumes because my friend Norman has access to all the costumes in the world. But that was really secondary, because I was going to do it anyway even if he hadn't had the costume. This just had a strength to it which surprised me. People saw this, they knew, they waved to me across the street, they came up to me and said, 'Oh, give me a blessing.' You know, 'Make my wish come true.'

"The costume was designed by someone who's done a lot of work for dance companies. It's sort of a take-off of a ballet dress from the eighteenth century. It was beautiful. Sort of a white satin with glitter and silver sequins. I wore a blond wig with glitter and a wonderful crown like a headress which actually was from the Snow Queen. I made the wings myself from foam that had been used as packing for a stereo. I used wire and glitter. When I glued the glitter I smiled because I thought, 'Yes, there's something so fanciful and frivolous about glitter that it's like the antithesis of being practical and down to earth. They looked kind of frumpy and weren't straight. It looked kind of like I had done a lot of flying around. I liked the bedraggled aspect. I wanted to be slightly frumpy as if I had gone through the mill a bit myself and had still come to the fact that goodness is the bottom line. And I wore white tennis sneakers sort of like yuppie women who go to the office in sneakers. I thought, 'Well, the good fairy has got to save her feet, too.' I made the wand from a wood dowel and an aluminum tin-foil Christmas tree ornament at the end.

"My friend Norman has all these costumes in his apartment because he ran a children's theater. It's sad to see all those costumes and realize that it's really the people that make the costumes come alive and not the other way around. Some of the jewels were falling off the crown. They looked sad in the apartment. But once I got it on and I got out there it came alive. I realize it is the spirit of the performer."

J. K.: "What kind of performance did you do in the parade?"

Fred: "I wasn't actually in the parade. Crowds make me nervous. In a sense conformity makes me nervous, too. So I thought I would just work on the peripheries and whoever needed me would find me. I went from Christopher Street to the MCC Church on Seventh Avenue where I met some friends and we went out to a coffee shop. And then I came back to Christopher Street and Bleeker and I just stood there and held court for a while. That's when I met you. None of my friends were in costume and I wasn't sure if I should enter the coffee shop because a meeting was in progress and it would disrupt the meeting. But I said, 'Screw it!' and went in. The meeting stopped and they all applauded. They loved it, and I was a big hit. Then we all went out for coffee and I granted a few wishes. They couldn't believe how into the character I was."

J. K.: "What kind of characters did you go as previously?"

Fred: "I was in the parade once and I went as King Frost. I felt I had to work up to this because I felt I needed to be there as a persona. As King Frost I was in a beautiful kaftan, multicolored in icy colors, with a full face mask and a beard and a big hat and big, long fingers in gloves. And I felt very protected as I was nervous about going out on the street in public. Then I realized how much children and people in general responded and the good will of the crowd. Last year I went as a reindeer. I had antlers. But I had lost two friends who died that month and I couldn't get into it. One died from AIDS and one from lung cancer. I was in grief. I wasn't going to do anything. But I had the antlers on hand for a show I had done. So I put it on and it made me feel a little better. But also I think this year having gone through a grief process and saying, 'Life is too short and this world needs some love and goodwill and some healing.' And I was ready to really go out there as a persona. I felt I was a persona. I wasn't holding back."

Fred relates some negative encounters during his performance, some of which he attributes to homophobia. I ask whether he sees the parade as a gay event.

Fred: "No, I don't see gay pride march as a gay parade either. I see it as a people's event. People just being themselves. I'm gay myself but I'm definitely a person first. For me the parade is an opportunity to explore sides to being human."

J. K.: "Which sides?"

Fred: "Whatever you've got to work on. A friend of mine went as the wicked sea hag witch and she said she'd never do it again. She went to McDonald's and pressed her face against the glass and was picking her nose. People hit her. They were negative toward her. She was, perhaps, getting out some of her anger and resentment. But it's sort of what you sow you reap. She said she would never do that again. But I think she had to do it that time. I see people getting out anger at the church. They cross-dress as nuns. There's a guy from that church on Christopher Street with a cross impaled through his neck and he's like this manic preacher. I'm at peace with the church. I think God is all around. So I don't need to make fun or work out anything with the religious world. I just felt so full of love and goodness this year. I think after going through the grief process, it was such a devastating experience, it's funny, the ironies of life, but it released so much goodness in me and so much love. I could have gotten cynical, too."

J. K.: "What does the parade mean on a collective level?"

Fred: "I suppose it really must be some sort of primal ritual for people, some kind of need to act out something."

J. K.: "And for the city?"

Fred: "For the city? I think it's becoming New York's holiday. And I think that's great. I think it's a chance for New York to celebrate its diversity of character. It's really a very creative city, even despite all the yuppification and gentrification. So I feel it's a chance to celebrate New York's creativity, its imagination. Also, you know New York is such a city which is in some ways perceived as a city of greed and of practicality. You know, money talks. That's what gets you ahead in this town is power and money. I think this is kind of perhaps a cleansing ritual for the city to recall sort of where its heart can be, too—one of fantasy and imagination. It can relinquish some of that hard edge of being practical and just money oriented."

J. K.: "Is this a peculiarly Greenwich Village vision of the city?"

Fred: "Well, the West Village is considered the gay capitol of the city. Gays have a lot of lessons to learn, but in a sense they have allowed themselves to break from some of the conventional images of personality. Some of it is what is gender, what are the roles a human being can be. The straight world has that more defined. In the gay world when someone comes out as a gay person they have to question all of that. They may come up with some stereotypical answers of their own, but there really is an opportunity to come out as a truer individual. I certainly don't think that's limited just to gay people, but it's something that gaypeople definitely have to deal with. The parade allowed me to act out for myself. I think the parade allows people to reveal a lot about themselves. I think working through any feeling, you have to admit it. And no feeling is bad because it's all part of being human."

J. K.: "What about the drag queens on Christopher Street? Why has the promenade become such a big post-parade scene?"

Fred: "Because I think there is an opportunity later for acting out those more ... it's almost like the adult parade. The Christopher Street promenade really is a magnet. I'm wondering if it isn't something about the ambivalent sexuality of it. This city is very alienated from its sexuality. I think that's why we have all the pornography and all the acting-out places in the city. It portrays a certain alienation from sexuality. Christopher Street is like a sex center and I think people are confused and fascinated like the homophobic boys about their sexuality, about what gender means, what role does sex play in our lives. I think it's been very alienated from our lives, very not integrated."

J. K.: "And you think that on this particular night people feel free to come and explore these issues?"

Fred: "I think so. I think there's a sexual charge in it. You know, men dress as women, flirting with straight men. I've seen straight men flirting with female impersonators. And they knew it's a man and they're enjoying it. They're flirting with it. It's titillating. I don't think it means they're necessarily gay either. But it allows them a release from these preconceived notions about what it means to be a straight man and a gay man."

J. K.: "Are most people who come to Christopher Street on Halloween straight?"

Fred: "No. There's a mix of everyone there. You can really feel the tourist aspect of it. I was a little initially resentful because I realized it's really not my part anymore. But I realized that on the other hand if this country is becoming more and more homogenized, people need to be reminded of this other side to life—this life of imagination. So I thought, 'Well, o.k. It's changed. It's not my ball game anymore, but let 'em be here and let me....' And I felt accepted by them. I felt they got something from me and that gave me something. I had to shift gears, though. I felt more like instead of being in an aquarium all on my own, it was more like being in an aquarium being watched. I was aware of all the outsiders."

Conclusions

Elsewhere, I have argued that the emergence of the Village Halloween parade is connected to the increasing gentrification of Greenwich Village and the decline of its bohemian character (1991). The parade attempts to rescue what, in fact, the neighborhood no longer is. In this essay, I would like to take another tack, and argue that the reason for its successful emergence as a city and even a regional holiday, rather than as a neighborhood festival, represents a decline in the relevance of festivals generally connected to America's civil religion, while there continues to be a profound need for public celebrations. The Halloween parade, as the interviews make clear, is for some, if not many, of its participants much more than a parade: it is a celebration through which individuals not only express their membership in a collective culture, but both experience that culture and, indeed, contribute to its formation through performance. And it is a culture whose cosmic vision is closely tied to the spiritualism of the New Age. The fact that such a vision has particular appeal to artists and gay people suggests their underlying discontent—a mood that has become particularly acute with the fluorescence of the new commercial city during the late 1970s and 1980s, along with the general turn during the Reagan years toward the corporate, indeed, toward the practical generally. Although there is much within the parade that speaks to similar mainstream turns in American culture—yuppies are as much a part of this event as are artists and drag queens—there are very vocal elements within it contesting such a turn, and attempting to reposition public culture toward spiritual, political, and otherwise countercultural directions. Moreover, recent developments in the parade are moving the event increasingly toward political and strongly environmental themes.

Of course, environmental as well as New Age themes reflect a broader constituency than gay people and artists, and it should come as no surprise that such themes are coloring public celebrations now. In an evocative assessment of the past and future meaning of festivals in European and American culture, William Johnston argues that anniversaries allow us to simultaneously acknowledge and tame the transience of existence, the fact that we are born, mature, and die. Very much like the annual calendar itself, anniversaries allow cultures to impose a sense of man-made order on the flow of time. Although all cultures have religious festivals that ratify the unchanging annual cycle, the more complex societies added to such celebrations the commemoration of heroes who surpassed the limitations of nature, either through physical prowess and stamina or through the life of the mind, as in the European tradition of humanism. Whereas the nineteenth century saw the rise of an artistic avant-garde that rebelled against the cult of commemoration and sought to celebrate the new, the late twentieth century has seen a decline in the avant-garde and a postmodern turn toward parody and allusion to the past.

With the decline of the avant-garde, there is no vocal opposition to the official calendar of commemorations. Not only does this detract from the volatility of celebrations, but there is a persistent lack of input by intellectuals in setting national cultural agendas: celebrations proliferate, but rarely do they make room for the offbeat, the unofficial. According to Johnston,

The challenge for innovators is to find ways either to redirect or to expand the offerings thrown up by the Great Calendar. Commemo-

rations need to address issues other than those of national identity, civil religion, and humanist continuity. One antidote to the
managers' monopoly of anniversaries involves devising what can
be called countercommemorations. Such subversive occasions
would question the ways in which official planners respond to the
Great Calendar. Countercommemorators can, for example, dissent
about which celebrants deserve recognition and which do not.
They can suggest juxtapositions that managers have overlooked,
and they can challenge the criteria of selection favored by cultural
ministries. In a word, countercommemorations should aim to re-
shape the offerings of the Great Calendar into counterimages of
official agendas. (115)

Johnston argues that given the waning of faith in progress and the future,
the role of countercommemorators is not to set themselves up as a
revolutionary avant-garde, but to act as cultural critics. Postmodernism's
pastiche quality demonstrates a degree of flexibility that is quite useful
to countercommemorators. But to use commemorations effectively, three
obstacles that are inherent limitations of celebrations must be overcome:
(1) their ephemeral quality, which works against the attempt at generat-
ing coherence; (2) postmodern representations tend toward a degree of
specialism and a turning away from panoramic or radical visions; and (3)
anniversaries occur at arbitrary moments without respect to planners'
needs and preferences. Each of these impediments can be circumvented:
ephemerality through annual repetition and replication of the central
message in related events; specialism by the fact that panoramic visions
address a widely felt need and, when well done, attract huge audiences;
arbitrariness by emphasizing the connections among each year's celebrants
or by pairing celebrants in provocative ways.

Although Johnston warns against countercommemorators turning
neo–avant-garde, by no means does he advocate a turning away from critical concerns with the present and future of society. Indeed, much as Kenneth Gergen argues in his recent book on the self in contemporary society,
Johnston sees a positive feature of postmodern culture as entertaining notions of the arbitrary in culture; countercommemorations may be useful in
promoting the idea of choice in the construction of self and group identities,
something that may be useful in breaking down national boundaries as we
move toward an increasingly interconnected global society (Johnston, 119).[2]

One obvious weakness in Johnston's model is the need to distinguish
more clearly between the official and the unofficial, between those events

organized from the streets and those that come about through the agency of local or state government. Countercommemorations are counter because they emerge in opposition to those that are brought about through the various agencies of public culture—both government and commercial. And because they are organized from the streets, countercommemorations have the peculiar ability to rescue public culture from the dead mindscape of regulation and discipline.

Although Johnston's formulation is insufficiently grounded in close readings of particular events to be an effective model for analyzing festivals, the issue he raises regarding the need for countercommemorations and the likelihood of their increasing value in the face of a bimillennial consciousness is a point worth considering. Indeed, the Halloween parade's annual nature and its nonarbitrary connection both to the changing seasons, its sweeping cosmic vista as well as its tie to a particular neighborhood certainly lends to this American festival a good deal of vitality. But whether it is truly bimillennial would suggest its ready replication in many other communities, both at home and abroad. Otherwise, the event is simply what so many believe it to be—a wonderful reflection of the diversity of peoples, cultures, and lifestyles that remain, despite gentrification in the heart of America's great metropolis. Clearly, if it is the latter, then the proper intellectual entry into the meaning of this festival is not the dimension of time, but that of space. Perhaps, the proper answer here is that festivals are as much about one as the other. And that is why New York's New Age festival locates itself in this very old neighborhood, Greenwich Village.

Notes

1. This issue is not as self-evident as it seems. Some festivals do commission scripts and proceed to act them out during the days of the festival. St. Paul Winter Carnival is a case in point. Although performers are given a certain degree of license to play with their parts, it is a limited one with all the parts assigned—even purchased—and the story itself performed as a play at the opening banquet.
2. Although earlier (1991) I attempted to connect its emergence like so many other counterparades (Lawrence) to the increasingly public nature of gay culture, perhaps its emergence should be seen within the broader scope of the transformation of the self and the arbitrariness of so many other cultural categories, with gender being only one of many.

References

Johnston, William M. *Celebrations: The Cult of Anniversaries in Europe and The United States Today.* New Brunswick, N.J.: Transaction Books, 1991.

Gergen, Kenneth J. *The Saturated Self: Dilemmas of Identity in Contemporary Life.* New York: Basic Books, 1992.

Kugelmass, Jack. "Wishes Come True. Designing the Greenwich Village Halloween Parade". *Journal of American Folklore* 104, (1991), 443–65.

———. "The Fun is in Dressing Up: The Greenwich Village Halloween Parade and the Reimagining of Urban Space," *Social Text* 36, (1993), 135–49.

Lawrence, Denise. "Parades, Politics, and Competing Urban Images: Doo Dah and Roses." *Urban Anthropology* 11 (1982), 155–76.

12

The "Caribbeanization" of New York City
West Indian Carnival in Brooklyn

Remco van Capelleveen

This essay focuses on the little known West Indian Carnival in Brooklyn, New York, as an element of the recent migration experience of African-Caribbean people in the United States, or more precisely, on the Carnival as a symbol and expression of an emerging transnational African-Caribbean identity and culture that has been the specific product of the migration experience. At the same time, the presence of African-Caribbean immigrants in New York City has had its impact on the city and has led to what has been dubbed the "Caribbeanization of New York City," a development that is part of a more general process which I have called "Third Worldization" of the metropolitan center.[2] The West Indian Carnival in Brooklyn is, in a way, the focus of both—the peculiar product of the recent migration experience as well as an outstanding expression of the impact of the immigrants on the host society.

As for the use of terminology, the term *West Indian* refers to the inhabitants of the English-speaking Caribbean islands, the mainland territories of Guyana and Belize, as well as the English-speaking Afro-creole enclaves in the predominantly Hispanic Caribbean countries along the East Coast of Central America. The term *African Caribbean* refers to the people of the Anglophone, Francophone, and Dutch-speaking (that is, the "non-Hispanic") regions of the Caribbean. The "African-Caribbean" societies share certain similarities, which distinguish them from the "Hispanic Caribbean": (1) the historically perpetual dominance of a plantation economy, (2) a population overwhelmingly of African descent (with the exceptions of Guyana and Trinidad), and (3) an Afro-creolized folk culture distinct and separated from

159

that of the Euro-creole dominant classes. The *Hispanic Caribbean,* on the other hand, has been historically characterized by (1) a more diversified settler economy, upon which plantation slavery was later imposed; (2) a greater mixing of peoples of Indian, African, and Spanish descent; and (3) a more unified syncretized culture dominated by the Spanish tradition, into which, nevertheless, African and Amerindian heritages have been synthesized.[3] Since the number of immigrants from the Dutch-speaking and Francophone Caribbean in New York City, except for those from Haiti, is negligible, the African-Caribbean population of New York City consists essentially of immigrants from the Anglophone Caribbean and from Haiti. The following analysis refers, strictly speaking, to "West Indians" in New York City, that is, migrants from the Anglophone Caribbean or what is known as the Commonwealth Caribbean. To a large degree, however, it is also valid for Haitian immigrants—thus the frequent use of the term *African Caribbean.*

I.

Since the turn of century, New York City, the immigrant city par excellence and the target of millions of mostly European immigrants in the past, has also become "the promised land" for a growing number of immigrants from the Caribbean. However, it was not until the passing of the Hart-Cellar Act of 1965 that African-Caribbean migration turned into a mass movement exceeding that of the previous seventy years and growing ever since. While legal black immigration to the U.S. was almost 142,000 or 0.7 percent of total immigration in 1900–1930, legal African-Caribbean immigration accounted for 838,300 or 8.5 percent of total immigration in the 1969–1987 period.[4] As with their predecessors, a majority of the recent immigrants settled in New York City. According to the 1980 census, there have been about 300,000 African-Caribbean immigrants in New York—more than four-fifths of whom arrived after 1965. Presently, the city has well over a million African-Caribbean inhabitants, including U.S.-born children of immigrants and so-called illegals. New York City has become the city with the largest number of African Caribbeans in the whole world—the metropolitan branch of the Caribbean archipelago, so to speak.

The massive influx of these new immigrants has been expressed in an infusion of African-Caribbean life-styles and culture into the social fabric of the city.[5] Whereas the early immigrants from the West Indies settled and merged (after a period of conflicts) with the U.S. black communities of Harlem and Bedford-Stuyvesant, the post-1965 migrants have moved to neighborhoods in central Brooklyn—and, to a lesser degree, in southeast Queens and the north Bronx—where they visibly exhibit their West Indian origin. Given the fragmentation of the Caribbean region (historically generated by the European colonial powers) and the corresponding trait of "insularity," which is still part of Caribbean consciousness today,[6] it is interesting that the immigrants have not separated from each other according to national or insular origin. However, they have moved away from Latinos and U.S. African Americans—as well as from white New Yorkers, a fact which, of course, has been due less to subjective preferences than to the widespread existence of white racism.[7]

Caribbean neighborhoods have offered to the newcomer not only protection and support and a piece of home "far from home," but they have increasingly developed into the center of a transnational African-Caribbean culture. Neighborhood institutions such as churches, schools, and day-care facilities, as well as street corners (as informal meeting places), have taken on decidedly African-Caribbean characteristics. As in the Caribbean itself, immigrant social life in New York City takes place, to a large degree, in the streets, that is, in public arenas. A balanced mix of commercial activities and residential areas has provided a public space that has been occupied by migrants displaying openly their African-Caribbean identity and that gives the neighborhood its specific vitality. It is this "security in ethnic identity" that migrants from the Caribbean did not develop during the first decades of this century.[8] Today, West Indian and Haitian groceries, bakers, and restaurants, which sell food and meals from the Caribbean exclusively; barber shops and beauty salons as places of social gatherings; record stores with their calypso, soca, and reggae sounds; and, most of all, the presence of African-Caribbean people in the streets, including the obligatory Rastas and domino players, has created a distinct atmosphere that has turned central Brooklyn into the "Third World within the metropole." As the West Indian–American novelist Paule Marshall so vividly describes it:

Whenever I . . . walk along Fulton Street or Nostrand Avenue, . . . I have to remind myself that I'm in Brooklyn and not in the middle of a teeming outdoor market in St. George's, Grenada, or Kingston, Jamaica, or on some other West Indian island. Because there, suddenly, are all the sights and sounds, colors, smells, and textures of the entire Caribbean archipelago, transplanted intact to the sidewalks of New York.[9]

Immigrants from the entire Anglophone Caribbean as well as from Haiti live in the same neighborhoods and interact and communicate in their daily lives. People who had little contact with each other before migrating to New York have been brought together spatially and socially in New York City, developing an African-Caribbean ethnicity and culture, a comprehensive African-Caribbean consciousness, which has overcome, to a large degree, the traditional insular and national barriers. At the same time, this African-Caribbean consciousness has been relayed back to the Caribbean—as a result of the immigrants maintaining close ties with home and the bidirectional migration process.

II.

The existence and importance of such a transnational African-Caribbean ethnicity and culture has been most clearly demonstrated in *the* African-Caribbean event in New York, the West Indian Carnival, which takes place every year during and before the Labor Day weekend in Brooklyn. Almost completely ignored by non-Caribbean New Yorkers and the non-Caribbean press, the "West Indian American Day Carnival" (as it is officially called) features several nights of concerts, steel band and calypso contests, and children's pageants on the grounds of the Brooklyn Museum, culminating on Labor Day in a massive street procession on Eastern Parkway with tens of thousands of masqueraders and musicians and, since the mid-1980s, more than a million revelling, participating spectators. These official events are accompanied by dozens of commercially and privately organized shows, dances, festivities, and parties in West Indian neighborhoods around the city. During Labor Day weekend, the West Indian population of Brooklyn doubles. West Indians come from nearby New York suburbs and neighboring New Jersey and from as far as Florida or California, from all parts of Canada, and even from the Caribbean and England to spend the West Indian Carnival with relatives and friends in Brooklyn.

The West Indian Carnival in New York City dates back to the 1920s, when "homesick" Trinidadian and eastern Caribbean immigrants organized masquerades and steel-band and calypso contests in large ballrooms in Harlem. When the crowds became too large for the indoor facilities, Carnival was moved to the streets in 1947 and, because of the cold winter weather in New York, held on Labor Day, at the begnning of September. In the mid-1960s, Carnival was moved to Brooklyn by Rufus Gorin, a Trinidad-born band leader and die-hard "mas man,"[10] because the majority of West Indian immigrants had begun to settle in the borough. Due to its bad reputation following "disturbances" in the past, Carnival was held for several years in small side streets as block parties. In 1969, Gorin's successor, Carlos Lezama, who still organizes today's Carnival as president of the West Indian American Day Carnival Association (WIADCA), obtained official permission from the city to celebrate Carnival on Eastern Parkway, a wide boulevard that runs through the center of Brooklyn's African-American neighborhoods. Despite repeated "disturbances" and "outbreaks of violence" as well as several attempts to give Carnival more "respectability" and "professionality" by moving it to Fifth Avenue in Manhattan, the West Indian Carnival continued to beheld in Brooklyn and developed into the largest ethnic and cultural spectacle in North America.[11]

The most important components of Brooklyn Carnival—calypso music, steel bands, and mas bands, as well as individual masquerades—have come out of the Carnival tradition in Trinidad.[12] A mas band consists of a king and a queen in highly sophisticated costumes, several other important characters, and a larger number of (sometimes several hundred) revellers in less-elaborate costumes. All costumes of a mas band are carefully designed around a Carnival theme and fabricated in the month ahead of Carnival in the so-called mas camps. Although the Brooklyn Carnival is still Trinidadian in its principal form, the music and masquerades have changed over time. On the one hand, non-Trinidadian elements have increased. During the past years, not only calypso and soca has been played—often from powerful sound systems mounted on trucks—but more and more ska and reggae from Jamaica, spouge from Barbados, cadence from Dominica, and merengue from Haiti. Since 1983, a "Reggae Night" has been added to the official events of the Labor Day weekend. And in 1986, after the fall of Francois Duvalier, Haitians were more visible than ever in the Carnival procession. On the other hand, traditional masquerade performances consisting of small groups and individuals have been replaced by large mas bands and more current performances, although in Brooklyn one can still see traditional masquerades such as the "Jab Molassi" (devil-men) or the "Moco Jumble" (stilt dancer). Though still Trinidadian in form and organization, the Brooklyn Carnival has developed into a genuinely pan–West Indian and African-Caribbean event, subtly transforming traditional allegiances to specific islands and home countries into a new feeling of West Indian collectivity and solidarity. As the anthropologists Donald Hill and Robert Abramson have noted:

Transplanted to Brooklyn, the great variety of dances seen in island performances has dwindled to two or three steps suitable for moving up Eastern

Parkway in huge crowds. In New York City, the local villager has a new identity: he or she is not just an islander but a West Indian.[13]

This new feeling of "West Indianness" has been expressed in a number of calypsos (for example, the Mighty Sparrow's popular 1976 calypso "Mas in Brooklyn"). And even Bob Marley—in whose home country, Jamaica, Carnival is not celebrated—stated that West Indians come out on Labor Day "to forget their troubles and dance, but more important, they come together to reaffirm their indigenous culture, their common identity."[14] The traditional Carnival's motto, "all of we is one," symbolizing the reversal and equalization of social hierarchies and differences, has taken on the new meaning of equalizing different national and insular origins. Instead of flags and symbols of national identity, the Brooklyn Carnival has displayed masquerades and costumes that have been turned into symbols of West Indian unity.[15] The West Indian Federation might have failed in the Caribbean; in Brooklyn on Labor Day, it has certainly been successful. However, as the Carnival brings together and merges African-Caribbean people from the different islands as well as the diaspora, black U.S. Americans and Latinos have been strikingly absent from the Brooklyn Carnival.

As distinct from most other ethnic street festivals in the United States—even the other "Caribbean" event in New York City, the Puerto Rican parade—the West Indian Carnival has lacked a centralized structure and leadership. "As a dramatic event, Carnival is strikingly leaderless," writes sociologist Philip Kasinitz. "There are themes, a certain ebb and flow to the activity, but no particular center or head."[16] The official organizing committee, WIADCA, secures the permission for the Labor Day procession on Eastern Parkway and makes sure that the various conditions (for example, sufficient sanitary facilities) are met. WIADCA also organizes official events such as the concert nights, the steel-band and calypso contests, and the "Kiddie's Carnival" on the Brooklyn Museum grounds. On the other hand, the organization of the steel bands and mas bands, the endless rehearsals in the mas camps, as well as the design and fabrication of the costumes have all remained relatively uncoordinated and totally independent from the official organizers. The lack of a centralized structure and leadership has been particularly evident, however, in the Carnival procession on Eastern Parkway itself.

The procession starts with the organizers of WIADCA, various dignitaries, and the grand marshals marching down the parkway. Nobody pays any attention to them. Most people are not even aware of their presence. At this stage, the main action is occurring on the sidelines. There, one meets friends and relatives from home or from other parts of the West Indian diaspora; eats curried goat, meat patties, or rôti; drinks beer and rum punch; dances to the music from the sound systems that have been installed everywhere; or simply browses through the displays of countless vendors, which have turned the sidelines of the parkway into a gigantic flea market.

With a delay of about half an hour, the 'second act' begins: Cadillac convertibles, carrying winners of a West Indian beauty contest attired in bathing suits, drive slowly down the parkway. Like the dignitaries before, these young women, although a more delightful sight, are peripheral to the Carnival.

Then it takes another one or two hours until the real Carnival procession begins—with the brass and steel bands, the pretty and colorful mas bands, the devil-men and stilt-dancers, and the floats with the blasting sound systems. Even now, spectators do not behave like regular spectators, that is, they do not stand back and watch. Instead, they intervene actively, "road march" (parade), "jump up" (dance), and "play mas" themselves and merge with the steel and mas bands, which, surrounded by a huge dancing and revelling crowd of people, are hardly able to move down the parkway.

Most of the bands and floats never reach the reviewing stand at the Brooklyn Museum, where the organizers and dignitaries have been waiting to inspect the Carnival parade. However, nobody seems to mind. Only the organizers, the dignitaries, and the press have regularly complained about the "chaos" and the "disgrace" of the Carnival. The official end of the Carnival procession, which was moved from 11:00 P.M. to 6:00 P.M. in 1979 as a result of "disturbances" in the past, is enforced by a martial-looking police phalanx and a battalion of street cleaners marching up Eastern Parkway against the flow of the Carnival procession. The bands and revellers withdraw into the side streets (not without little skirmishes with the police), where the Carnival continues until late in the night.

Like other cultural events, Carnival is a highly contested terrain, determined by different interests and social forces. According to the anthropologist Abner Cohen, Carnival contains a "potentially for political articulation, serving in some situations as 'rituals of rebellion,' whose function is cathartic and is ultimately a mechanism helping in the maintenance of the established order; and in other situations as expressions of resistance, protest, and violence."[17] At the same time, the dialectical character of Carnival is hidden by its formal definition and by popular ideas about it: Carnival is regarded as a festival characterized by revelling, playfulness, merrymaking, and overindulgence in eating, drinking, and sex, culminating in massive street processions by individual as well as bands of masqueraders, playing and dancing ecstatically to the accompaniment of loud and cheerful music. Carnival's special attraction is that it allows for temporary release from the constraints of the social order, enabling relationships even among strangers as well as usually forbidden excesses.[18]

The concrete historical reality of Carnival, of course, is more complex—and contradictory. Through most of its history, Carnival has been a period of ritualized role reversal and—to use Victor Turner's phrase—"lampooning liberty" for the lower classes.[19] In Trinidad, where it was brought by French colonialists but, after emancipation, appropriated and transformed by the freed slaves to preserve African traditions and to oppose the ruling classes, Carnival developed into a "symbol of freedom for the broad mass of the population."[20] Although the rebellious and subversive elements of Carnival usually remain wrapped up in the form of a festival and thus defused, Carnival has to be understood as an unstable and precarious balance of compromise between contradictory forces and potentialities, between consensus and conflict, control and spontaneity, compliance and subversion, cosmos and chaos. Both elements are present in Carnival, at one and the same time as well as within (an ambiguous) unity of form.

In the case of the Brooklyn Carnival, both the "chaos" and the appearance of a massive police force point to its potentially explosive character. As particularly the "riots" during the West Indian Carnival in London have shown in the past, Carnival can be an accurate gauge of social deprivation as well as of potential for resistance by the immigrants in the host society. Because West Indians' traditional suspicion of authority (generated by the historical experience of colonialist violence, slavery, and neocolonial dependency), which has carried over into the "chaos" of Carnival, tends to undermine organized political mobilization, the "ritualized resistance" to the social order,[21] playfully displayed during Carnival celebration, constantly bears the potential of getting out of the organizers' and the police's control. As Donald Hill and Robert Abramson have put it:

At present, Carnival in Brooklyn is a huge party where guests indulge themselves with food, liquor, music, and camaraderie. But, in light of it's [sic] history, Carnival's spectacle must be regarded as potential rebellion, the other face of communitas.[22]

However, what is special about the Brooklyn Carnival is not so much the "ritualized resistance" and reversal of social roles, but, as I have mentioned before, the creation of West Indian collective identity, the equalizing and merging of different national and insular origins by turning masquerades and costumes into symbols of West Indian unity. In Brooklyn on Labor Day (but not only on Labor Day), a collective African-Caribbean identity and culture, a comprehensive African-Caribbean consciousness has become reality.

III.

While the Brooklyn Carnival symbolizes, on the one hand, the emergent collective identity of the African-Caribbean community in New York City, it has exposed, on the other, the West Indian community's ambivalent relationship to black U.S. Americans. Despite frequent emphasis on the necessity of "black unity" and reference to the common history of slavery and racism of all African Americans in the "New World," the immigration experience and Caribbean life in New York City has generated a form of collective identity that is defined in ethnic (*not* racial) terms—in a way following the New York and American tradition of ethnic politics.[23] This not only implies a cultural distinction between Caribbean and U.S. African Americans; it tends to contribute to their political division. At the same time, West Indians are regarded by white America, without distinction, as part of the African-American community—defined on the basis of racial classification, not of ethnic and cultural affiliation. As Roy Bryce-Laporte pointed out, African Caribbean immigrants "suffer double invisibility, . . . as *blacks* and as *black foreigners*."[24] Moreover, Caribbean and U.S. African Americans have both been exposed to racism and discrimination and to social and political marginalization, which has considerably limited their options in American society. In fact, West Indian incorporation into African America has been the only viable path to political and economic success in the past. Therefore, it is not surprising that West Indians have remained ambiguous about their relationship with "native" African Americans, avoiding open dissociation from them. Instead, West Indian identity has been defined in cultural rather than explicitly political terms, which has made possible the continuation of the ambivalent and contradictory relationship toward U.S. African Americans allowing for both dissociation and solidarity, depending on the concrete situation.[25]

The new African-Caribbean immigrants came to New York City, bringing with them a consciousness not of being "black" but of their specific (insular) Caribbean origin. In New York City, this national or insular self-definition has been transformed into a comprehensive African-Caribbean identity and culture. Similar to their European predecessors, West Indian immigrants have developed an *ethnic* consciousness, although on a *transnational* scale. As distinct from their European predecessors, the migrants from the African Caribbean (as well as from the whole Circum-Caribbean) do not really move from one nation state to another. As the U.S. and the Circum-Caribbean have developed into one, however asymmetric, "West Atlantic system," with the United States as its center and the Caribbean as its periphery,[26] the communities of the region have spread across political boundaries. Jamaican society, for example, encompasses not only the two million–plus Jamaicans who live in Jamaica but also the more than a million Jamaicans who live on the North American mainland. The same is true for most West Indian societies, as they have substantial populations in the United States and Canada. Caribbean migrants "do not recognize the need to become new citizens, not out of disrespect for American citizenship but because the idea of citizenship has lost meaning. Nor have they changed their community. They simply have changed from the periphery to the center of their own communities."[27] Crown Heights or East Flatbush in Central Brooklyn is as much a remote urban section of any West Indian society as it is an ethnic neighborhood of New York City. Correspondingly, African-Caribbean migrants are less inclined toward assimilation, but have kept alive the option to return to the periphery, which has become in itself a vehicle and expression of the immigrants' holding on to their West Indian identity. Moreover, the geographical closeness between the Caribbean and New York City has allowed for continuous commuting not only of people but also of ideas, culture, life-styles, consumer goods, and money to and from New York City, contributing to the preservation of strong familial, cultural, and material links to the Caribbean.

Nevertheless, life in New York City has confronted African-Caribbean immigrants with a racially divided society. The African-Caribbean response to this situation has been ambivalent. On the one hand, they have tried to avoid the 'inferior' status of U.S. African Americans by insisting on their difference and stressing their "West Indianness." On the other, experience of widespread racism has generated an understanding of a common "black fate" that might develop into a pan-African consciousness. Such a comprehensive "black consciousness" has been particularly expressed vis-à-vis white America.[28] Whatever forms of "black consciousness" will come forth in the future, for the time being we do witness the "Caribbeanization" of New York City, developing the increasing African-Caribbean community into an emerging cultural and political force that has already left its distinct marks on the city.

Notes

1. Former prime minister of Trinidad and Tobago, Eric Williams (see Archie W. Singham, "Coalition Building: Race, Culture Play Critical Roles," *The City Sun,* Apr. 17–23, 1985, 19).
2. Constance Sutton, "The Caribbeanization of New York City and the Emergence of a Transnational Socio-Cultural System," *Caribbean Life in New York City: Sociocultural Dimensions,* ed. Constance Sutton and Elsa Chaney (New York: Center for Migration Studies, 1987), 15–30; Remco van Capelleveen, "Give me your tired, your poor, and your huddled masses?—'Dritte Welt'—Migration in die USA," *Prokla* 74 (March 1989): 68.
3. Sutton, "Caribbeanization," 16; Orlando Patterson, "Migration in Caribbean Societies: Socioeconomic and Symbolic Resources," *Human Migration: Patterns and Policies,* ed. William McNeill and Ruth Adams (Bloomington: Indiana University Press, 1978), 108–10; H. Hoetink, "'Race' and Color in the Caribbean," *Caribbean Contours,* ed. Sidney Mintz and Sally Price (Baltimore: Johns Hopkins University Press, 1985), 55–84.
4. Ira A. deReid, *The Negro Immigrant: His Background, Characteristics and Social Adjustment, 1899–1937* (New York: Columbia University Press, 1939), 235; U.S. Immigration and Naturalization Service, *Statistical Yearbook* and *Annual Report,* various years; see also Remco van Capelleveen, *Amerikanische Odyssee: Afrokaribische Migranten in New York City,* Habilitationsschrift (Freie Universität Berlin, 1991), chap. 4 (forthcoming).
5. The influx of African-Caribbean immigrants has also shown in the recent transformation of the metropolitan economy. The immigrants have played an important role in the process of economic restructuring by providing cheap and abundant labor for the growing service economy as well as the downgraded manufacturing industries (see Remco van Capelleveen, "Caribbean Immigrants in New York City and the Transformation of the Metropolitan Economy," in *El Caribe y Américana Latina—The Caribbean and Latin America,* ed. Ulrich Fleischmann and Ineke Phaf (Frankfurt: Vervuert, 1987), 260–71; van Capelleveen, *Amerikanische Odyssee,* chap. 6). This economic position of the immigrants is important because, unlike the ghetto economy of the first half of this century, it provides a material basis for the development of a distinct African-Caribbean community and identity.
6. David Lowenthal, "'An Island Is a World': The Problem of Caribbean Insularity," *Perspectives on Caribbean Regional Identity,* ed. Elizabeth Thomas-Hope (University of Liverpool monograph series 11, 1984), 109–21; the Caribbean poet and historian Edward Brathwaite has called this fragmented consciousness the "inner plantation." Edward Kamau Brathwaite, "Caribbean Man in Space and Time," *Savacou* 11–12 (1975): 1–11, 106–8.
7. Dennis Conway and Ualthan Bigby, "Where Caribbean People Live in New York City," in *Caribbean Life in New York City,* 74–83; Roger Waldinger, "Beyond Nos-

talgia: The Old Neighborhood Revisited," *New York Affairs* 10, no. 1 (1987): 1–12.

8. Phillip Kasinitz, *West Indian Diaspora: Race, Ethnicity, and Politics in New York City* (Ann Harbor, Mich.: UMI, 1988), 118.

9. "Rising Islanders of Bed-Stuy," *New York Times Magazine*, Nov. 3, 1985, 67.

10. *Mas* is the West Indian term for masquerade or costumed revellers. "Playing mas" means to participate in a "mas band."

11. Carnival also has been celebrated in other parts of the West Indian diaspora: for example, in Notting Hill, London; Toronto; Montreal; Boston; Washington, D.C.; Los Angeles; Miami; Baltimore; Hartford, Conn.; and elsewhere. None of these (not even the Toronto "Caribana," which drew up to 500,000 spectators in 1985) has reached the scale and importance of the Brooklyn Carnival.

12. Donald Hill and Robert Abramson, "West Indian Carnival in Brooklyn," *Natural History* (August-September 1979): 77; for the Carnival in Trinidad, see Errol Hill, *The Trinidad Carnival: Mandate for a National Theatre* (Austin: University of Texas Press, 1972); Ruth Wuest, "Der Karneval in Trinidad: ein vergängliches Kunstwerk," in *Anglophone Karibik—USA: Peripherie und Zentrum in der'neuen Welt'*, ed. Michael Hoenisch und Remco van Capelleveen (Hamburg: Argument-Verlag, 1991), 68–80.

13. Hill and Abramson, "West Indian Carnival," 83.

14. New York *Amsterdam News*, Sept. 10, 1977; see Monica Gordon, "Carnival in Brooklyn: A West Indian Cultural Extravaganza," (New York, n.d.), 2.

15. Philip Kasinitz and Judith Freidenberg-Herbstein, "The Puerto Rican Parade and West Indian Carnival: Public Celebrations in New York City," in *Caribbean Life in New York City*, 343.

16. Philip Kasinitz and Judith Freidenberg-Herbstein, "The Puerto Rican Parade and West Indian Carnival: Public Celebrations in New York City," in *Caribbean Life in New York City*, 341.

17. Abner Cohen, "A Polyethnic London Carnival as a Contested Cultural Performance," *Ethnic and Racial Studies* 5, no. 1 (1982): 24.

18. Ibid., 34.

19. Victor Turner, "The Spirit of Celebration," in *The Celebration of Society: Perspectives on Contemporary Cultural Performance*, ed. Frank Manning (Bowling Green, Ohio: Bowling Green University Press, 1983), 190.

20. Hill, *Trinidad Carnival*, 24.

21. Angelita Reyes, "Carnival: Ritual Dance of Past and Present in Earl Lovelace's *The Dragon Can't Dance*," *World Literature Written in English* 24, no. 1 (1983): 108.

22. Hill and Abramson, "West Indian Carnival," 85.

23. See Philip Kasinitz, "Brokers in Babylon?" The Changing Role of Afro-Caribbean Immigrants in New York City Politics," in *Anglophone Karibik—USA*, 95–109.

24. Roy Bryce-Laporte, "Black Immigrants: The Experience of Invisibility and Inequality," *Journal of Black Studies* (September 1972): 31.

25. Kasinitz and Freidenberg-Herbstein "Puerto Rican Parade," 345.
26. See Orlando Patterson, "The Emerging West Atlantic System: Migration, Culture, and Underdevelopment in the United States and the Circum-Caribbean Region," *Population in an Interacting World,* ed. William Alonso (Cambridge, Mass.: Harvard University Press, 1987), 227–60.
27. Ibid., 257–58.
28. Constance Sutton and Susan Makiesky-Barrow, "Migration and West Indian Racial and Ethnic Consciousness," in *Caribbean Life in New York City,* 104–5.

Contributors

NORMA E. CANTÚ is a professor of English at Texas A&M International University in Laredo, Texas, and is currently on an Intergovernmental Personnel Act position at the National Endowment for the Arts, Folk Arts Program in Washington, D.C. Her publications include critical articles, poetry and fiction. Her research interests center on Chicana literature and Chicano literary culture.

ANNA LOU DEHAVENON is an Adjunct Assistant Professor of Anthropology in Community Medicine at the Mt. Sinai School of Medicine of the City University of New York. She is the founder and director of the Action Research Project on Hunger, Homelessness, and Family Health. She received her Ph.D. in anthropology from Columbia University.

GENEVIÈVE FABRE is a professor of American Studies at the Université Denis Diderot, in Paris, and is the founder and co-president of ADECLAN (Association for the Development of the Study of Latino Cultures of North America). She is the author of *Drumbeats, Masks and Metaphor, The Configurations of Ethnicity, Parcours Identitaire,* and co-editor of *European Perspectives on Hispanic Literature in the U.S.A.* and a collection of essays, *History and Memory in African American Culture.*

ROLAND L. GUYOTTE is Associate Professor of History at the University of Minnesota, Morris. Educated at Brown and Northwestern Universities, he is a specialist in the history of American higher education. With his wife, Barbara M. Posadas, he has co-authored several articles on Chicago's Filipino old-timers' community.

173

RAMÓN A. GUTIÉRREZ is a professor of History and the founding chair of the Ethnic Studies Department at the University of California, San Diego. He is the author of *When Jesus Came, the Corn Mothers Went Away: Marriage, Sexuality and Power in New Mexico, 1500–1846*, and the co-editor of the *Encyclopedia of the North American Colonies*, and *Recovering the U.S. Hispanic Literary Heritage*. He is currently at work on a cultural history of the Chicano Movement in the United States.

MARÍA HERRERA-SOBEK is a professor of Spanish at the University of California, Irvine. She is the author of *The Bracero Experience: Elitelore Versus Folklore*, *The Mexican Corrido: A Feminist Analysis*, *Northward Bound: The Mexican Immigrant Experience in Ballad and Song*, and the editor of *Beyond Stereotypes: The Critical Analysis of Chicana Literature*, *Gender and Print Culture: New Perspectives on International Ballad Studies*, *Chicana Creativity and Criticism: Charting New Frontiers in American Literature*.

SYBIL KEIN is a professor of English at the University of Michigan and a New Orleans creole poet, playwright and musician. She is the author of *Gombo People*, *Delta Dancer*, *Serenade Creole*, and *An American South*.

JACK KUGELMASS is an Associate Professor of Anthropology and the Director of the Folklore Program at the University of Wisconsin, Madison. He is the author of *The Miracle of Intervale Avenue: Aging with Dignity in the South Bronx*, *Masking Culture: The Greenwich Village Halloween Parade*, editor of *Between Two Worlds: Ethnographic Essays on American Jewry*, and *Going Home: How Jews Invent Their Old Countries*, and co-editor of *From a Ruined Garden: The Memorial Books of Polish Jewry*.

ALESSANDRA LORINI is a professor of history at the University of Florence, Italy. She received her Ph.D. from Columbia University and has published on the history of American social science, on public space in urban America, and on gender, nationalism and cultural identity.

TED OWNBY is an Assistant Professor of History and Southern Studies at the University of Mississippi. He is the author of *Subduing Satan: Religion, Recreation, and Manhood in the Rural South, 1865–1920*, the editor of *Black and White: Cultural Interaction in the Antebellum South*, and is currently at work on a study of the development of consumer culture in Mississippi history.

BARBARA M. POSADAS is Associate Professor of History and Director of the M.S. Option in Historical Administration at Northern Illinois University.

Educated at DePaul and Northwestern Universities, her essays have appeared in *Labor History, Amerasia Journal,* the *Journal of American Ethnic History,* and the *Illinois Historical Journal.*

REMCO VAN CAPELLEVEEN is a professor of Sociology at the Free University of Berlin, Germany. He received his Ph.D. at the University of Frankfurt and has published, among other topics, on minorities, ethnic relations, and migration.

Index

177

Bongo as banda, 104–5
Boundaries, political, communities cross, 168
Bourgeoisie, black, sociologists on, 36
Boys: in county fair, 135; in Sunday Pentecostal ritual, 89
British West Indies, blacks from, 38
Bronx: African-Caribbeans in, 161; Hudson-Fulton Festival and, 41
Brooklyn: African-American Masonic lodges in, 36; African-Caribbeans in, 161, 162, 168; Hudson-Fulton Festival and, 41; West Indian Carnival in, 159–69;
Burial society and African culture, 102. See also Organizations, self-help; Societies, benevolent
Burials, African American, 102–3, 107

Calypso: pan-West Indian identity and, 164; in West Indian Carnival, 163
Campaigns, moral purity, and county fairs, xiii
Caribbean: African-Caribbean consciousness in, 162; blacks from, 38; in West Atlantic system, 168
Caribbeanization of New York, 159–69
Carnival: of African-Americans, 102; in diaspora, 170n11; function of, 166; in New York, 147
Carnival, Caribbean, Halloween parade compared to, 142
Carnival, West Indian: activities of, 164–65; African-Caribbean culture, ethnicity and identity in, xiv, 159, 162, 167; black unity and, xiv; in Brooklyn, 159–69; chaos of, 166; compared to ethnic festivals, 164; cultural traditions of, 163; diaspora and, 164, 165; food of, 165, 166; function of, 165–67; history and description of, 162–63; immigrants and, 166; motto, organization and structure of, 164; police and resistance in, 166; U.S. and Latino

blacks, African-Caribbean unity and, 164
Carnivals: nature and function of, 4–6; compared with religious feasts, 6–7. See also Masquerades
Carrizo and matachines costumes, 59, 61, 64
Cat shaking, 131, 132
Categories, cultural, and Halloween parade, 156n2
Celebration: of abolition, 31–32; of Fourth of July, 34–35; organizer's role in, 147–48; pan-West Indian, 163–64; of Rizal Day, 116–17, 125
Celebration, harvest: and agricultural commercialization and technological innovations, 133; change in, 136–37; county fair as, 133–34; forbidden and accepted activities of, 131; human sexuality and, 133; traditional culture, mass culture and, 129; transition of, xiii. See also Work sharing; Work, group
Celebrations: affect indigenous populations, xi; analysis of, ix, 2; appropriateness of, 27n7; art forms in, 26; avant-garde role in, 154; binary oppositions and, 8–9; of blacks, 29; civic, ludic, religious compared, 7; community power and, 9; cultural anthropologists on, 29; of Emancipation Day, 31–32; environmental and New Age themes in, 154; ethnicity and, 2–3; functions of, 26–27; harvest, 129–37; intellectuals and, 154; issues addressed and limitations of, 155; men in, 130; national cultural agendas and, 154–56; parades in, 4; political significance of, 26; self, community and, xi; sex roles in, 130; significance of, 1, 8; signs in, 26; Spaniards use, xi; William Johnston on, 154–55; women in, 130–31. See also Celebration; Feasts; Festivals